MAGICK CITY:
TRAVELLERS TO ROME
FROM THE MIDDLE AGES
TO 1900

VOLUME III:
THE NINETEENTH CENTURY

ABOUT THE AUTHOR

Inaugural Teaching Fellow in Ancient History, University of
Sydney (1962-4), Lecturer in History, University of Melbourne
(1965-2005), retiring from a Personal Chair. MA (Syd.), DLitt
(Melb.), Hon.DLitt (Macquarie), Fellow of Society of Antiquaries,
Royal Historical Society, Australian Academy of the Humanities,
and Corresponding fellow of Pontifical Roman Academy of
Archæology. Awarded the Princess Daria Borghese gold
medal (2019) and honorary Italian citizenship (2022)
for contributions to the history of Rome

BY THE SAME AUTHOR

Pharaonic Egypt in Victorian Libraries
University of Melbourne, 1970

The Unification of Egypt
Refulgence Press, 1973

Zosimus: New History, translated with commentary
Australian Society for Byzantine Studies, 1982

Gibbon's Complement: Louis de Beaufort
Istituto Veneto, 1986

The History of Rome: A Documented Analysis
Bretschneider, 1987

The Historical Observations of Jacob Perizonius
Accademia Nazionale dei Lincei, 1991

*The Eagle and the Spade: The Archæology of Rome
During the Napoleonic Era*
Cambridge University Press, 1992

Jessie Webb, A Memoir
University of Melbourne, 1994

Melbourne's Monuments
University of Melbourne, 1997

*Napoleon's Proconsul: The Life and Times
of Bernardino Drovetti (1776-1852)*
Rubicon Press, 1998

The Infancy of Historiography
University of Melbourne, 1998

The Pope's Archæologist: The Life and Times of Carlo Fea
Quasar, 2000

(ed.) Raymond Priestley, *The Diary of a Vice-Chancellor:
University of Melbourne 1935-1938*
University of Melbourne, 2002

*The Emperor's Retrospect: Augustus' Res Gestæ in
Epigraphy, Historiography and Commentary*
Peeters, 2003

What an Historian Knows
University of Melbourne, 2008

The Prince as Poisoner: The Trial of Prince Sigismondo Chigi (1790)
(with Dino Bressan), Tipografia Vaticana, 2015

(ed.) *Fifty Treasures: Classical Antiquities in Australian
and New Zealand Universities*
Australasian Society of Classical Studies, 2016

Rome, Twenty-nine Centuries: A Chronological Guide
Gangemi, 2017

The Prince of Antiquarians: Francesco de Ficoroni
Quasar, 2017

Akhenaten: An Historian's View
American University (Cairo), 2018

MAGICK CITY

TRAVELLERS TO ROME
FROM THE MIDDLE AGES
TO 1900

VOLUME III:

THE NINETEENTH CENTURY

BY RONALD T. RIDLEY

PALLAS ATHENE

Christoffer Wilhelm Eckersberg, The Colosseum, *1816*

CONTENTS

NOTE ON MODERN WORKS OF ART

Travellers often mention modern paintings in various collections. Every effort has been made to trace these; they have often been moved. Where a new location is known it is indicated; where nothing of any such work can be found in modern catalogues of the artist in question – and the attributions are often fanciful – nothing more is said; where the work is still in the same collection, it is asterisked.

CURRENCY

One other thing is indispensable for understanding the many references to prices: the CURRENCY system. For most of the time the following is valid:

10 *bajocchi* (copper) = 1 *paolo* (silver) = 6*d* Eng.
100 *bajocchi* = 1 *scudo* (silver) = 5 *livres* / francs
2 *scudi* = 1 sequin (gold) = 10/- stg = 1 ducat
4 *scudi* (4.5 by 1780s) = £1 stg.

Previous pages: J. M. W. Turner, Modern Rome – Campo Vaccino, 1839

THE NINETEENTH CENTURY: THE FIRST HALF

THE TRAVELLERS

Travellers from the British Isles open with Stephen, second EARL MOUNTCASHELL (1770-1822), an Irishman, who was in Rome at the end of December 1803. SAMUEL TAYLOR COLERIDGE (1772-1834), poet and philosopher, who had already published with Wordsworth *Lyrical Ballads* (1798), visited Rome from December 1805 to May 1806. George, LORD BYRON (1788-1824) had already had his famous feud with the *Edinburgh Review*, and made an Eastern tour which produced *Childe Harold*; he made a brief visit in May 1817. PERCY BYSSHE SHELLEY (1792-1822), after being expelled from Oxford and after the tragedy of his first marriage, travelled to Italy with his second wife, Mary Godwin; he was in Rome in late November 1818 and March-June 1819. WILLIAM HAZLITT (1778-1830), the essayist, visited Rome March-April 1825. SIR WALTER SCOTT (1771-1832) came to Rome in the year of his death, April-May. WILLIAM WORDSWORTH (1770-1850) had already in his youth visited France and later Germany, and reached his poetic peak by 1807; he visited the city in his late sixties, April-May 1837. THOMAS BABINGTON MACAULAY (1800-1859), MP from 1830, had already published his *Lays of Ancient Rome* (1842); he was in Rome November-December 1838; from 1848 he turned to history. WILLIAM MAKEPEACE THACKERAY (1811-1863) stayed from late November 1844 until early 1845 (the great novels began with *Vanity Fair*, 1847) and again December 1853-February 1854. CHARLES DICKENS (1812-1870) arrived on 30 January and left in March 1845; he had already published *Pickwick Papers* (1836), *Oliver Twist* (1837), *Nicholas Nickleby* (1838) and *Martin Chuzzlewit* (1843). FLORENCE NIGHTINGALE (1820-1910) visited Rome between 9 November 1847 and 26 March 1848; she was to train as a nurse in 1851 and serve in the

Crimean War, 1854. ROBERT BROWNING (1812-1889), already a famous poet and married to Elizabeth, made three visits: November 1853-May 1854, March-May 1859 and December 1859-June 1860. JOHN (later LORD) ACTON (1834-1902), leading English liberal Catholic, opponent of papal infallibility, friend of Döllinger and Gladstone, was in Rome for the first time in 1857; he was to be Regius Professor of History at Cambridge from 1895. PAULINE DE LA FERRONAYS (1808-1891) was French by birth but was in Rome for Easter 1858 as Mme Augustus Craven. GEORGE ELIOT (1819-1880), Mary Ann Evans, had already translated Strauss' *Leben Jesu* and published her first novel, *Scenes of Clerical Life*, and was mistress of George Lewes; she spent April 1860 in Rome. Frances Dickinson (1820-1898), better known as FRANCES ELLIOT, novelist and writer of memoirs, about whom little is known, but her second husband was dean of Bristol, seems to have been in Rome *c*. 1870. OSCAR WILDE (1854-1900), visited very briefly in 1877, but his main visit was after his great successes, *The Portrait of Dorian Grey* (1891) and *The Importance of Being Earnest* (1895), in April-May 1900, not long before his death. THOMAS HARDY (1840-1928), who trained as an architect, but began as a novelist with *Far from the Madding Crowd* (1874), was in Rome for a week, *c*. 24 March-2 April 1887. Finally the historian GEORGE TREVELYAN (1876-1962) spent Christmas 1897 in Rome; perhaps one result was the wonderful Garibaldi trilogy (1907-1911); he was to become Regius Professor of History at Cambridge in 1927.

There is one English visitor more famous than most others, who never left, but of whom no impressions of Rome from his own hand remain. JOHN KEATS arrived on 15 November 1820. One letter written by him survives, but, understandably, it is entirely concerned with his health. He died on 23 February 1823, and was buried in the 'Protestant' cemetery on the 26th.

FRANÇOIS RENÉ DE CHATEAUBRIAND (1768-1848), 'the outstanding literary genius of the early nineteenth century' in France, historian, diplomat and traveller, was in Rome June 1803-January 1804 as secretary to the French embassy. Anne Louise Germaine Necker, MME DE STAËL (1766-1817), the daughter of Gibbon's old flame Suzanne Curchod, visited Rome in February and March-May 1805 while in

Anne-Louis Girodet de Roussy-Trioson, Sketch for Chateaubriand
Meditating on the Ruins of Rome, *1808*

exile from Napoleon; she was inspired to write *Corinne* (1807). JEAN-
AUGUSTE-DOMINIQUE INGRES (1780-1867), the leading French
portraitist and historical painter of his generation, made two long
sojourns in Rome: October 1806-June 1819, January 1835-April 1841.
ALPHONSE DE LAMARTINE (1790-1869), the Romantic poet and French
Foreign Minister in 1848, was in Rome in November 1811. Henri Beyle,
better known as STENDHAL (1783-1842), novelist and critic, spent four
or five days in Rome at the beginning of October 1811; he was to serve
in the Russian campaign in 1812, and was French consul at Civitavecchia 1831-42. PHILIPPE PETIT-RADEL (1749-1815), professor of surgery
in Paris, of patriotic and anti-ecclesiastical views, was in Rome 1811-
1812. JEANNE RÉCAMIER (1777-1849), *née* Bernard, who conducted one
of the most famous Parisian salons from 1819, visited Rome

April-December 1813 and April-May 1814. JEAN-FRANÇOIS CHAMPOL-
LION (1790-1842), decipherer of hieroglyphs, was in Rome 11-17 March
and 19 April-17 June 1825. JEAN-BAPTISTE-CAMILLE COROT (1796-1875),
the famous landscapist, painted in Rome at the beginning of his
artistic career, from late 1825 until September 1828. ANTOINE CLAUDE
PASQUIN (1789-1847), who wrote under the pseudonym Antoine
Valéry, the devout Royal Librarian at Versailles, was in Rome 1826-
1828(?). JULES MICHELET (1798-1874), historian of man and the
natural world, spent 5-15 April 1830 in Rome. HECTOR BERLIOZ (1803-
1869) was in Rome for a characteristically turbulent time as winner
of the Prix de Rome, March 1831-May 1832. HONORÉ DE BALZAC (1799-
1850), author of the ninety-volume *Comédie humaine* (1829-1848),
visited Rome from 25 March to 20 April 1846. The brothers Edmond
(1822-1896) and Jules (1830-1870) Goncourt, art historians, novelists
and critics, were in Rome February-March 1856. ERNEST RENAN (1823-
1892), historian, philologist and author of the most famous biography
of Jesus in this century (1863) after having renounced an ecclesiastical
career, was in Rome for most of October 1849 until April 1850.
HIPPOLYTE TAINE (1828-1893), professor of Fine Arts, who wrote on
everything and who dabbled in disturbing social theory, visited Rome
March-April 1864.

ELISA VON DER RECKE (1754-1833), born in Kurland, a poet who
exposed Cagliostro, was in Rome November 1804-May 1805 with her
lover Christoph Tiedge. *AUGUST VON KOTZEBUE (1761-1819), born at
Weimar, prolific but superficial playwright and journalist and one-time
convict, also visited Rome 1804-5. *WILHELM MÜLLER (1794-1827),
born at Dessau, poet, author of *Die schöne Müllerin* (1821) and *Die
Winterreise* (1823) spent January-August 1818 in Rome. *LEOPOLD VON
RANKE (1793-1886), born in Saxony, one of the most influential historians of the century and professor in Berlin from 1825, was in Rome
March 1829-April 1830, concentrating on the archives, work that was
to result in the *History of the Papacy* (1834-7). *FELIX MENDELSSOHN
(1809-1847) visited Rome November 1830-April 1831. THEODOR
MOMMSEN (1817-1903), born at Garding in Schleswig, rationalist and
the greatest Roman historian of all time, came to Rome on a study
tour December 1844-May 1845. *FERDINAND GREGOROVIUS (1821-1891),

Ludwig Knaus, Portrait of Theodor Mommsen, *1881*

born at Neidenburg, East Prussia, classic historian of Rome in the Middle Ages, stayed in Rome from October 1852 until June 1860. LUDWIG VON PASTOR (1854-1928), born at Aachen, classic historian of the Papacy, made his first visit to Rome March-April 1876 (those asterisked are Protestant).

The nineteenth century saw a sharp rise in the number of American visitors to Rome. WASHINGTON IRVING (1783-1859), humorist, historian and diplomat, travelled to Europe for his health and was in Rome March-April 1805. GEORGE TICKNOR (1791-1871), professor of French and Spanish at Harvard, visited Rome November 1817-March 1818, December 1836-April 1837, and January-March 1857; his is one of the most valuable intellectual journals. HENRY WADSWORTH LONGFELLOW (1807-1882) came to Rome in 1828, sent by Bowdoin College to study

Margaret Fuller Ossoli, photographed by Albert Sands Southworth, 1846

languages, but he was appointed to Harvard on his return; his poetry was to begin appearing in 1839. JAMES FENIMORE COOPER (1789-1851) had been a naval lieutenant, begun his career as a novelist, and served as consul at Lyons; he was in Rome December 1829-April 1830. RALPH WALDO EMERSON (1803-1882), a Unitarian minister disowned by his congregation, philosopher and essayist, visited the city in March-April 1833 following the death of his first wife. JULIA WARD HOWE (1819-1910), humanitarian and female suffragist and author of *The Battle Hymn of the Republic*, made three visits: winter 1843-spring 1844, October 1850-summer 1851, and 1877. GEORGE HILLARD (1808-1879), Boston lawyer and anti-slavery politician, was the author of 'probably the most popular book about Italy by an American' (*Six Months in Italy*), based on a visit to Rome 1847-48. MARGARET FULLER OSSOLI (1810-1850), feminist, philosopher and journalist, is the main witness as a traveller of the Roman Republic. In Rome she married marchese Ossoli, and was in charge of a hospital during the siege. On Rome's fall, she and her husband and infant sailed for America, but were all drowned when their ship was wrecked. Julia Howe wrote her biography. HARRIET HOSMER (1830-1908), the sculptor, was in Rome from November 1852 for most of the rest of her life. CHARLES ELIOT NORTON (1827-1908), later professor of Fine Arts at Harvard, was in Rome December 1855-April 1857. HERMAN MELVILLE (1819-1891) had already spent much time in the South Seas (*Typee, Omoo, Moby Dick*) when he visited Rome in February-March 1857. His fellow-novelist NATHANIEL HAWTHORNE (1804-1864) followed the next year, January-May 1858; *The Marble Faun* was one result. HENRY JAMES (1843-1916) stayed from 30 October until 28 December 1869; *Roderick Random* and *Daisy Miller* followed.

Other nations were represented by smaller numbers. Of Russians, NICOLAI VASILIEVICH GOGOL (1809-1852) had already published *The Inspector-General* and *Dead Souls*; he spent most of 1837-1846 in Rome. FYODOR MIKHAYLOVICH DOSTOYEVSKY (1821-1881), who had been an exile in Siberia 1849-1859, and begun *Crime and Punishment* in 1866, was in Rome September-October 1863. PIOTR ILLYICH TCHAIKOVSKY (1840-1893), who had published his first symphony in 1866, visited Rome in May 1874, November 1877 (his marriage had broken down, but *Swan Lake* was published this year), from December 1879 to March 1880 (his *Italian Capriccio* was published in this latter year), from December 1881 to January 1882, and in April 1890.

The Swiss were represented by CHARLES DE BONSTETTEN (1745-1832), a naturalist, who visited Rome *c.* 1805; JEAN MALLET DE HAUTEVILLE (1787-1865) from Geneva, an historian, who was in Rome for Easter 1815; and JACOB BURCKHARDT (1818-1897) from Basel, the famous art historian (*The Civilisation of the Renaissance in Italy*, 1860), in Rome from early April to mid June 1846.

The Scandinavians have two famous representatives: HANS CHRISTIAN ANDERSEN (1805-1875): Italy was 'the land of his longing', and he visited Rome a number of times: most of October 1833-March 1834 (with a travelling scholarship from Frederick VI; the resulting

Improvisatore (1835) made his European reputation), December 1840-February 1841, April 1846, April-May 1861. HENRIK IBSEN (1828-1906) was already a theatre director, but enraged at Norway's neutrality in Denmark's war with Germany, went into a kind of exile, living in Italy and Germany until 1891; he stayed in Rome 1864–1868. From Poland came HENRYK SIENKIEWICZ (1846-1916), author of *Quo Vadis*, and Nobel laureate for Literature 1905, who was in the city in 1879, 1886, 1890, and 1893. From Hungary, finally, the most famous visitor was FRANZ LISZT (1811-1886), who spent many years in Rome: January-June 1839 (he had lived with comtesse d'Agoult 1835-9), from October 1861 for most of the next seven years, 1875, and some months in the second half of each year from 1877 to 1885. As a concert virtuoso until 1847 he was constantly on tour, but then turned to composition, and after taking minor Franciscan orders in 1865, spent most of his life in Rome or Weimar.

INTRODUCTION

The eighteenth century ended very badly for Rome. The pope's authority was challenged all over Europe, with many states following the demands made by France since the seventeenth century for an independent Church, or worse, one subordinate to the will of the State (as in Austria). State control meant the restriction of ecclesiastical jurisdiction, refusal of dues, abolition of the Inquisition, confiscation of Church property and closing of religious institutions. Worse came with the French Revolution, when the armies of the secular Republic swarmed across Europe. Anti-French military coalitions failed one after another, and Rome was defenceless. On 13 January 1793, the French ambassador to Rome, Hugo de Bassville, was stabbed to death. This was avenged four years later with the submission of Rome and the Treaty of Tolentino in February 1797. With the killing of General Duphot on 28 December of the same year, however, the punishment had to be much more severe. The city surrendered to the French on 10 February 1798, a republic was declared, and on 20 February Pius VI was arrested and deported to die in exile at Valence. This republic was overthrown by the Neapolitans in September 1799.

Pius VII was elected in Venice in 1800, and the French again occupied Rome in 1808. The pope was kidnapped from the Quirinal on 6 July 1809 and imprisoned at Savona and Fontainbleau. Rome became a prefecture until the collapse of the Napoleonic empire in 1814, and the restoration of the papacy. Pius' successors, Leo XII and Gregory XVI, were both intransigent reactionaries, who reimposed ecclesiastical domination and brutally repressed political liberalism and the beginnings of the reunification of the peninsula. Pius IX came to the throne in 1846 with hopes for a more liberal approach, but events moved too quickly. In January 1848 Sicily rose against the Bourbons in Naples; in February revolution in Paris overthrew Louis-Philippe; in March Charles Albert of Piedmont proclaimed a constitution, and the Milanese drove out the Austrians, but the Piedmontese attempt to expel the Austrians from northern Italy failed by August. Pius had issued a constitution for Rome on 14 March, but the next month denounced the drive for Italian unification. On 24 November he was forced to flee Rome.

Visitors of all nationalities continued to flood into Rome during the first half of the century through all these upheavals. Their LODGING continued to find its centre in the piazza di Spagna, or nearby. Some travellers gave their address simply as the piazza: Mme de Staël 1805 and William Wordsworth 1837; near the Spanish steps for Elisa von der Recke 1804. More precise addresses in the piazza were the Pio (Earl Montcashell 1803), Serni's (Mme Jeanne Récamier 1813), the Allemagna (William Thackeray 1844) and no. 5 in the piazza (Felix Mendelssohn 1830). Nearby was via Condotti: Damon's (Alphonse de Lamartine 1811), simply that street (Jean-François Champollion 1825). Above the piazza was Trinità de Monti (Philippe Petit-Radel 1811), the villa Medici (Hector Berlioz 1831), the via Sistina (Wilhelm Müller 1818) and via Gregoriana (no. 33, the house of Salvatore Rosa: William Hazlitt 1825). Leading up to Trinità was via S Sebastianello (no. 8: Florence Nightingale 1847). A few minutes to the south-east was piazza Barberini, closer to which others stayed: via della Purificazione (Hans

Christian Andersen 1840; at no. 80, Franz Liszt 1839), via di S Nicola da Tolentino (Julia Howe 1844) and via delle Quattro Fontane (no. 11, Jacob Burckhardt 1846). A few minutes to the west from piazza di Spagna, across the Corso, was piazza S Lorenzo in Lucina, where the palazzo Fiano was located. Here Mme Récamier moved to the first floor in 1813 after Serni's; it was quite a French centre, housing also the comte de Forbin, soon to be director of national museums, the painter François Granet, and the police chief Jacques Norvins. Another new centre was the Campo Marzio: in the piazza Navona, opposite Sant'Agnese (Longfellow 1820), via della Ripetta (Hotel de Paris, James Cooper 1828), and via Campo Marzio (no. 33, Jules Michelet 1830). Theodor Mommsen, finally, enjoyed the splendour of the German Archæological Institute in the palazzo Caffarelli on the Capitol in 1844.

We have as usual some information about COSTS. Visitors naturally commented on the food available in Rome. In 1805 August von Kotzebue stated that Rome was generally cheaper than Naples, contrary to ordinary opinion. Vegetables were 'very fine', bread 'might be better', while coffee and sugar were 'exorbitantly dear'. Six years later, Petit-Radel still found bread poor and expensive (the grain came from Tuscany and there were few mills at Rome), while fruit was good, but not as flavoursome as French; meat was cheaper than France but not as good (beef was 7 *sous* for 12 ozs [340 grams], but the youngest veal cost 13-15), fish was expensive, but pork and boar were good. Wines were poor: the best came from Gensano, Albano and Velletri (about 8 *sous* a bottle). There were no good restaurants, and Petit-Radel wickedly commented that Romans tucked in when others were paying, but were very frugal at home. In 1818 Müller declared that the best *trattoria* was the Hermelin in piazza Sciarra, but that Franz in via Condotti served lunch and dinner. Good Orvieto wine could be found near S Agostino. He also pointed out that apart from his nationals he preferred English company when he ate: the French talked too much and ate too quickly. Ralph Waldo Emerson in 1833 ate well and cheaply:

At Rome at the best *trattoria* you may eat a good dinner for 15

Franz Ludwig Catel, Crown Prince Ludwig in the Spanish Wine Tavern, 29 February 1824.
The Crown Prince is at the far end of the bench, next to Thorwaldsen.
Standing to the left is the innkeeper Rafaele Anglada, with some of his wine collection—
see the well loaded shelves above

bajocchi. Thus today and yesterday I have dined at the Lepri
[via Condotti] on this fashion:
  'Macaroni a la Napolitana', 3
  'Mongana con spinnagio', 5
  'crema in piatta', 5, and
  two bread rolls to eat with it, 2
  [totals] 15 cents for a good dinner in the best house. Add one
or two for the waiter. My breakfast at the most expensive caffé
in Rome costs 16 cents.
  Coffee in the evening 5.[1]

Burckhardt in 1846 priced food at one gulder a day (*c. 65 bajocchi*). Florence Nightingale in 1847 spent 5 *paoli* (50 *bajocchi*) on dinner from a *trattoria* opposite. As for accommodation, Emerson spent 50 cents a day at the Gran Bretagna, while Burckhardt, who tended to live spartanly – to say the least – claimed that a good room could be had for 4 *scudi* per month. Emerson claimed that a visit to the pope cost $5; Burckhardt stated that the visit to each gallery cost 1 *paoli* (10 *bajocchi*). As Honoré de Balzac noted in 1846: 'Unfortunately Rome is expensive, she has as many beggars as inhabitants, which makes visits to palaces and galleries a major impossibility.'

There were, of course, seasons, as Longfellow graphically described:

> The masks and mummeries of Carnival are over; the imposing ceremonies of Holy Week have become a tale of the times of old; the illumination of St Peter's and the Girandola are no longer the theme of gentle and simple [sic]; and finally, the barbarians of the North have retreated from the gates of Rome, and left the Eternal City silent and deserted. The cicerone stands at the corner of the street with his hands in his pockets; the artist has shut himself up in his studio to muse upon antiquity; and the idle *facchino* [porter] lounges in the marketplace, and plays at *mora* by the fountain. Midsummer has come, and you may now hire a palace for what, a few weeks ago, would hardly have paid your night's lodging in its garret.[2]

The *scudo* was slightly devalued in comparison with the last century. Charles Dickens in 1845 gave 10 *scudi* as £2/2/6d, so that 1 *scudo* = 4/3d, while Nightingale made it 4/4d. The *scudo* also equalle 5.3 francs and 1.5 gulders (150 kreuzer, or farthings).

CICERONI or guides, where they are known to us, are impressive. The famous Danish antiquarian Georg Zoëga served Elisa von der Recke in 1804; an actress-friend showed Lamartine around in 1811, while again the leading antiquarians Alessandro Nibby and Christian Bunsen conducted George Ticknor in 1818, Feliciano Scarpellini and Eduard Gerhard (founder of the German Archæological Institute) initiated Michelet in 1830, and William Gell did the honours to Sir Walter Scott in 1832. Henry Colyar guided both Thomas Macaulay

Antoine Sergent-Marceau, Georg Zoëga, *c. 1815-18*

in 1838 and Florence Nightingale in 1847, while the diarist Henry Crabb Robinson and the sculptor John Giblin served Wordsworth in 1837.

Some travellers gave advice to their fellows. The American George Hillard in 1847 wrote about psychological preparation:

> As Rome cannot be comprehended without previous preparation, so it cannot be felt without a certain congeniality of temperament. Something of the imaginative principle; the power of going out of one's self, and forgetting the actual in the ideal, and the present in the past; the capacity to sympathize with the dreamer, if not to dream; a willingness to be acted upon, and not to act, – these must be wrought into the being of him who would catch all the inspiration of the place. The traveller must leave all his notions of progress and reform at the gates, or he will be kept in a constant state of protest and

rebellion; as unfit to receive the impressions which are around him as a lake ruffled by the storm, to reflect the heavens. He must try to forget such things as a representative government, town-meetings, public schools, railways, and steam-engines. He must learn to look upon pope, cardinal, and monk, not with a puritan scowl, but as parts of an imposing pageant, which he may contemplate without self-reproach, though without approving; as the man of peace may be innocently amused with the splendid evolutions of a review. He whose spirit is so restless and evanescent as to forbid repose, whose zeal for progress admits neither compromise nor delay, – who sees, not the landscape, but the monastery which blots it, not the church, but the beggar on its steps, – who, in the kneeling peasant, finds all idolatry and no devotion, – may have many good and great qualities, but he is out of his place in Rome. He is an exotic, and will only languish and pine in its uncongenial soil.[3]

In the same category come remarks about the POST OFFICE and BANKS. More recent travellers would recognise Thackeray's revelations:

Although I looked 35 days running at the Post Office until I was sick and ashamed of applying, the beasts would not give me your letters because they were supposed to be for Mr Jackeray instead of Thackeray, and I have only just got the letters – the money was quite safe at Tortoni's, where the clerks had declined to have anything to do with my bills, and where as soon as they found them covered they invited me to a ball – but I was too much enraged and disgusted to accept the invitation...[4]

For northern Europeans an adjustment of diet was necessary: the summer of 1829 was especially hot, so Leopold von Ranke abandoned his meat breakfast (*Schinkenfrühstück*), reduced his consumption of wine from one-and-a-half *fogliette* (¾ litre) of wine to half of one, and exchanged his afternoon coffee for a lemonade.[5]

Some other disappointments were eternal. Wordsworth was, admittedly, sixty-seven:

But of churches and pictures and statues in them I am fairly tired – in fact I am old in head, limbs and eyesight for such hard work, such toiling and such straining and so many disappointments either in finding the most celebrated picture covered up with curtains, a service going on so that one cannot ask to have a sight, or the church closed when one arrives at the door.

Sightseeing was indeed hard work. Patience and humility were also required. The Swiss Jean George Mallet de Hauteville in 1815 identified the eternal pest, the ignorant critic:

Does he believe, after a few minutes' examination, that he has the right to criticise a work which may well have cost months of meditation and examination from a painter whose reputation has already long been made?[6]

The various NATIONALITIES of visitors could as always be distinguished. The American Ticknor in 1817 offered notes on many groups.

[Johann] Winckelmann [the famous eighteenth century antiquarian, see Vol. II] says, in one of his curious letters to [Hieronymus] Berendis, 'A Frenchman is not to be improved here. Antiquity and he contradict one another'; and since I have been here I have seen and felt a thousand proofs of the justness of the remark… Simond himself, though I think him in general a cool, impartial man, stands up a mere Frenchman as soon as you get him upon the subject of antiquities, of which he seems to have about as just notions as divines have of the world before the flood.

Of the Russians there are a good many that circulate in general society, and talk French and English fluently; but, really, wherever I have seen this people, I have found them so abdicating their nationality and taking the hue of the society they are among, that I have lost much of my respect for them…

The English everywhere, and in all great collections, formed a substantial part of society in Rome during the whole winter. The greatest gaiety was among them, and the greatest show…

The wealthier English by 1838 seemed to have created for themselves a rather comfortable life, as Macaulay described it:

> The Government treats us very well. The Pope winks at a Protestant chapel, and indulges us in a reading-room, where the *Times* and *Morning Chronicle* make their appearance twelve days after they are published in London. It is a pleasant city for an English traveller. He is not harassed or restrained. He lives as he likes, and reads what he likes, and suffers little from the vices of the administration.

And the incomparable talents of Dickens in devastating characterisation found more than enough grist for their mill:

> We often encountered, in these expeditions, a company of English Tourists, with whom I had an ardent, but ungratified longing, to establish a speaking acquaintance. They were one Mr Davis, and a small circle of friends. It was impossible not to know Mrs Davis's name, for her being always in great request among her party, and her party being everywhere. During the Holy Week, they were in every part of every scene of every ceremony. For a fortnight or three weeks before it, they were in every tomb, and every church, and every ruin, and every Picture Gallery; and I hardly ever observed Mrs Davis to be silent for a moment. Deep underground, high up in St Peter's, out on the Campagna, and stifling in the Jews' quarter, Mrs Davis turned up, all the same. I don't think she ever saw anything, or ever looked at anything; and she had always lost something out of a straw hand basket, and was trying to find it, with all her might and main, among an immense quantity of English halfpence, which lay, like sands upon the seashore, at the bottom of it. There was a professional Cicerone always attached to the party (which had been brought over from London, fifteen or twenty strong, by contract), and if he so much as looked at Mrs Davis, she invariably cut him short by saying, 'There, God bless the man, don't worrit me! I don't understand a word you say, and shouldn't if you was to talk 'till you was black in the face!' Mr Davis always had a snuff

Carl Spitzweg, English Tourists in the Campagna, *c. 1840*

coloured great coat on, and carried a great green umbrella in his hand, and had a slow curiosity constantly devouring him, which prompted him to do extraordinary things, such as taking the covers off urns in tombs, and looking in at the ashes as if they were pickles – and tracing out inscriptions with the ferule of his umbrella, and saying, with intense thoughtfulness, 'Here's a B you see, and there's a R, and this is the way we goes on in; is it!' His antiquarian habits occasioned his being frequently in the rear of the rest; and one of the agonies of Mrs Davis, and the party in general, was an ever present fear that Davis would be lost. This caused them to scream for him, in the strangest places, and at the most improper seasons. And when he came, slowly emerging out of some Sepulchre or other, like a peaceful Ghoule, saying 'Here I am!' Mrs Davis invariably replied, 'You'll be buried alive in a foreign country Davis, and it's no use trying to prevent you!'

Mr and Mrs Davis, and their party, had, probably, been brought from London in about nine or ten days. Eighteen hundred years ago, the Roman legions under Claudius, protested against being led into Mr and Mrs Davis's country, urging that it lay beyond the limits of the world.

The most insightful observations, however, were offered by Margaret Fuller Ossoli on her fellow Americans:

> Thus it is that the American, on many points, becomes more ignorant for coming abroad, because he attaches some value to his crude impressions and frequent blunders. It is not thus that any seed corn can be gathered from foreign gardens. Without modest scrutiny, patient study, and observation, he spends his money and goes home, with a new coat perhaps, but a mind befooled rather than instructed. It is necessary to speak the languages of these countries, and know personally some of their inhabitants, in order to form any accurate impressions.[7]

Hillard noted special problems for women: 'From many places they are absolutely excluded, and the guide books will make the cool announcement that this or that spot is so holy that no woman is allowed to approach it.'[8]

The classic WAYS TO VISIT were still in vogue. Chateaubriand, as a Frenchman, began his moonlight walk at Trinità de Monti.

> From its height the bell-towers and far off buildings seemed like obliterated sketches of a painter, or like irregular coasts seen from the sea, on board a ship at anchor. The shadow of the obelisk: how many people had observed this shadow in Egypt and in Rome? Trinità de Monti is deserted; a dog barks in this French retreat. There is a small light in a lofty room of the villa Medici. The Corso: the calm and whiteness of its buildings. In piazza Colonna the column of Antoninus is half lit…

Ticknor also began with a moonlight tour, starting from ponte Sant'Angelo. From here he naturally went on to the Colosseum and the Forum. Burckhardt, on the other hand, was entranced by the view from his residence on the Quirinal:

Franz Ludwig Catel, The Colosseum by moonlight, *1833*

it has become here literally a dream of youth, the palaces in the moonlight, then on the left an enormous panorama from the Pantheon to monte Pincio, now submerged in the most beautiful silver light, and finally on the right, way beyond some

peaceful cloisters and fallen walls, the black pine groves of the
villa Ludovisi; but below in piazza Barberini, down at my feet,
'my friend the Triton' sprays his glittering jet in the moonlight
night. (NB All this is without a word of a lie, and literally so).

Then there were the visits to the museums and galleries by torchlight. A group of young Germans, including Mommsen, went to the
Vatican in March 1845. He noted that the cleaned statues, especially
the *Mercury*, had lost a lot, but that particularly the *Laocoön* became
much 'clearer'. They were so philistine, however, as to burst into
laughter at the sight of Canova's *Gladiator*. After seeing the Vatican
collection by torchlight, Julia Howe, seeing the statues again by
daylight, thought that they had died.[9]

REACTIONS to the Eternal City were not always unanimous. Hazlitt
was in a minority.

This is not the Rome I expected to see. No one from being in it
would know he was in the place that had been twice mistress of
the world. I do not understand how Nicolas Poussin could tell,
taking up a handful of earth, that it was 'a part of the eternal
city'. In Oxford an air of learning breathes from the very walls:
halls and colleges meet your eye in every direction; you cannot
for a moment forget where you are. In London there is a look of
wealth and populousness which is to be found nowhere else. In
Rome you are for the most part lost in a mass of tawdry, fulsome
common places. It is not the contrast of pig styes and palaces that
I complain of, the distinction between the old and new; what I
object to is the want of any such striking contrast, but an almost
uninterrupted succession of narrow, vulgar looking streets, where
the smell of garlic prevails over the odour of antiquity, with
the dingy, melancholy flat fronts of modern built houses, that
seem in search of an owner. A dunghill, an outhouse, the weeds
growing under an imperial arch offend me not; but what has a
green grocer's stall, a stupid English china warehouse, a putrid
trattoria, a barber's sign, an old clothes or old picture shop or
a Gothic palace, with two or three lacqueys in modern liveries
lounging at the gate, to do with ancient Rome? No! this is not

Wilhelm Marstrand, A charlatan sells ink in the Piazza Barberni, *1840-49*

the wall that Romulus leaped over: this is not the Capitol where Julius Cæsar fell: instead of standing on seven hills, it is situated in a low valley; the golden Tiber is a muddy stream: St Peter's is not equal to St Paul's: the Vatican falls short of the Louvre, as it was in my time; but I thought that here were works immoveable, immortal, inimitable on earth, and lifting the soul halfway to heaven. I find them not, or only what I had seen before in different ways: the Stanzas of Raphael are faded, or no better than the prints; and the mind of Michael Angelo's figures, of which no traces are to be found in the copies, is equally absent from the walls of the Sistine Chapel. Rome is great only in ruins: the Coliseum, the Pantheon, the Arch of Constantine fully answered my expectations; and an air breathes round her stately avenues, serene, blissful, like the mingled breath of spring and winter, betwixt life and death, betwixt hope and despair. The country about Rome is cheerless and barren. There is little verdure, nor are any trees planted, on account of their bad effects on the air. Happy climate! in which shade and sunshine are alike fatal.

Hazlitt admitted that there were contrasts. As Mme de Staël put it,
'In Rome, all impressions are contradicted: the most beautiful monuments are raised in honour of the most superstitious ideas, the
grandest memories are alongside the deepest misery.' Moonlight, as
usual, emphasised those contrasts. Dickens viewed 'the narrow streets,
devoid of footways, and choked, in every obscure corner, by heaps of
dunghill rubbish... in their cramped dimensions, and their filth'
counterposed by 'the broad square before some haughty church'. It
was also the fusion and adaptation which were striking:

> But whether, in this ride, you pass by obelisks, or columns:
> ancient temples, theatres, houses, porticoes, or forums: it is
> strange to see, how every fragment, whenever it is possible, has
> been blended into some modern structure, and made to serve
> some modern purpose – a wall, a dwelling place, a granary, a
> stable – some use for which it never was designed, and asso-
> ciated with which it cannot otherwise than lamely assort. It
> is stranger still, to see how many ruins of the old mythology:
> how many fragments of obsolete legend and observance: have
> been incorporated into the worship of Christian altars here;
> and how, in numberless respects, the false faith and the true
> are fused into a monstrous union.[10]

What, then, was the MEANING OF ROME, her attraction, for these
visitors? Chateaubriand in 1803 could provide a whole list: 'the unpar-
alleled mixture of architecture and ruins' from the Pantheon to the
dome of St Peter's, the beauty of the women ('one would think that
one saw ancient statues of Juno or Pallas descended from their pedestal'), the skin colours (which was why painters loved them as models),
'the herds of goats and especially the yokes of great oxen with enormous horns, lying at the feet of the Egyptian obelisks, amid the ruins
of the Forum, and under the arches where once passed the Roman
triumphant generals', and the sound everywhere of water. Mme de
Staël was generally critical, but admitted to being awoken to new ideas
and feelings: 'all the masterpieces of art which revive the soul when
it is down, the harmonious sounds which resound at night in all the
streets, this social freedom which is not as worthy as political freedom,

but which has its charm, the Italians witty, inoffensively cheerful, amorous as soon as you allow it'. She was charmed by the language and its grace, and the imagination of the literary class. There was weakness of character and political degradation, 'but no vanity, not much wickedness, and a tendency to enthusiasm which always makes people, at least momentarily, good and lovable'. There was, however, one aspect of Roman life she could not tolerate: the ubiquitous idea of death. Shelley, of course, noticed the same, but turned the observation on its head: 'Rome is a city as it were of the dead, or rather of those who cannot die, and who survive the puny generations which inhabit and pass over the spot which they have made sacred for eternity.' Burckhardt was more phlegmatic:

> The delight of Rome is a constant guessing game and combination; the ruins of time lie in puzzling layers one on top of another. I miss here a beautiful, complete building, to whose towers and niches the excited soul could fly: 'Rome is heavy and too colourful,' said [the poet August] Platen rightly. But all in all she is still Queen of the World, and gives one from her memory and charm a more wonderful combined impression than any other city.

Pasquin was most insightful: 'Simple contemplation and prolonged stay in Rome can take the place of long studies and much travelling.' Balzac summed up thus:

> Truly, you have to save up and go once in a lifetime to Rome, otherwise you will know nothing of antiquity, architecture, splendour, or of the impossible realised. Rome in the short time that I stayed there will be one of the grandest and most beautiful memories of my life.

No wonder that some expressed themselves ecstatically. In Byron's words, 'I am delighted with Rome – as I would be with a bandbox.' At the thought of being there, Mommsen could only cry: 'World, don't collapse! Sky, don't fall down!'[11]

Overleaf: Attributed to Ippolito Caffi, View of Saint Peter's Square and Basilica in Rome, c. 1846

BASILICAS, CHURCHES AND CATACOMBS

ST PETER's basilica generally called forth unalloyed admiration. A striking exception was Elisa von der Recke in 1804. She compared the church constantly and unfavourably with the Pantheon. 'One does not find this dignity, this sublime simplicity… [T]his sweet harmony which, at first glance, fills the mind with a unique idea and which struck me so forcibly entering the Pantheon, was absolutely lacking in St Peter's.' 'A diversity of pompous images' defeated devotion. Her guide Zoëga told her that the bronze statue of St Peter was in fact a Roman senator. She did, however, like Alessandro Algardi's relief of Leo and Attila on the former's tomb, and Antonio Canova's tomb for Clement XIII. Another German visitor at the same time was similarly unimpressed. Augustus von Kotzebue declared that

there is but one monument in the church that represents a sensible action of a pope; it is the correction of the calendar by Gregory XIII: the rest are devoted to remind us only of wonders or revolting cruelties.

For the colonnade he pardoned Bernini 'many incongruities', but he thought that the obelisk was a great mistake, being too large for the facade. Stendhal in 1811 disapproved of the facade, because the columns were engaged, but he liked the interior. He was especially taken with the tomb of Clement XIII (which he misnamed that of Benedict XIV) and Canova's figure of *Religion*. Jean George Mallet de Hauteville, the Swiss historian, was one of the few to comment on the outrageous inscription on the facade, where after a century of building, only the name of Paul V appears. The older jokes about the Pole seeing St Peter's were now being supplemented. Byron would, of course, pick them up.

I'll tell you a story. – The other day a man here – an English – mistaking the statues of Charlemagne and Constantine – which are *Equestrian* for those of Peter and Paul – asked another – which was Paul of these same horsemen? – to which the reply

Raffaello Sanzio Morghen, *The tomb of Pope Clement XIII by Canova*, c. 1800

was, 'I thought Sir that St Paul had never got on horseback since his *accident*?'

Shelley took up the critical approach. 'Externally it is inferior in architectural beauty to St Pauls, although it is not wholly devoid of it: internally it exhibits littleness on a large scale.' The colonnade he found 'wonderfully fine' but the dome was concealed by the facade (the fault of Carlo Maderno) and 'that diabolical contrivance they call an attic'. In April 1819 he saw a remarkable sight:

> In the square of *St Peters* there are about 300 fettered criminals at work, hoeing out the weeds that grow between the stones of the pavement. Their legs are heavily ironed, & some are chained two by two. They sit in long rows hoeing out the weeds, dressed

in party coloured clothes. Near them sit or saunter, groupes
of soldiers armed with loaded muskets. The iron discord of
those innumerable chains clanks up into the sonorous air, and
produces, contrasted with the musical dashing of the fountains,
& the deep azure beauty of the sky & the magnif[ic]ence of the
architecture around a conflict of sensations allied to madness.
It is the emblem of Italy: moral degradation contrasted with
the glory of nature & the arts.

One becomes used to the English comparisons between St Peter's
and St Paul's in London. William Hazlitt went further:

> After all, St Peter's does not seem to me the chief boast or
> most imposing display of the Catholic religion. Old Melrose
> Abbey, battered to pieces and in ruins, as it is, impresses me
> much more than the collective pride and pomp of Michael
> Angelo's great work. Popery is here at home, and may strut
> and swell and deck itself out as it pleases, on the spot and for
> the occasion. It is the pageant of an hour. But to stretch out its
> arm fifteen hundred miles, to create a voice in the wilderness,
> to have left its monuments standing by the Teviot side, or to
> send the midnight hymn through the shades of Vallombrosa,
> or to make it echo among Alpine solitudes, that is faith, and
> that is power. The rest is a puppet-shew!

Such British criticisms may be expected, but the French royal librarian, Antoine Claude Pasquin, in 1828 could find barely a good word
for the basilica. The statues in the portico were in bad taste or mediocre. In the interior bad taste and exaggeration abounded. In the main
body of the basilica, most of the statues were 'horribly mannered': St
Andrew was the best and he retold the joke about the movement in
Veronica's clothes being caused by the wind created by Bernini's
interference with Michelangelo's pilasters. The doctors of the Church
supporting Peter's chair were of 'detestable execution'. Algardi's relief
of Attila, so universally praised, was 'pitiful in style and design', and
Camillo Rusconi's tomb of Gregory XIII was 'beneath even this
detestable artist'! Hector Berlioz in 1831 made particular use of the

Hortense Lescot, Kissing the Foot of St Peter, *1812*

church. 'Nor did I ever see St Peter's without a thrill. It is so grand, so noble, so beautiful, so majestically calm!' During the hot summer he would spend whole days there, in a confessional, reading Byron! He imagined where the poet must have walked and stood, perhaps with Countess Guiccioli. The sight of a peasant kissing the toe of St Peter (in reality Jupiter the Thunderer, he thought) caused him to contrast this man's modest contentment with his own despair and bitterness. Ralph Waldo Emerson visited the piazza with artistic friends in the moonlight: 'the finest fountain [*sic*] in the world'. He thought that when he returned home he would remember few statues better than the head of *Justice* on the tomb of Paul III. The stories of the amorous Spaniard seem to have been forgotten. Wordsworth declared that 'of all things that I have seen at Rome the inside of St Peter's has most moved me', but he does not elaborate. The first thing that Thomas Babington Macaulay did on arriving in November 1838 was to walk to the basilica. 'The colonnade in front is noble – very, very noble; yet it disappointed me.' Then he entered. 'I never in my life saw, and never, I suppose, shall see again, anything so astonishingly beautiful. I really could have cried with pleasure.' Poor Bernini was still being denounced. Franz Liszt declared the next year 'As regards St Peter's, I go there very rarely; with those innumerable works of his, Bernini has desecrated and defiled it. Apart from the two lions, Canova's tomb [of Clement XIII] is detestably mediocre. His, incidentally, is a very much usurped reputation. I'll gladly say the same of Thorwaldsen, who has done a papal tomb in St Peter's: the whole thing very cold and stiff.' This was the tomb of Pius VII, described by Gregorovius as 'a work of great delicacy, grace and simplicity'. Theodor Mommsen preferred the piazza to the basilica. Charles Dickens similarly found the piazza's beauty 'so fresh, so broad, and free and beautiful – nothing can exaggerate'. The interior of the church was disturbed for him by preparations for some festival. 'I had a much greater sense of mystery and wonder in the Cathedral of St Mark in Venice.'

Only a few days after his arrival, the first Sunday (2 February 1845), Dickens attended mass in St Peter's. His description of the varied congregation is memorable.

A large space behind the altar, was fitted up with boxes, shaped like those at the Italian Opera in England, but in their decoration much more gaudy. In the centre of the kind of theatre thus railed off, was a canopied dais with the Pope's chair upon it. The pavement was covered with a carpet of the brightest green; and what with this green, and the intolerable reds and crimsons, and gold borders of the hangings, the whole concern looked like a stupendous bonbon. On either side of the altar, was a large box for lady strangers. These were filled with ladies in black dresses and black veils. The gentlemen of the Pope's guard, in red coats, leather breeches, and jack boots, guarded all this reserved space, with drawn swords, that were very flashy in every sense; and from the altar all down the nave, a broad lane was kept clear by the Pope's Swiss guard, who wear a quaint striped surcoat, and striped tight legs, and carry halberds like those which are usually shouldered by those theatrical supernumeraries, who never *can* get off the stage fast enough, and who may be generally observed to linger in the enemy's camp after the open country, held by the opposite forces, has been split up the middle by a convulsion of Nature.

I got upon the border of the green carpet, in company with a great many other gentlemen, attired in black (no other passport is necessary), and stood there at my ease, during the performance of mass. The singers were in a crib of wire-work (like a large meat safe or bird cage) in one corner; and sang most atrociously. All about the green carpet, there was a slowly moving crowd of people: talking to each other: staring at the Pope through eye glasses: defrauding one another, in moments of partial curiosity, out of precarious seats on the bases of pillars: and grinning hideously at the ladies. Dotted here and there, were little knots of friars (Francescáni, or Cappuccíni, in their coarse brown dresses and peaked hoods) making a strange contrast to the gaudy ecclesiastics of higher degree, and having their humility gratified to the utmost, by being shouldered about, and elbowed right and left, on all sides. Some of these had muddy sandals and umbrellas, and stained garments: having trudged in from the country. The faces of the greater part were as coarse and heavy as their dress; their dogged, stupid, monotonous stare at all the glory and splendour, having something in it, half miserable, and half ridiculous.

Upon the green carpet itself, and gathered round the altar, was a perfect army of cardinals and priests, in red, gold, purple, violet, white, and fine linen. Stragglers from these, went to and fro among the crowd, conversing two and two, or giving and receiving introductions, and exchanging salutations; other functionaries in black gowns, and other functionaries in court dresses, were similarly engaged. In the midst of all these, and stealthy Jesuits creeping in and out, and the extreme restlessness of the Youth of England, who were perpetually wandering

Jean-Auguste-Dominique Ingres, Pontifical Mass in St Peter's, *c. 1832*

about, some few steady persons in black cassocks, who had knelt down with their faces to the wall, and were poring over their missals, became, unintentionally a sort of humane man traps, and with their own devout legs tripped up other people's by the dozen.

There was a great pile of candles lying down on the floor near me, which a very old man in a rusty black gown with an open-work tippet, like a summer ornament for a fireplace in tissue paper, made himself very busy in dispensing to all the ecclesiastics: one apiece. They loitered about with these for some time, under their arms like walking sticks, or in their hands like truncheons. At a certain period of the ceremony, however, each carried his candle up to the Pope [Gregory XVI], laid it across his two knees to be blessed, took it back again, and filed off. This was done in a very attenuated procession, as you may suppose, and occupied a long time. Not because it takes long to bless a candle through and through, but because there were so many candles to be blessed. At last they were all blessed; and then they were all lighted; and then the Pope was taken up, chair and all, and carried round the church.

I must say, that I never saw anything, out of November, so

like the popular English commemoration of the fifth of that month. A bundle of matches and a lantern, would have made it perfect. Nor did the Pope, himself, at all mar the resemblance, though he has a pleasant and venerable face; for, as this part of the ceremony makes him giddy and sick, he shuts his eyes when it is performed: and having his eyes shut, and a great mitre on his head, and his head itself wagging to and fro as they shook him in carrying, he looked as if his mask were going to tumble off. The two immense fans which are always borne, one on either side of him, accompanied him, of course, on this occasion. As they carried him along, he blessed the people with the mystic sign; and as he passed them, they kneeled down. When he had made the round of the church, he was brought back again, and if I am not mistaken, this performance was repeated, in the whole, three times. There was, certainly, nothing solemn or effective in it; and certainly very much that was droll and tawdry. But this remark applies to the whole ceremony, except the raising of the Host, when every man in the guard dropped on one knee instantly, and dashed his naked sword on the ground; which had a fine effect.

The American George Hillard devoted most attention to the papal monuments, and found them wanting: this was 'the Alexandrian age of art'. The form of the tombs was fairly identical: pyramidal, with the pope kneeling, sitting or standing, a sarcophagus with reliefs, flanked with statues: 'Prudence, Justice, Charity and Religion lean, sprawl, or recline; and all endeavour, with more or less of ill success, to do what marble never can do.' No other visitor of the earlier nineteenth century, however, has given us such enthusiastic responses as Florence Nightingale. 'No event in my life,' she declared at the age of twenty-seven, 'except my death can ever be greater than that first entrance into St Peter's, the concentrated spirit of the Christianity of so many years.' On a later visit on a Sunday afternoon, she described the English promenade. Some friends always came then to walk their dog! Another dog came in through the Sacristy door 'and soon a skirmish began, and a stiff canine tow wow'. Most memorable, however, is her ascent to the ball.

I have been up the dome of St Peter's with the good-natured old [Henry] Colyar, as X [Selina, Mrs Bracebridge, her companion] did not wish to go. I went thinking it was to be a sight, and sight seeing, you know, I abaw, but oh that mighty shrine, I have dreamed of nothing else since. And to begin, we went up the steps, I in a rage all the way because they were all lined with inscriptions commemorating the event that this crowned head and that, onorò la basilica Vaticana in such and such a year with his presence – honoured St Peter's, honoured M. Angelo! Can the human love of baseness and slavery any further go? – but it is a passionate love, we all know – so let that pass. We reached the roof, and here we saw other parties of English going up, so my dear old friend would not let me go, but kept me on the roof, till the plagues of Egypt had passed by – and when I saw what it was when we did go up, I was very glad he had done so. So we walked up and down behind the cloud of witnesses on the roof, that little heavenly city – and then we walked along the top of the great golden roof of the nave, which lies there like a long back of some sleeping leviathan, and is so thick that even if the wooden roof above were to burn, it could not. He opened a trap door to shew me its thickness, and the dome is 2 feet thicker – and through this little hole we looked down upon the pavement of the church itself – worlds below us it seemed, but that was nothing.

Presently we began to mount, and came out upon the first gallery in the dome, below the great oblong windows, and we walked slowly round it. I looked down, and I saw a world, an earth in the far distance, little figures as it were men, kneeling and praying, and their priests standing between them and every altar – and I saw glow-worms round St Peter's shrine, but no sound came up to me – and it seemed to me as if I had flown up from the earth, and the world had passed away, and I looked up and saw the Padre Eterno – above our heads – and it took away all power of thought – my mind was too much out of breath to speak to me, and all it could say was Sancte Michael Angele, ora pro nobis – as Erasmus did of Socrates.

Then we went up to the second gallery, above that range

of windows, where the dome begins to spring. And here it seemed as if we were at once in the company of heaven – all those Angels and Archangels, and the Apostles, and the little Cherubim and Seraphim and all the host of heaven – and just below them, in the lunettes, those beautiful Mosaics of the Doctors of the Church all looking up. No Jewish woman going up to her first passover at Jerusalem ever felt a deeper and more awful conviction of the presence of God there than this, the greatest offering of the greatest Christian genius, inspires. And again I thought that architecture was perhaps the worthiest tribute – (because the farthest from actual imitation – which must fall, oh so far short of even our ideal,) from Man to God. The exquisite, the wonderfully beautiful curve of that dome, I should have had no idea of if I had not gone up – it is incomparably elegant – it gives one such an idea of grace and of strength, that it is like one of the works of God himself – surely so beautiful a line was never imagined before. It looks as if it must have been so easy to have made it, because it must have grown so – it was natural for the stones to have formed themselves into that shape, and they must have liked it. But when you look down and see where you are, see that dome resting mid-heaven, only supported by these four arches, and such arches, with their mighty span, then you realize something of the genius which, coming from God, walked upon the winds and planted its temple there. St Peter walked upon the waters, and he fainted and sunk – his courage failed him – why did [not] Michael Angelo. When he placed his dome, let alone, one poor body upon the airs, and looked down and saw the space between him and the earth, he neither trembled nor shook, but left his daring flight a wonder and an inspiration to all the nations of the world. He laid the beams of God's chambers in the airs, and if he was afraid, we have not seen it.

We went up another story, and looked into the lantern, and up at the Padre Eterno – and then we came out upon the little gallery *outside* round the lantern, and seemed to look upon all Italy – and the lovely windings of the Tiber, and Soracte no longer lone, but the last pearl of the string of the Apennines – and no sound of pain or pleasure came up from the mighty land, nothing but the plashing of the Eternal fountains – as we stood upon this solitary witness, making the clouds its chariot, we did seem flapped by the wings of the wind, which hold up this mighty emblem of the Unseen, and we were obliged to go in.

We went up to the top of the little tent above the lantern, and then the Colyar asked me if I would go into the ball. I was a little frightened, I own, and when I got up I thought nothing on earth would get me down again, but I thought it would be disrespectful to M. Angelo not to see all that he had built to show us – so I scrambled up a perpendicular iron ladder which goes, you know, through the neck of the ball, and where there is not room to put your hands on each side of the ladder so you must hold on to the step above you – and I stood in the ball itself – just under the highest cross, the emblem of our earthly faith, which has been raised the nearest heaven in the world. Can a human soul ever forget such a moment? My dear old patient friend let me walk round both galleries again (in the inside of the dome) as we came down, and, unwearied ever, waited till I had done, or at least till I was ashamed of not having done, and took me out upon a ledge which, you know, runs all round the church just below where the golden roof of the nave begins. It coasts along under the Evangelists which occupy the 4 corners (?) of the dome – and there I saw the enormous scale they were upon – all the little jewels in the tiara (and keys under) were enormous bumps, and the pen in St Matthew's hand was 6 feet long – and yet when I looked across at St John opposite, so beautiful is the effect of the Mosaic at a distance, so perfect the proportions of the dome, that I could not persuade myself he was companion to the one I was standing under – not all one's reason can convince one – the pieces of Mosaic look like Wooden pavement bits – both here and in the dome.[12]

One wonders what she was wearing while making this daring climb.

Andrew Wilson, S Giovanni in Laterano, *first half of nineteenth century, showing the great basilica still surrounded by the campagna, with the Aurelianic wall to the south*

Elisa von der Recke in 1805 was struck by the desolation of the area surrounding S GIOVANNI IN LATERANO, but was also delighted with the view of the aqueducts and tombs. Pasquin was most impressed with the ceiling: 'one of the most splendid known'. The figures of the twelve apostles were not clothed but draped, 'and they could not take a step without this covering falling to the ground'! The story still circulated of the four bronze columns of the Chapel of the Holy Sacrament being made from vessels captured at the battle of Actium between Antony and Octavian. Most impressed of all was Florence Nightingale: 'What a pomp of platform... The inside is the most brilliant interpretation of Christianity one ever saw.' No one, however, brought more historical reality to this place than the Swiss, Jean George Mallet de Hauteville:

from the palace the impetuous Innocent III launches his thunderbolts on almost all the contemporary princes and fills France with blood; Gregory IX and Innocent IV follow his example: from the court set out the legates who levy taxes on nations, who interfere in the quarrels of kings, halt the march of their armies, and set out for sovereigns the conduct they must adopt; from Rome depart the decrees which dispose of thrones which are not at all vacant, which undo the subject of their sermons, and which renders the monarch an object of horror in the eyes of his people.[13]

It was also, he noted, the seat of no fewer than five councils.

Another picture of desolation surrounded s PAOLO. Elisa von der Recke never had such a melancholy impression as on the road here. The air was so bad that the priests had to leave the monastery from July to October, and the country between Rome and Ostia was raided by African pirates. The basilica was frequently flooded. That was in 1805. Pasquin more than twenty years later observed the rebuilding

Luigi Rossini, S Paolo after the fire, *1823*

after the basilica's destruction by fire in 1823. He regretted the enormous expense in this desert which would, he thought, result in only a poor substitute, while the old basilica would have made a superb ruin![14]

S MARIA MAGGIORE produced mixed reactions in Florence Nightingale: 'its gay and merry front crowning the laughing Esquiline, the most cheerful of all the churches – and inside, its long perspective of columns, with the beautiful sober harmony of its colouring. There is such a brilliancy about the outside that it makes amends for the bad taste.'[15]

Following the basilicas, the other churches may be mentioned in order. Pasquin praised the sculpture of SANTA BIBIANA in her church by Bernini: 'one of the most pleasing modern sculptures... before he took so much trouble to do badly' (*sic*). Pasquin, later the royal librarian, was a very religious man, and he took more trouble than most others to comment on the churches; his notes will be often quoted. About the GESÙ he told an amusing story. The area was very windy. This was explained by the fact that the Devil and the Wind were walking here together and the former said: 'I have something to do in there, wait for me.' And the Wind has been waiting ever since. This story came shortly after the restoration of the Jesuits in 1814. In S GREGORIO on the Cælian, Washington Irving recorded the fine frescoes, Domenichino's *Flagellation of St Andrew*, and Reni's *Crucifixion* of the same, although he noted that they were much damaged by damp. That attitude was epitomised by Florence Nightingale:

> my favourite S Gregorio, which looks so merry and proud at the top of its never ending flight of steps, fronting the gay and laughing Palatine, with generally a Benedictine in his nice clean white gown and cowl standing just within this Cortile at the top of the steps. But we did not want to see the Church, only just our favourite Guido in S Agnes's Chapel, (the fresco in the ceiling) of the Gloria and the Padre Eterno, which, always excepting the Sistine, I had rather see than anything else in Rome, and X thinks it has not its compeer. Oh how often I shall see it floating by in a summer evening – for though none of the colours are precisely those of clouds, yet the whole effect

Bartolomeo Pinelli, S Gregorio Magno, c. 1820

is that of a sunset glory. With every possible disadvantage – all the angels have instruments, and the very notes of music (from which they are playing) are hanging over the Orchestra – there is not a material idea connected with it. The Eternal Father looks like a vision of Omnipotence floating by, which will be gone in a moment, and has only just tarried for an instant to bless.

At S IGNAZIO, Pasquin was shocked by the grandeur, riches and ornaments. Young women were apparently in the habit of writing to the saint. Longfellow noticed this:

> I saw a large pile of these letters a few weeks ago in Gonzaga's chapel, at the church of St Ignatius. They were lying at the foot of the altar, prettily written on smooth paper, and tied with silken ribands of various colors. Leaning over the marble balustrade, I read the following superscription upon one of them: '*All' Angelico Giovane S Luigi Gonzaga, Paradiso*, – To the angelic youth St Louis Gonzaga, Paradise.' A soldier, with

a musket kept guard over this treasure, and I had the audacity to ask him at what hour the mail went out; for which heretical impertinence he cocked his moustache at me with the most savage look imaginable, as much as to say, 'Get thee gone': –

S MARIA IN ARACŒLI was famous above all for the Bambino, the doll representing Jesus, and Dickens was present when he was displayed to a small group. A monk who had donned a pair of gold gloves lifted down the coffer.

Then, with many genuflexions, and muttering certain prayers, he opened it, and let down the front, and took off sundry coverings of satin and lace from the inside. The ladies had been on their knees from the commencement; and the gentlemen now dropped down devoutly, as he exposed to view, a little wooden doll, in face very like General Tom Thumb, the American Dwarf: gorgeously dressed in satin and gold lace, and actually blazing with rich jewels. There was scarcely a spot upon its little breast, or neck, or stomach, but was sparkling with the costly offerings of the Faithful. Presently, he lifted it out of the box,

The Santo Bambino *(S Maria in Aracœli); nineteenth century woodcut*

and, carrying it round among the kneelers, set its face against the forehead of every one, and tendered its clumsy foot to them to kiss – a ceremony which they all performed, down to a dirty little ragamuffin of a boy who had walked in from the street. When this was done, he laid it in the box again: and the company, rising, drew near, and commended the jewels in whispers. In good time, he replaced the coverings, shut up the box, put it back in its place, locked up the whole concern (Holy Family and all) behind a pair of folding doors; took off his priestly vestments; and received the customary 'small charge', while his companion, by means of an extinguisher fastened to the end of a long stick, put out the lights, one after another. The candles being all extinguished, and the money all collected, they retired, and so did the spectators.

Dickens recorded the varying results of the image's interventions: sometimes frightening the sick to death and sometimes (especially with women in childbirth) performing wonders. Florence Nightingale recorded the other thing for which the church was memorable, the preaching of children in December.

[T]o hear the little children preach – four we heard – the first, a little girl, was a miniature compendium, a diamond Edition of the preacher at the Gesù, (you never saw any thing so droll.) gests, inflections of voice, everything – she said her lesson quite perfectly, very distinctly, without fear, and yet apparently without vanity – the matter was common place enough, but her audience was all attention. The second was very shy, and not a word was audible, but it was the prettiest picture – the mother who brought her, stood behind, her hands clasped, her eyes raised, every feature strained with anxiety, and yet with a sort of reverence for her child who was to preach to the multitude, evidently praying to God for her. I longed to get through the crowd to her, and tell her that her child had said the best, but there was such a crowd I could not. Then came another little fearless thing, and the contrast between her proud father, and the last mother was curious. The last was a little boy about 5,

Antoine Thomas, Children Preaching in S Maria del Popolo, *c. 1817*

who said his with real dignity – they were all dressed in their
own dirty clothes – the church was crowded with children.

The Capucchin cemetery in s MARIA DELLA CONCEZIONE on via
Veneto had its macabre fascination. Montcashell in 1804 stated that
a visit required papal permission. A year later Kotzebue urged every
visitor not to neglect 'these last retreats of humanity'. It is Nightingale
also who gives the most detailed reaction to Raphael's famous Sibyls
in s MARIA DELLA PACE:

> I have now seen these Sibyls twice, they are lovely, passing lovely
> in their faces. You cannot conceive of anything so exquisite as
> the colouring and grouping of them – the grace of the figures
> is beyond anything I ever saw but you cannot get beyond the
> picture, the art – you do not realize the people, and you never
> speak of them as anything but a picture. *Du reste,* they have a

John White Abbott, Study after Raphael's Sibyls in S Maria della Pace, *c. 1805*

great deal more of the old Grecian grace of Guido than of the virgin earnestness of Raphael. You would never fancy them inspired women, even the angels hovering over them might be Amorini, and one of the Sybils even looks discontented that she does not know more. But no description can do justice to the glory of the colouring.

The most controversial sculpture in any church remained Bernini's *Santa Teresa* (see ill. Vol. II) in s MARIA DELLA VITTORIA. Elisa von der Recke preferred not to speak of her: there was 'no sign of saintliness to be seen'. A rival of Santa Teresa was Michelangelo's *Moses* (see ill. Vol. II) in s PIETRO IN VINCOLI. Elisa von der Recke implied that the sculptor's supremacy was now challenged by Canova, but Pasquin judged the tomb of Julius II 'the most important created by modern art': Moses' clothing was wrong, but the anatomy of the statue was equal to that of the Laocoön. Franz Liszt similarly found the sculpture 'sublime. Sculptors reproach him (Michelangelo) with many things, but the impression he creates is simply prodigious.' Florence Nightingale's reactions, however, were on the whole negative.

How you honour this inspiration in Moses – can this be the man who shrunk back, who said he was slow of speech, who was loath to be chosen of the Lord, – how altered he is, how a life of action may change the very nature of a man, reverse the very leopard's spots. And yet for all this, it is not interesting to me. I feel only surprise. It looks much better however, if you conceal those horrid horns which, you know, come entirely from a mistranslation in the Vulgate – the same word in the Hebrew signifying 'shinings' and 'horns', the Vulgate makes it 'Et ignorabat quod *cornuta* esset facies sua,' which we have 'And he wist not that the skin of his face *shone*.' It is very disgusting to be so unmoved by what all the world so reverences – one is afraid that one's power of appreciation is becoming exhausted.

S STEFANO ROTONDO was infamous for its frescoes, which generally called forth Protestant revulsion. Dickens will suffice:

a damp mildewed vault of an old church in the outskirts of Rome, will always struggle uppermost in my mind, by reason of the hideous paintings with which its walls are covered. These represent the martyrdoms of saints and early Christians; and such a panorama of horror and butchery no man could imagine in his sleep, though he were to eat a whole pig, raw, for supper. Grey bearded men being boiled, fried, grilled, crimped, singed, eaten by wild beasts, worried by dogs, buried alive, torn asunder by horses, chopped up small with hatchets: women having their breasts torn with iron pincers, their tongues cut out, their ears screwed off, their jaws broken, their bodies stretched upon the rack, or skinned upon the stake, or crackled up and melted in the fire: these are among the mildest subjects. So insisted on, and laboured at, besides, that every sufferer gives you the same occasion for wonder as poor old Duncan awoke, in Lady Macbeth, when she marvelled at his having so much blood in him.[16]

In conclusion, some general notes are occasionally offered. When Kotzebue was in Rome 1804-5, he commented on the last years of old habits before the French occupation enforced new standards of hygiene in matters such as cemeteries and abattoirs. There were two hundred and fifty churches and thirteen basilicas: 'there is a stench of putrid bodies in every one' (some were not even placed in coffins, he stated, because of a shortage of wood). The most extended comment comes from Dickens:

> The scene in all the churches is the strangest possible. The same monotonous, heartless, drowsy chaunting, always going on; the same dark building, darker from the brightness of the street without; the same lamps dimly burning; the self-same people kneeling here and there; turned towards you, from one altar or other, the same priest's back, with the same large cross embroidered on it; however different in size, in shape, in wealth, in architecture, this church is from that, it is the same thing still. There are the same dirty beggars stopping in their muttered prayers to beg; the same miserable cripples exhibiting their deformity at the doors; the same blind men, rattling little pots like kitchen pepper castors, their depositories for alms; the same preposterous crowns of silver stuck upon the painted heads of single saints and Virgins in crowded pictures, so that a little figure on a mountain has a head dress bigger than the temple in the foreground, or adjacent miles of landscape; the same favourite shrine or figure, smothered with little silver hearts and crosses, and the like: the staple trade and show of all the jewellers; the same odd mixture of respect and indecorum, faith and phlegm: kneeling on the stones, and spitting on them, loudly; getting up from prayers to beg a little, or to pursue some other worldly matter: and then kneeling down again, to resume the contrite supplication at the point where it was interrupted. In one church, a kneeling lady got up from her prayers, for a moment, to offer us her card, as a teacher of Music; and in another, a sedate gentleman with a very thick walking staff, arose from his devotions to belabour his dog, who was growling at another dog: and whose yelps and howls resounded through the church, as his master quietly relapsed into his former trains of meditation – keeping his eye upon the dog, at the same time, nevertheless.[17]

Discounting his English prejudices, there is still many an accurate

Antoine Thomas, Disabled and paralysed people lying outside a wall of the cemetery
Santo Spirito in Rome begging for alms from passers-by, *1823*

picture here of both atmosphere and individuals. In general, however,
there is a notable decline in insightful comments about churches in
the nineteenth century in comparison with earlier times.

Visitors described many ECCLESIASTICAL FESTIVALS. English affection
for animals made ST ANTHONY'S DAY (17 January) and the blessing of
the horses always a favourite. The ceremony of sprinkling them with
holy water was done by Camaldolese monks.

> On Sunday afternoon was the blessing of the Papal horses at St
> Antonio, behind Sta. Maria Maggiore. X. and I walked there,
> very much preferring to see it as *one* of the crowd – which
> filled all that great Piazza. It was very pretty, the Camaldolese
> all in white (with his great red brush) raised 2 or 3 steps above
> that immense crowd – he was flanked on either side by a pink
> bonnet – and the horses galloping in from the Campagna,
> either ridden or in a little Carritelle. I never laughed so

much – the horse had nothing on but his hat and shoe strings, no bridle nor sort of saddle – the favourite head dress was a pheasant's tail stuck in his ear, if of the very jaunty kind – if of the dignified, a bunch of cock's plumes sticking right out of the top of his head. Tie up my tail with ribbons rare, and my toilette was completed – my tail was generally wound like a swaddled baby with pink ribbons and terminated near the root with a handsome satin knot, but if this was unattainable, an elegant, but not expensive, tail was obtained by painting it with a graceful corkscrew of pink, yellow and white stripes of *ruddle* – the brush being wiped upon the ribs to carry the colour and complete the effect – so that the animal resembled those little wooden performances in the windows of Romsey High St which are supposed to receive the ultimate likeness to a horse by dashes of scarlet and white paint on the sides – which, speaking of *traditional* likenesses, (my study of late) is a circumstance of great importance for determining the first type of horse under Adam.

We arrived just in the nick of time to see the 42 Papal horses drive up, 5 carriages and 6, three carriages and 4, all black of course – but where the white mule was, unless he was inside, I could not see – perhaps he is so good that he does not want blessing. The horses were so delighted with themselves that they galloped down that steep hill from S Maria Maggiore to the Quirinal after the blessing to the infinite terror of the postilions, who each the size of a Mrs Lockhart, will be in bed for a week I should think with that jolting. The coachmen and footmen were of a corresponding size, and each seemed to have got into somebody else's coat, for the tails barely reached to the middles of their waists – and looked as if they were pulled out once in 300 years for some such occasion as this. But away trotted the horses regardless of every thing but the proverb that even the horse shall have its day, and quite con[s]cious that this was the day of St Antonio, the day for horses and not for men.[18]

The central event of the Church calendar was EASTER. Anne Louise de Staël in 1805: 'I have just spent three days almost constantly in

John Frederick Lewis, Easter in Rome, *1840*

church. I liked the music very much, also the illuminated cross, the sombre vaults, everything which is vague and undefined like lofty religious thoughts; but the ceremonies of washing of feet, the processions of the Holy Supper, have not affected me at all. All this becomes a spectacle and is judged as such.' Jeanne Récamier informs us that during the French occupation and the absence of the pope (1809-14), Holy Week was not celebrated in the Sistine Chapel, but only in St Peter's. Dickens counselled visitors to avoid Rome at Easter: 'The ceremonies are, in general, of the most tedious and wearisome kind; the heat and crowd at every one of them, painfully oppressive; the noise, hubbub, and confusion, quite distracting.' Honoré de Balzac in 1846 found that there were 50,000 foreigners at Rome for Easter, and all wanted to leave at the same time: the roads were impassable.[19]

Theodor Mommsen in 1845 found PALM SUNDAY horrible. 'The palms are interwoven with straw, not green as one imagines, and without any taste, like everything, clothing, behaviour etc. The voices of the castrati are intolerable.' The ceremony of the washing of the Apostles' feet on EASTER THURSDAY had always featured in travellers' accounts, but few had the eye of Dickens:

I think the most popular and most crowded sight (excepting those of Easter Sunday and Monday, which are open to all classes of people) was the Pope washing the feet of Thirteen men, representing the twelve apostles, and Judas Iscariot. The place in which this pious office is performed, is one of the chapels of St Peter's, which is gaily decorated for the occasion; the thirteen sitting 'all of a row', on a very high bench, and looking particularly uncomfortable, with the eyes of Heaven knows how many English, French, Americans, Swiss, Germans, Russians, Swedes, Norwegians, and other foreigners, nailed to their faces all the time. They are robed in white; and on their heads they wear a stiff white cap, like a large English porter-pot, without a handle. Each carries in his hand, a nosegay, of the size of a fine cauliflower; and two of them, on this occasion, wore spectacles: which, remembering the characters they sustained, I thought a droll appendage to the costume. There was a great eye to character. St John was represented by a good-looking young man. St Peter, by a grave looking old gentleman, with a flowing brown beard; and Judas Iscariot by such an enormous hypocrite (I could not make out, though, whether the expression of his face was real or assumed) that if he had acted the part to the death and had gone away and hanged himself, he would have left nothing to be desired.

As the two large boxes, appropriated to ladies, at this sight, were full to the throat, and getting near was hopeless, we posted off, along with a great crowd, to be in time at the Table, where the Pope, in person, waits on these Thirteen; and after a prodigious struggle at the Vatican staircase, and several personal conflicts with the Swiss guard, the whole crowd swept into the room. It was a long gallery hung with drapery of white and red, with another great box for ladies (who are obliged to dress in black at these ceremonies, and to wear black veils), a royal box for the King of Naples, and his party; and the table itself, which, set out like a ball supper, and ornamented with golden figures of the real apostles, was arranged on an elevated platform on one side of the gallery. The counterfeit apostles' knives and forks were laid out on that side of the table which was nearest to the wall, so that they might be stared at again, without let or hindrance.

The body of the room was full of male strangers; the crowd immense; the heat very great; and the pressure sometimes frightful. It was at its height when the stream came pouring in, from the feet washing; and then there were such shrieks and outcries, that a party of Piedmontese dragoons went to the rescue of the Swiss guard, and helped them to calm the tumult.

The ladies were particularly ferocious, in their struggles for places. One lady of my acquaintance was seized round the waist, in the ladies' box, by a strong matron, and hoisted out of her place; and there was another lady (in the back row in the same box) who improved her position by sticking a large pin into the ladies before her.

The gentlemen about me were remarkably anxious to see what was on the table; and one Englishman seemed to have embarked the whole energy of his nature in the determination to discover whether there was any mustard. 'By Jupiter there's vinegar!' I heard him say to his friend, after he had stood on tiptoe an immense time, and had been crushed and beaten on all sides. 'And there's oil!! I saw them distinctly, in cruets! Can any gentleman, in front there, see mustard on the table? Sir, will you oblige me! *Do* you see a Mustard Pot?'

The apostles and Judas appearing on the platform, after much expectation, were marshalled, in line, in front of the table, with Peter at the top; and a good long stare was taken at them by the company, while twelve of them took a long smell at their nosegays, and Judas – moving his lips very obtrusively – engaged in inward prayer. Then, the Pope [Gregory XVI], clad in a scarlet robe, and wearing on his head a skull cap of white satin, appeared in the midst of a crowd of Cardinals and other dignitaries, and took in his hand a little golden ewer, from which he poured a little water over one of Peter's hands, while one attendant held a golden basin; a second, a fine cloth; a third, Peter's nosegay, which was taken from him during the operation. This His Holiness performed, with considerable expedition, on every man in the line (Judas, I observed, to be particularly overcome by his condescension); and then the whole Thirteen sat down to dinner. Grace said by the Pope. Peter in the chair. There was white wine, and red wine; and the dinner looked very good. The courses appeared in portions, one for each apostle; and these being presented to the Pope, by Cardinals upon their knees, were by him handed to the Thirteen. The manner in which Judas grew more white-livered over his victuals, and languished, with his head on one side, as if he had no appetite, defies all description. Peter was a good, sound, old man, and went in, as the saying is, 'to win'; eating everything that was given him (he got the best: being first in the row) and saying nothing to anybody. The dishes appeared to be chiefly composed of fish and vegetables. The Pope helped the Thirteen to wine also; and, during the whole dinner, somebody read something aloud, out of a large book – the Bible, I presume – which nobody could hear, and to which nobody paid the least attention. The Cardinals, and other attendants, smiled to each other, from time to time, as if the thing were a great farce; and if they thought so, there is little doubt they were perfectly right. His Holiness did what he had to do, as a sensible man gets through a troublesome ceremony, and seemed very glad when it was all over.[20]

GOOD FRIDAY was the day of the *Miserere*. Elisa von der Recke described the whole event in 1805. It commenced about five in the afternoon with very simple hymns sung by a high alto and a bass. Then came psalms, half-recited, half-sung, and between each, a candle was extinguished until only the dusk was visible through the high windows. This was followed by a deep silence for a few moments, until a voice which seemed celestial intoned the *Miserere* sweetly in crescendo, with other voices gradually joining in. Jeanne Récamier, who was present in 1813 during the last year of the French occupation, vouchsafes us the information that during the performance that year the Chief of Police, Jacques Norvins (see p. 145), broke out into sobs. Dickens described the confusion caused by having a heavy curtain in the doorway of the Sistine chapel and the vast crowding. Balzac at the same time declared that the *Miserere* of St Peter's was so superior to that of the Sistine that he went to hear it twice, once conducted by the maestro di cappella Pietro Guglielmi ('music of the angels') and once by his colleague Valentino Fioravanti ('a scholarly performance').[21] EASTER SUNDAY was marked by the papal benediction and the illumination of St Peter's. Emerson gives the best description of the former, in 1833, under Gregory XVI:

> At twelve o'clock the benediction was given. A canopy was hung over the great window that is above the principal door of St Peter's, and there sat the Pope. The troops were all under arms and in uniform in the piazza below, and all Rome and much of England and Germany and France and America was gathered there also. The great bell of the church tolled, drums beat, and trumpets sounded over the vast congregation.
>
> Presently, at a signal, there was silence, and a book was brought to the Pope, out of which he read a moment and then rose and spread out his hands and blessed the people. All knelt as one man. He repeated his action (for no words could be heard), stretching his arms gracefully to the north and south and east and west, pronouncing a benediction on the whole world. It was a sublime spectacle. Then sounded drums and trumpets, then rose the people, and everyone went his way.

For the illuminations we turn again to Dickens, in 1845:

> But, when the night came on, without a cloud to dim the full moon, what a sight it was to see the Great Square full once more, and the whole church, from the cross to the ground, lighted with innumerable lanterns, tracing out the architecture, and winking and shining all round the colonnade of the piazza! And what a sense of exultation, joy, delight, it was, when the great bell struck half past seven – on the instant – to behold one bright red mass of fire, soar gallantly from the top of the cupola to the extremest summit of the cross, and the moment it leaped into its place, become the signal of a bursting out of countless lights, as great, and red, and blazing as itself, from every part of the gigantic church; so that every cornice, capital, and smallest ornament of stone, expressed itself in fire: and the

Unknown artist, St Peter's Basilica and square lit up by torches, *c. 1830-1850*

black solid groundwork of the enormous dome, seemed to grow transparent as an egg shell!

A train of gunpowder, and electric chain – nothing could be fired, more suddenly and swiftly, than this second illumination; and when we had got away, and gone upon a distant height, and looked towards it two hours afterwards, there it still stood, shining and glittering in the calm night like a Jewel! Not a line of its proportions wanting; not an angle blunted; not an atom of its radiance lost.

The next night – Easter Monday – there was a great display of fireworks from the Castle of St Angelo. We hired a room in an opposite house, and made our way to our places, in good time, through a dense mob of people choking up the square in front, and all the avenues leading to it; and so loading the bridge by which the castle is approached, that it seemed ready to sink into the rapid Tiber below. There are statues on this bridge (execrable works) [Bernini's Angels!] and, among them, great vessels full of burning tow were placed: glaring strangely on the faces of the crowd, and not less strangely on the stone counterfeits above them.

The show began with a tremendous discharge of cannon; and then, for twenty minutes, or half an hour, the whole castle was one incessant sheet of fire, and labyrinth of blazing wheels of every colour, size, and speed: while rockets streamed into the sky, not by ones or twos, or scores, but hundreds at a time. The concluding burst – the Girandola – was like the blowing up into the air, of the whole massive castle, without smoke or dust.

In half an hour afterwards, the immense concourse had dispersed; the moon was looking calmly down upon her wrinkled image in the river; and half a dozen men and boys, with bits of lighted candle in their hands: moving here and there, in search of anything worth having, that might have been dropped in the press: had the whole scene to themselves.[22]

A CHRISTMAS celebration is described at S Maria Maggiore by Elisa von der Recke in 1804:

At midnight the church is opened to the crowd of impatient pilgrims. Three chandeliers and a few scattered lamps attached to the top of the columns spread a soft light in the vast building, similar to dusk, and the crowd which moves in all directions seems like wandering shadows. Everything moves: the 'beau monde' elegantly dressed, ecclesiastics of different orders, variously dressed, country folk in their coarse and simple clothes, and the beggars in rags. The spectacle changes continually and lasts until three in the morning. Then the processions begin, men and women converse in loud voices; the tired pilgrims sleep scattered among the high marble columns; those who are hungry and thirsty eat and drink; the penitents in the open confessionals obtain absolution for their sins; strangers observe and painters take advantage of this mélange, choosing groups for sketches.

Finally the solemn march begins; the crucifix is carried from altar to altar; the cardinals in all their pomp; the prelates and priests follow. The cross rises very high, everyone kneels, then the crucifix returns to the sacristy. Soon after the spectacle of the crib begins with the same solemnities. The infant Jesus in a crib, radiating glory, stretches out his little hand and gives the blessing, a great murmur of joy goes up, and the multitude swirls in the beautiful church until nine in the morning.[23]

The CATACOMBS continued their morbid fascination. Julia Howe on her first visit to Rome 1843-4 was guided through S Callisto by 'Padre Machi' (sic). This was Giuseppe Marchi (1795-1860), a Jesuit who was 'Conservatore dei cimiteri sotterranei' and who directed excavations at S Agnese and S Callisto. The usual stories were told of parties being lost, even though, in one case, a musical band was sent in in the hope of guiding them to safety. A mischievous youth picked his mark, saying to Julia 'Has it ever occurred to you that if our guide should suddenly die here of apoplexy, we should never be able to find our way out?' The most commonly visited catacomb remained, of course, S Sebastiano. Once again Dickens gives us the most memorable picture:

A gaunt Franciscan friar, with a wild bright eye, was our only guide, down into this profound and dreadful place. The narrow ways and openings hither and thither, coupled with the dead and heavy air, soon blotted out, in all of us, any recollection of the track by which we had come; and I could not help thinking, 'Good Heaven, if, in a sudden fit of madness he should dash the torches out, or if he should be seized with a fit, what would become of us!' On we wandered, among martyrs' graves: passing great subterranean vaulted roads, diverging in all directions, and choked up with heaps of stones, that thieves and murderers may not take refuge there, and form a population under Rome, even worse than that which lives between it and the sun. Graves, graves, graves; graves of men, of women, of their little children, who ran crying to the persecutors, 'We are Christians! We are Christians!' that they might be murdered with their parents; Graves with the palm of martyrdom roughly

Entrance to the Catacombs of S Sebastiano, in a magazine illustration of 1849

cut into their stone boundaries, and little niches, made to hold a vessel of the martyrs' blood; Graves of some who lived down here, for years together, ministering to the rest, and preaching truth, and hope, and comfort, from the rude altars, that bear witness to their fortitude at this hour; more roomy graves, but far more terrible, where hundreds, being surprised, were hemmed in and walled up: buried before Death, and killed by slow starvation[!].

'The Triumphs of the Faith are not above ground in our splendid churches,' said the friar, looking round upon us, as we stopped to rest in one of the low passages, with bones and dust surrounding us on every side. 'They are here! Among the Martyrs' Graves!' He was a gentle, earnest man, and said it from his heart; but when I thought how Christian men have dealt with one another; how, perverting our most merciful religion, they have hunted down and tortured, burnt and beheaded, strangled, slaughtered, and oppressed each other; I pictured to myself an agony surpassing any that this Dust had suffered

with the breath of life yet lingering in it, and how these great
and constant hearts would have been shaken – how they would
have quailed and drooped – if a fore knowledge of the deeds
that professing Christians would commit in the Great Name
for which they died, could have rent them with its own unutterable anguish, on the cruel wheel, and bitter cross, and in
the fearful fire.

Florence Nightingale and a female companion insisted intrepidly in
'making another little turn' by themselves, which they did, armed with
candles. She commented on the clearing of these tombs for saints' bones
and coyly asked the old Dominican with her if she could obtain any.
'You must go to the custodian of Sant'Apollinare; write the name of
the saint you want. There are some of all kinds.' Guided by Padre
Marchi, Florence also visited S Agnese fuori le mura, and her extended
commentary obviously reflects his views. There was a separate entrance
for men and women – who knew what wickedness the darkness might
conceal among the faithful. The catacombs originated in quarries for
sand and tufa. The Christians lived in the upper levels, worshipped and
were buried on the second or third levels. A scratched palm indicated
the grave of a martyr, Marchi stated. Florence brought away several
bones, including the knee of a child. Depictions of the saints showed
them with arms raised in adoration: Marchi explained that this meant
that they were not to be worshipped. He also claimed that men and
women attended services on opposite sides of the passageway.[24]

PALACES

Visitors often continued to be critical of the great Roman palaces.
Augustus von Kotzebue warned: 'We must expect a great deal of
trash, for the great families here are contented with one or two good
pieces in a room and are indifferent as to all the rest.' Antoine Pasquin described the common features as windows grilled like prisons, unwashed marble stairs, columns covered in cobwebs, the

Room in the Palazzo Borghese, in a magazine illustration of 1847

antechamber on the first floor containing a huge baldaquin carved with the family arms, dirty servants – who sometimes knew a lot about the art works – brick floors, horrible furniture, and the total absence of flowers, in short, 'monuments to vanished glory'. George Hillard said much the same and summed up: 'A melancholy air of decay and neglect hangs over the scene. Broken windows, dilapidated furniture, tarnished gilding, niches without statues, spaces on the wall where once were pictures, betray to the hasty glance the forlorn condition of the impoverished nobleman.' It is, then, striking that James Fenimore Cooper raised a protest. The traveller

gets to be too critical in his distinctions to satisfy even himself. Thus, the English cockney, who has never seen a house with more than two drawing rooms, fancies it extraordinary that an Italian, with a palace larger than St James's, should not always occupy its state apartments, although his own king is guilty of the same act of neglect. Instead of saying that the Princes Doria, Chigi, Borghese, Colonna, Corsini, &c. have vast palaces like George IV and that their state apartments are liberally thrown open to the public, while, like King George and all other kings, they occupy, in every day life, rooms of less pretension and of more comfort, they say, that these Roman nobles have huge palaces, – a fact that cannot be denied, – while they live in corners of them. This false account of the real state of the case arises simply from the circumstance that an English nobleman occupies *his* best rooms. The question whether the second rate rooms of an Italian palace are not equal to the best apartments of an ordinary English dwelling, never suggests itself.[25]

As usual, where the work remains in the named collection it will be asterisked, and where present but different locations are known they will be indicated, but that is often hard, given the predilection of the owners to ascribe as many works as possible to artists such as Raphael, many of which are now reassigned. At the PALAZZO BARBERINI Washington Irving in 1805 stated that many of the best paintings had been sold, but he most liked *Reni's *Magdalen* (see ill. Vol. II) 'the countenance mild and gentle, the eyes cast up to heaven with an expression of languor – of grief – of devotion, rapture etc that gives an indescribable interest in it'. Pasquin revealed his profession as a librarian by his interests here: the library contained 50,000 volumes and one thousand Greek manuscripts, drawings by Sangallo, twenty manuscripts of Dante, a French translation by Guyot Desmoulins of Pierre Cornestor's *Scolastica Historia super Novum Testamentum* (1473), an eleventh century Exultet, letters of Bembo, Galileo, Pieresc, Bellarmine, and correspondence of English catholics with Urban VIII, and volumes with scholia by the Manutii, Giuseppe Scaliger, Lucas Holsten, David Hoerschel, and especially Tasso. The first librarian had been Leone Allacci (d. 1689); the current one was Rizzi. The young German classicist Theodor Mommsen found the *Fornarina* 'not beautiful, the expression of the head very unpleasant, absolutely without Raphael's nobility', but praised Titian's Paul I – presumably *Paul III* (see ill. Vol. I) – Dürer's *Mago*, and what he liked best, *Beatrice Cenci* for the 'most beautiful expression of the melancholy girl'. Mommsen rejected Reni's authorship of the last, and it is now attributed to Elizabetta

'Guido Reni's Beatrice Cenci', in a magazine illustration of 1849

Sirani. The same painting alone captured Dickens' attention:

> She has suddenly turned towards you; and there is an expression
> in the eyes – although they are very tender and gentle – as if
> the wildness of a momentary terror, or distraction, had been
> struggled with and overcome, that instant; and nothing but a
> celestial hope, and a beautiful sorrow, and a desolate helpless-
> ness remained.

Hillard was another who did not care for the *Fornarina*: 'The eyes
are black and bright, and the countenance has some animal beauty,
but an expression the reverse of elevated or intellectual. The arms and
bosom are beautifully and carefully painted, but it is not a pleasing
work, nor does it represent an attractive person.'[26]

William Hazlitt declared that the PALAZZO BORGHESE contained
three fine pictures – and only three: *Domenichino's *Diana and
Actæon* (see ill. Vol. II), *Raphael's *Descent from the Cross*, and *Titian's
Sacred and Profane Love. Pasquin recorded that the palace was called
'il cembalo' (the harpsichord) from its shape. Of the paintings he
listed *Garofalo's *Descent from the Cross*, *Domenichino's *Diana and
Actæon* ('eternally copied'), *Veronese's *St Anthony preaching to the
fishes* and **St John in the desert*, *Raphael's *Deposition*, Rubens'

Visitation, Giorgione's *David*, *Titian's *Return of the Prodigal*, **Sacred and Profane Love*, and *Three Graces*, del Sarto's *Holy Family*, *Bellini's *Virgin and Child*, and Correggio's *Dance*.[27] Hillard described the palace in the late 1840s as very attractive:

> The Palazzo Borghese, a building of immense size, contains the finest private collection of pictures in Rome, upwards of six hundred in number, distributed through nine apartments on the ground floor. The public are freely admitted, for several hours of every day, to view the collection, and artists are allowed to make copies. In short, every visitor, of decent appearance and decent behavior, can get as much satisfaction out of these pictures as the owner himself. The Borghese family is still rich, and the suite of apartments devoted to the collection is taken good care of.

Hillard reduced Hazlitt's choice to one: 'the gem of this collection is the *Entombment of Christ*, by Raphael, painted by him in his twenty-fourth year'. He admitted, however, that judgements varied, with some finding it 'stiff and feeble, at least in comparison with the artist's later works'.[28] One notes here three separate titles for the same painting by Raphael: Calvary is in the distant top right, so it is not a Deposition, and there is no sign of a tomb.

At the PALAZZO CHIGI, Pasquin in the 1820s listed a Venus, an Apollo, Caravaggio's *John the Baptist drinking at a fountain*, *Garofalo's *Ascension,* Pietro da Cortona's *Guardian Angel*, Guercino's *Flagellation* (Galleria Nazionale), Carracci's *Dead Christ* (Stuttgart), and Rosa's *Poet and Satyr*. The library he described as brilliant, and the librarian was the 'celebrated' Carlo Fea, who showed him round. His study contained piles of brick fragments, of cornices, of inscriptions, all pell-mell on the floor, alongside piles of books, maps, and rolls covered in dust. Pasquin was very touched by the kindness and zeal of Fea, who loaded him with brochures, plans and dissertations.[29]

Of the PALAZZO COLONNA Kotzebue stated that the statues could not claim great attention but that, unlike most other palaces ('fit only for owls to dwell in'), it had a 'truly royal saloon'. That was in 1805. Forty years later, Florence Nightingale painted the same gloomy picture:

In that grand gallery of the Colonna palace, there is scarce a
picture of value remaining – the Cenci is gone to the Barberini – but the Gallery is still the finest coup d'œil of any palace
in Rome, rising by three steps into a sort of regal oratory at the
end which looks upon one of the bridges by which you cross
the river, from every window – a truly princely plan – into the
Colonna gardens on the other side.[30]

Similar problems are revealed at the PALAZZO CORSINI at the foot of
the Janiculum. Elisa von der Recke in 1805 noted that it was unin-
habited, and that she was shown around by the *portiere*, but there
were paintings by Poussin, Rosa, Reni, Titian, Guercino and Carracci.
Twenty years later Hazlitt called the pictures 'another large and indifferent collection. All I can recall worth mentioning are a very sweet
and silvery toned *Herodias* by Guido; a fine landscape by Gaspar
Poussin; an excellent sketch from Ariosto of the Giant Orgagna; and
the *Plague of Milan* by a modern artist, a work of great invention and
judgement.' At the same time Pasquin listed *Guercino's *Ecce Homo*,
Caravaggio's *Virgin*, Fra Bartolomeo's *Holy Family*, Raphael's *Julius II*
(one now in the Uffizi), Titian's *Philip II* (now in Cincinnati), Dürer's
Rabbit, *Reni's *Salome with the head of John the Baptist*, Rubens' *Tiger
Hunt*, a Poussin landscape, and Murillo's *Virgin*.[31]

The gallery in the PALAZZO DORIA received much attention from
Chateaubriand, who provided a lengthy catalogue, but he commented
on few paintings: Claude Lorrain's *Flight into Egypt* ('the calm of the
light is marvellous'), and *Marriage in a Wood* ('perhaps the most
finished work of this great painter'), landscapes of Domenichino
('something remarkable! French eyes have seen best the light of Italy'),
and Rubens' *Diana and Endymion* ('he draws well, but paints badly').
Hazlitt declared that here 'there is nothing remarkable but the two
Claudes, and these are much injured in colour... There are several
Garofalos, which are held in esteem here (not unjustly) and one fine
head by Titian. The Velázquez (*Innocent X*), so much esteemed by
Sir Joshua [Reynolds], is a spirited sketch'! Pasquin singled out also
the two landscapes by Claude and Dürer's *Avarus* (The Greedy Man).
Hans Christian Andersen also provided a lengthy catalogue, but his

comments are jejune in the extreme: in Vasari's *Deposition*, Mary is too young, in Carracci's *Pietà* Christ is too young, and in Breughel's *Four Elements* the naked woman particularly perplexed him. He seemed to like best *Claude's *Flight into Egypt* ('everything is alive').[32]

The sculptures at the PALAZZO FARNESE had been one of its major glories, but they had been transferred to Naples in 1787. In 1805 Elisa von der Recke reported the palace unoccupied, save for a few rooms by the directors of the coach service to Naples. She complained that the architecture of the building was too heavy and the entrance mean. Regarding the Carracci frescoes, 'the lover of fine arts finds there abundant pleasure and the artist an inexhaustible source of study and improvement' was her uninspired observation. At the same time Irving waxed eloquent at the destruction of the Colosseum to build this edifice, but agreed with Recke: 'The palace has at present a melancholy and deserted appearance in the interior.' The collection of antiquities having been removed to Naples, the 'sole object worthy of attention at present' was the fresco, and he particularly liked the procession of Bacchus and Ariadne. In the late 1820s Pasquin found the palace the most beautiful in Rome for good reasons: its pure and proud style, so different from the Florentine rustic style and the Neapolitan and Genoese 'architecture of pomp'; moreover, Paul III did not demolish the Colosseum to build it – rather he appointed Latino Manetti as the first Commissioner of Antiquities to protect the monuments. There was nothing so perfect as the courtyard since the Romans. Mommsen went to see the frescoes with his friend Wilhelm Hentzen: 'the figures are worthy of Raphael, but the composition is much more modest and barely succeeds; he is a dilettante by comparison'.[33]

The great collections at the PALAZZO GIUSTINIANI (via della Dogana Vecchia) had now been dispersed. Kotzebue in 1805 provided some of the background. The palace was now 'a lumber room for antiquarians', with the best pieces sold to Lucien Bonaparte, Napoleon's brother. Vincenzo Pacetti had worked as a restorer for Prince Vincenzo Giustiniani, the last of his line (he was most famous for the restoration of the Barberini *Faun*), and in return asked not for money but for any 'indifferent' head. The Prince knew 'as little about art as a negro', and gave him a head of Apollo, which Pacetti then sold to Lord Bristol for 150 ducats. When Bristol met Giustiniani, he boasted that he had obtained a masterpiece for his collection. Giustiniani was 'almost raving', so Bristol returned it for the sum which he had paid. Kotzebue should be credited for finally specifying the basic centuries-old problem: 'in this gallery, as indeed everywhere in Rome, they give what names (of artists) they please to pictures'.[34]

At the PALAZZO ROSPIGLIOSI on the Quirinal there were still things to be seen. Elisa von der Recke in 1805 judged the most valued antiquities to be the bust of Scipio Africanus (in green basalt) and frescoes from the Baths of Constantine. Reni's *Aurora* in the garden pavillion continued to be celebrated. Hazlitt decided to be contrary. He declared the *Aurora* to be 'a most splendid composition' but that Reni had 'failed through want of practice in the grace and colouring of most of the figures'. It was the *Andromeda* in the same collection that won his admiration:

> The Andromeda has all the charm and sweetness of his pencil, in its pearly tones, its graceful timid action, and its lovely expression of gentleness and terror. The face, every part of the figure, has a beauty and softness not to be described. This one figure is worth all the other group, and the Apollo, the horses and the azure sea to boot. People talk of the insipidity of Guido. Oh! let me drink long, repeated, relishing draughts of such insipidity! If delicacy, beauty, and grace are insipidity, I too profess myself an idolizer of insipidity: I will venture one assertion, which is, that no other painter has expressed the female character so well, so truly, so entirely in its fragile, lovely essence, neither Raphael, nor Titian, nor Correggio; and, after these, it is needless to mention any more. Raphael's women are Saints; Titian's are courtesans; Correggio's an affected mixture of both; Guido's are the true heroines of romance, the brides of the fancy, such as 'youthful *poets* dream of when they love'.

Hazlitt also praised Poussin's *Infant Cupid* or *Bacchus*, the *Dead Christ* by Annibale Carracci (Stockholm) and Guercino's *Diana and Endymion*. Florence Nightingale was also a little disappointed by the

English school, Copy after Guido Reni's Aurora, *c. 1820*

colouring of the *Aurora*: Reni put the green and red hours first and the white and grey last – 'but probably Guido knew best'.[35]

It is to Pasquin in the 1820s that we owe some description of the 'ravishing collection of paintings' in the PALAZZO SCIARRA: Valentin's *Beheading of John the Baptist* and *Rome Triumphant*; Garofalo's *Claudia pulling Cybele into Rome* and *Circe metamorphising Ulysses' companions* (both now Barberini); Lanfranco's *Cleopatra*; Raphael's *Young Musicians, Leonada,* and *Modesty and Vanity*; Caravaggio's *Cardsharps* (from the Barberini collection in 1812, probably the painting now in the Kimbell Art Museum), Reni's *Two Magdalens* (previously Barberini, now private collection); Bronzino's *Portrait of a Woman*; Titian's *Holy Family*; and a landscape by Poussin.[36] This collection was sold in 1896.

Elisa von der Recke selected highlights of the PALAZZO SPADA collection in 1805: Barocci's *Madonna*, Caravaggio's *Revolt of Maniello*, Poussin's *Rebecca at the fountain*, and *Guercino's *Death of Dido*. As well there were half life size reliefs from S Agnese fuori le mura of Diomedes and Ulysses, Adrastus killing the serpent, Paris with a cupid on Mt Ida, and Paris and Helen by the sea. The statues included an infant in a cloak and Aristides. Twenty years later Pasquin listed the remarkable paintings: Guercino's *David with Goliath's head*,[37] a Titian portrait, Carracci's *Charity*, Caravaggio's *St Anne and the Virgin*, *Guercino's *Dido* (the best thing in the gallery), and *Reni's *Cardinal*

Bernardino Spada. He also mentioned the statue of Aristides (or Aristotle) and the reliefs (perhaps the best from antiquity) and, of course, the Pompey, about which he tells that the Republicans in 1798 took it to the Colosseum when they acted a play of Voltaire! Pasquin realised that the statue was Imperial – but that had been proven by Carlo Fea in 1812. Dickens, however, would not give up the romantic version of Cæsar's dying at its feet:

> A stern, tremendous figure! I imagined one of greater finish: of the last refinement: full of delicate touches: losing its distinctness, in the giddy eyes of one whose blood was ebbing before it, and settling into some such rigid majesty as this, as Death came creeping over the upturned face.

Nightingale also believed it to be genuine, but for a different reason: 'that great ugly Pompey... It is quite hideous enough to be authentic, and I believe is.'[38]

We turn, finally, to the VATICAN. Chateaubriand had, of course, a sense of what had passed there:

> A beautiful day, brilliant sun, and very gentle air. The solitude of these great stairways, or rather of these ramps, which one can climb with mules. The solitude of these galleries, decorated with masterpieces of genius, where popes of earlier times passed in full pomp. The solitude of these loggie which so many illustrious men have admired: Tasso, Ariosto, Montaigne, Milton, Montesquieu, kings and queens, both reigning and deposed, and all the pilgrims from all parts of the world.

From the Treaty of Tolentino (1797) until 1815 the masterpieces of the museum were absent, having been ceded to France, and were replaced by plaster casts. During the same period, a French traveller, Philippe Petit-Radel, ironically complained that the exhibits were not numbered and keyed to a guide book. It was a low point in the museum's existence: there were only one or two attendants in 1811 or 1812, and one had to ring repeatedly to gain entrance, and then ransack one's purse on leaving.[39]

Pietro Paoletti, Canova presenting recovered Roman treasures to the Pope in 1816, *1830.*
Paoletti sets this scene before the relatively new entrance to the Vatican Museums;, but in
reality there was no welcoming ceremony for the great works retrieved from Paris by Canova.
The stars of the show are Raphael's Transfiguration *and the* Laocoön; *
the* Apollo Belvedere *stares forlornly off to the right*

In the BELVEDERE Elisa von der Recke told the story of the country
girl who fell in love with the Apollo and brought it flowers. She herself
was 'ravished by ecstasy' before the Melpomene. Petit-Radel declared
the Apollo 'the masterpiece of the most perfect in the Greek genre' –
but the Laocoön was 'sublime, superior to all other work' in its
composition and expression. Byron could not be restrained: 'The
Apollo is the image of Lady Adelaide Forbes', with whom a friend
had tried to make a match with the poet. Hazlitt did not like the
Apollo, but found the Laocoön 'admirable'. Pasquin was provoking:
how could Laocoön and his sons be naked when they had been sacrificing to Minerva? Emerson was contrary. The masterpieces had been
restored to the galleries by the time of his visit (1833): ''Tis false to say
that the casts give no idea of the originals. I found I knew these fine
statues by heart and had admired the casts long since much more than
I ever can the originals.[!] Here too was the Torso Hercules, as

familiar to the eyes as some old revolutionary cripple,' with the oblig-atory parochial reference. Young Mommsen was accompanied by Emil Braun, secretary of the German Institute and an art historian. One wonders whose views he was quoting when he drew attention to 'the pure ideal form of the Torso, the dramatic animation of the Apollo, full of faults, the full effect of the very agitated nature of the Laocoön, without caricature'. Florence Nightingale was bound to have decided preferences. In the case of Apollo, 'I had not the least expectation of him, the sublime repose, after he has shot off his arrow, without excitement, without anxiety, as to whether it will hit its mark, the supernatural lightness, and here too, the almost feminine delicacy and softness of the mouth – the same as the Christian idea of super human strength – and yet how different.' She realised that the Christian ideal was a 'worship of grief', while for the classical world it was a worship of heroic happiness. On the other hand, she could not bear the Laoc-oön. 'That eternal marble ought to perpetuate only eternal feelings seems a truism, and here it is, perpetuating a transitory expression of physical pain.' And the BRACCIO NUOVO also was not neglected by her. It was 'not very inspiring' except for three pieces: Demosthenes was 'glorious', although the body was not what she expected (seeming to

English school, Study after the Laocoön, *c. 1825*

lack 'thunder and storm'), but the 'excessive simplicity' was wonderful. The children of the Nile caught her fancy: 'the one on his shoulder so triumphant, and that little pert fellow, evidently the spoilt child, who is highest of all, and sticks out of the lotus'. And the Ganymede was 'the very image of grace'. Wilhelm Müller brings everything to life as though we were on a Sunday morning in February 1818 in the Belvedere:

> The clear, warm Sunday has filled the museum with strollers, Roman men and women go arm in arm, without a lingering glance at the statuary as if they were strolling in their own garden. The room with the animals and monsters charms the common people above all others; the peasants who come from outside Rome will recount at home the marvels in coloured and mottled marble, the springing hare and the crawling crab. A pair of shepherds from the Abruzzi, still quite hot from this rare enjoyment of art, opened the door leading to the chamber of the Apollo. I was hidden from their gaze behind a corner. The god stood with outstretched arm and threatening gaze before the astonished pair. Both instantly doffed their hats, withdrew over the threshhold, and timidly peeped from a respectful distance. Motionless and dumb they stood there for a few minutes, then one took the other by the hand and said: 'Let's go, let's go, we are lost. This is for the pope and cardinals.'[40]

The Tempietto of the Laocöon, in a magazine illustration of 1849

Then to the SISTINE. Elisa von der Recke was unsettled. It left no 'agreeable and consoling feeling', because the blessed were in a 'most unnatural state of repose' and the damned in the 'greatest disorder', so extreme as to be a caricature. Hazlitt also was shocked at the *Last Judgement*. In the ceiling Michelangelo's 'Adam receiving life from his Creator... for boldness and freedom, is more like the Elgin Theseus than any other figure I have seen'. The faces near the bottom of the *Last Judgement*, on the other hand, 'are hideous, vulgar caricatures of demons and cardinals, and the whole is a mass of extravagance and confusion'. He admitted, however, that to shake Michelangelo was to pull down Fame itself. Michelet offered more personal insights: 'The chapel has a terrible effect. Michelangelo is more pagan and Jew than Christian, the thought is not at all evangelical any more than the figure of Christ in the central picture. This thought is resumed in the paintings of the vault. It is the lair of the Christian Sibyls. The Virgin herself is afraid and presses up against Christ.' In the *Last Judgement* Dickens could discern no 'general idea or one pervading thought in harmony with the stupendous subject'. Florence Nightingale was most taken with the prophets and sibyls, whom she found utterly convincing. Her favourite was Daniel, 'opening his window, and praying to the God of his fathers three times a day, in defiance of fear. You see the young and noble head, like an eagle's, disdaining danger, those glorious eyes, undazzled by all the honours of Babylon.' The Delphic Sybil was the most beautiful and most inspired. 'I cannot tell you how affecting this anxious look of her far reaching eye is to the poor mortals standing on the pavement below, while the Prophets ride secure on the storm of Inspiration.' Of the *Last Judgement*, she had a particularly Protestant interpretation: all the figures are isolated, even though they are in groups. 'The sentiment that strikes one as uppermost in the picture is that of individual responsibility... and if the feeling of awe and terror with which the picture fills one could be defined, it might perhaps be this, the ghastly impression of spiritual solitude which it leaves.'[41]

The early nineteenth century visitors often recorded with horror the use of the RAPHAEL STANZE as barracks by the troops of Charles V in 1527. Elisa von der Recke was not alone also in liking best the *Freeing of St Peter*. Petit-Radel in 1811 found the rooms always full of easels and ladders of the artists every day who came to copy the frescoes. His favourite was the *School of Athens*, because artists so admired its invention, composition and perspective. Hazlitt was more eclectic: 'his Stanzas there appear to me divine, more particularly the Heliodorus, the School of Athens, and the Miracle of Bolsena, with all the truth and force of Titian's portraits (I see nothing, however, of his colouring) and his own purity, sweetness and lofty invention added to them'. Pasquin agreed: 'never has art appeared so grand, so powerful', especially in the *Mass at Bolsena* and the *School of Athens*. How then can one account for such a philistine reaction as Emerson's? 'It was a poor way of using so great a genius to set him to paint the walls of rooms that have no beauty and, as far as I can see, no purpose.' For once Florence Nightingale did not record her own reactions, but those of her artist friend Col. James Lindsay, who averred that the Stanze 'are the first pictures in the world and a never ending study... Col. Lindsay thinks that the Disputa del Sacramento beats all the rest, then comes the Heliodorus, and that Raphael never painted anything like them afterwards.'[42]

The LOGGIE were less visited. Stendhal in his one letter from Rome made no bones: 'I have seen the Loggie of Raphael, and decided that you should sell your shirt to see them if you haven't, or to see them again if you have already admired them.' Hazlitt also found them 'divine in form, relief, conception – above all, the figure of Eve at the forbidden tree'. Florence Nightingale had favourites: 'the first four of the Creator I do not like at all'; she much admired the *Finding of Moses* ('they all look so innocent, so surprised, so interested, as if they had never seen a baby before') but disliked the *Fall* 'and the Angel pushing Adam and Eve out of Paradise by the shoulders I think is positively vulgar'. She thought it was 'the whole exquisite effect' Raphael sought, 'looking down that lovely perspective of fairy vignettes'.[43]

Then to the PINACOTECA. Hazlitt turned to the masterpiece:

> The Transfiguration is a wonderful collection of fine heads and figures: their fault is, that they are too detached and bare, but it is not true that it embraces two distinct points of time. The event below is going on in the Gospel account, at the

J. M. W. Turner, Rome, from the Vatican. Raffaelle, Accompanied by La Fornarina, Preparing his Pictures for the Decoration of the Loggia, *c. 1820*

same time with the miracle of the Transfiguration above. But I almost prefer to this the Foligno picture: the child with the casket below is of all things the most Raphaelesque, for the sweetness of expression, and the rich pulpy texture of the flesh; and perhaps I prefer even to this the Crowning of the Virgin, with that pure dignified figure of the Madonna sitting in the clouds, and that wonderous emanation of sentiment in the crowd below, near the vase of flowers, all those faces are bathed in one feeling of ecstatic devotion, as the stream of inspiration flows over them. There is a singular effect of colouring in the lower part of this picture, as if it were painted on slate, and from this cold chilly ground the glow of sentiment comes out perhaps the more strong and effectual. In the same suite of apartments (accessible to students and copyists) are the Death of St Jerome, by Domenichino; and the Vision of St Romuald, by Andrea Sacchi, the last of the Italian painters. Five nobler or more impressive pictures are not in the world.

Pasquin counted in *c.* 1828 only fifty paintings in the gallery, but opined that three or four made it the first gallery in Europe: the *Transfiguration* and Domenichino's *St Jerome* are the two he names. Correggio's *Christ on a Rainbow* had only recently been acquired, and also Lawrence's *George IV* ('looks like an actor at his toilet'). Reni's *Fortune* was removed in 1826 because of its nudity, as were the *Three Graces* from the Museum, but the idea of a secret cabinet for such things was worse, he rightly observed: they would be unnoticed here. On his second visit in 1836, George Ticknor was alarmed. He noted that Raphael's *Madonna of Foligno* had suffered since he saw it last twenty years earlier, and the German artist August Temmel, who had been copying there for ten years, agreed that the paintings were deteriorating. They had first suffered from the heat, and now from damp.[44]

Ticknor, as a Harvard professor of languages, was very interested in the LIBRARY. He found only a dozen people using it, all studying manuscripts. The same old treasures were being shown to visitors: the Virgil, the Terence, texts of Petrarch and Tasso, Boccaccio's copy of Dante and others of the same poet, Henry VIII's work against Luther and letters to Anne Boleyn. He was struck by seeing Sixtus V's edict threatening excommunication of anyone who took away a book

Attributed to August Temmel, Copy after detail of Raphael's Madonna of Foligno, *c. 1835*

without the pope's permission: 'can anything more plainly show the spirit of the government and religion?' Macaulay was astounded. 'I had walked a hundred feet through the library without the faintest notion that I was in it. No books, no shelves were visible. All was light and brilliant; nothing but white, and red, and gold.' The books were all hidden away in cupboards painted in light colours.[45]

VILLAS

Antoine Claude Pasquin in 1828 declared the VILLA ALBANI the third museum of Rome, after the Vatican and the Capitoline. The collection had been rebuilt following sales in 1728 and 1733 to Saxony and Clement XII and in 1815 to Bavaria, and depredations by the French in 1799. Pasquin listed the Niobids, Apollo Sauroctonos, a relief of Hercules at rest, the relief of Antinoüs (the most admirable sculpture in the collection), Pallas, a herm of Mercury, the seated Faustina, the sarcophagus with the marriage of Peleus and Thetis, the relief of Diogenes, another in *rosso antico* of Dædalus making wings, another of Achilles and Memnon, and of Berenice offering her hair for the return of her husband Ptolemy. In December 1836 George Ticknor attended the celebration of Winckelmann's birthday there (he had been Alessandro Albani's librarian):

> The villa is neglected, but its palazzo, a fine building, is well preserved; the collection of antiques, stolen, literally stolen by the French – has been replaced, and the whole is much in the state in which it was when Winckelmann lived there…[46]

Of the VILLA BORGHESE Augustus von Kotzebue told the story of how Pauline Bonaparte tried to close 'the greatest and most beautiful' part of the gallery, 'scandalized' by Bernini's hermaphrodite: 'he has again [*sic*] sinned most grievously,' noted Kotzebue. In 1811 Philippe Petit-Radel found the villa denuded, containing only some 'rejects'. Even the reliefs on the façade had been removed. In 1828 Pasquin could make a more encouraging report. The collection had been sold to France for thirteen millions (not fourteen, as Canova told Napoleon), but had almost entirely been replaced within three years. He singled out a head of Vespasian, a colossal head of Isis, the relief of Curtius, colossal heads of Hadrian, Antoninus Pius, a life size Ceres (the most beautiful in existence), a herm of Apollo, and of Mercury, a portrait of Alcibiades, Leda, a relief of Telephus, and a statue of Hercules. George Hillard in 1847 drew attention to a long-standing famous feature of this villa:

> The grounds, which are three miles in circuit, are thrown open to the public as freely as if they belonged to it. At all times numerous parties will be found availing themselves of this generous privilege, some in carriages, some on horseback, but mostly on foot; for as a place of resort, it is more popular with persons of modest condition among the Romans than with the favoured classes... It is pleasant to note that the hospitality of the prince was never abused. Often as I was there, I never saw the smallest act of spoliation or indecorum.[47]

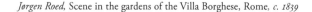

Jørgen Roed, Scene in the gardens of the Villa Borghese, Rome, *c. 1839*

The VILLA FARNESINA attracted little insightful comment. William Hazlitt is an exception:

> The little Farnese contains the Galatea and the Cupid and Psyche. If any thing could have raised my idea of Raphael higher, it would have been some of these frescoes. I would mention the group of the Graces in particular; they are true Goddesses. The fine flowing outline of the limbs, the variety of attitudes, the unconscious grace, the charming unaffected glow of the expression, are inimitable. Raphael never perhaps escaped so completely from the trammels of his first manner, as in this noble series of designs. The Galatea has been injured in colour by the stoves which the Germans, who were quartered there, lighted in the apartment.[48]

The reference to the Germans is the sack of 1527.

One collection which was not sold and dispersed was that of the VILLA LUDOVISI (acquired by the state in 1902). Elisa von der Recke noted the colossal head of Juno (the most beautiful piece), the bust of Cæsar, a statue of Theseus or Mars, and the by now highly debated identity of Orestes and Electra/Hippolytus and Phædra/Papirius and his mother (see ill. Vol. II) (the first is now accepted). At the same time, Kotzebue claimed that the collection was difficult to see. To Electra and Orestes and the head of Juno, he added Pætus and Arria (the Gallic couple) (see ill. Vol. II) and the seated Gladiator. Irving noted also Bernini's Pluto and Proserpine.

In 1812 Petit-Radel found it one of the best maintained villas, and described the arrangement of its main pieces. In the first room were busts of Pyrrhus, Antinoüs, Cæsar and Apollo; in the second, Mars in repose, Diana and Apollo, Pan and Syrinx; in the third, Agrippina, the head of Bacchus, and an Egyptian relief in red marble; in the fourth, Papirius and his mother, Arria and Pætus, Bernini's Proserpine, the head of Juno, and a relief of the Judgement of Paris. In the garden was the famous casino with Guercino's *Aurora*, but Petit-Radel also listed the main trees as cypress, laurel and oak, and in the middle of four cypress trees was the sarcophagus with the battle of Romans and Dacians. 'The garden is a real museum.' In 1828 Pasquin echoed

Kotzebue's remark: although the villa was 'impenetrable', he gained permission to see the collection, and listed the same masterpieces. Theodor Mommsen in 1844 also implied difficulty of access: he had the luck to be admitted 'thanks to Mr Henry'. He thought that the Arria and Pætus were Gauls belonging with the dying Gaul in the Capitoline; the hero with the sword across his knees he suggested might be Achilles; he noted also Penelope and Telemachus, and a bronze bust of Cæsar, but the Juno was 'incomparably beautiful'. Florence Nightingale, finally, was of course much taken with the Juno: 'the only goddess I ever saw... but I should not call her a Juno, but the Goddess of Liberty... noble and calm, strong but not stern, smiling but no exultation'. 'The gallery has hardly anything but treasures' – but the other group which caught her fancy was Arrius and Pætus or the Gaul and his Wife 'or fifty other names which it is called'.[49]

The picture of the VILLA MADAMA at this time is horrifying. Elisa von der Recke described it in 1805 as totally wild and untended, with rooms seeming ready to crumble, and serving as nesting places for night birds. Nothing had changed by 1811. Petit-Radel wrote of its state as that of 'the greatest abandon', with the peristyle used as stables, and in 1828 Pasquin described it as 'in its present degradation a sort of modern antiquity which artists never cease to study and admire'.[50]

The VILLA MATTEI had sold its masterpieces to Clement XIV in 1770, and they went to enrich the new Museo Pio-Clementino. It was therefore described by Petit-Radel in 1812 as denuded, with only a few rejects on show.

Josephus Augustus Knip, Five Capitals from the Villa Mattei, *c. 1809-12*

Joseph-Eugène Lacroix, A Studio in the Villa Medici, Rome, *1835*

We owe to Hector Berlioz an insider's description of the VILLA MEDICI, the French Academy in Rome for artists on the Pincian, in 1831:

The director's apartments are sumptuous, and an ambassador might envy them; but the pupils' rooms, with the exception of two or three, are small, inconvenient, and very badly furnished. A quartermaster in the Popincourt Barracks, at Paris, is better off in this respect than I was in the Palace of the Accademia di Francia. Most of the painters' and sculptors' studios are in the gardens; the others are scattered about the interior of the palace, and some are built out on a raised balcony overlooking the garden of the Ursuline Convent, with the Sabine Hills, Monte Cavo, and Hannibal's Camp in the distance. The library contains a fair collection of classical works, but absolutely no modern books. It is open to the students till three, and is a great resource for those who have nothing to do; for it is only fair to say that they enjoy the most complete liberty, and, beyond sending a picture, drawing, engraving, or piece of music once a year to the Académie at Paris, nothing is required of them; they may work as much or as little as they choose. The director's duties are confined to seeing that the rules of the establishment are not infringed; he exercises no sort of control over the students' work.[51]

The director at the time was Horace Vernet (see Portraits).

Almost our last view of the VILLA PERETTI, one of the masterpieces of Sixtus V, now the villa Massimo, is provided by Elisa von der Recke in 1805. It once stretched from the Esquiline to the Viminal and was famous for its antiquities. It had been bought in 1784 by Giuseppe Staderini, who sold the antiques, mostly to Thomas Jenkins, the notorious art dealer, from whom they were repurchased for the Pio-Clementino. Now essentially only the views remained: to the Sabine mountains, Frascati, the aqueducts of the campagna, the Minerva Medica, Santa Maria Maggiore, the baths of Caracalla, the pines of the villa Ludovisi and the villa Pamphili.[52] It was the coming of the railway which removed forever this marvel of old Rome and indeed the whole quarter.

The VILLA PAMPHILI on the Janiculum was, in Kotzebue's words, only 'a lazaretto of antiques', exhibiting only fragments. 'We must drive a great way in our carriage to see very little.' Here at least the park remained, and its condition in 1812 was evoked by Petit-Radel:

> The park is open always for public enjoyment, and from various places, one sees the campagna to the sea. Its arrangement is picturesque, varied and of different shades, so as to link it with the surrounding nature. That symmetry commanded by pride is not found here, to display instantly all the owner's wealth. The rake and the chalk line are used only for the parterre, where Flora makes the most modest display; the rest is given over to indulgent nature, which clothes the valleys and slopes with the finest grass and mottles them with a thousand different flowers…

Carl Frederich Heinrich Werner, Grand Cricket match in Rome at the
Doria Pamphili Villa between Eton and the rest of the world, *1850*

He paid special attention to the fountains. Everywhere were jets
and cascades falling into receptacles of all kinds, bordered with lush
and verdant plants and statues and busts, with seating everywhere for
conversation.

> Finally this villa offers plantations of very high pines, which
> spread like an umbrella over the green, groves of box, ordinary
> laurel and cherry laurel, some myrtles in the sunniest places,
> ceilings of green oaks, arranged in long avenues, almost impen-
> etrable to rain, and everywhere in every shape, fountains of very
> transparent water.

The modern visitor would hardly believe that all this had so recently
existed. Pasquin summed up in 1828: 'it is the most varied, the most
delightful of the Roman villas'.[53]
What a contrast these observations make with the eighteenth-
century picture! The era of the great villas was over, and Rome was
being converted from one of the greenest cities to one of the great
cities most lacking in parks. Development and speculation in the
nineteenth century devoured the space, and political upheavals
dispersed the artworks.

J. M. W. Turner, View of the Baths of Caracalla, *1819*

ANTIQUITIES

The period most commonly associated with romanticism was now in full bloom. The attraction of the ruins of classical Rome was strong. No one gives us a more extended insight into this than Elisa von der Recke's reaction to the Baths of Caracalla in 1805:

> It has disappeared, this magnificence associated with odious vices, accumulated by the spoils of cohorts which overran the world in order to devastate it. The terrible law of retaliation finally destroyed the execrable pride; men called barbarians who were less so that than those who called them so delivered the earth from the true barbarism of a general subjugation. Nature has now retaken the space where once art displayed its sumptuous products; there where the most noisy life inspired the country, now there reign solitude and silence; there where were heard incessant cries of joy and pain, one hears now only the lugubrious whistling of birds of prey, withdrawn into the

hovels. The solitary cricket reveals himself by his monotonous chant in the grass which grows in the midst of what were once superb chambers. Innocent nature acts openly, with sweetness and kindness in the same places which resounded with the sighs of thousands of victims, where treachery and wickedness plotted the death and destruction of men. The wild vine covers the grottoes where tyrants exhausted by pleasures voluptuously bathed. The walls once covered with gold of conquered peoples are now covered with ivy, which grows there abundantly, and which clings to the degraded walls as if to cover their decadence, the wild fig thrusts its vigorous roots into the cracks, and the aloe raises its covering above the ruins. Thus the sumptuous ornaments of art are replaced by those of a rich and powerful vegetation. The openings of the lofty arcades offer a romantic aspect: the branches of the bushes and parasitic plants fall in festoons and seem to seek their native soil and give the idea of a mysterious creation of green, of an ærial forest. Wherever one casts a glance, one finds a picturesque and romantic view.

Franz Liszt put it more prosaically in 1839:

> Rome suits me, above all the Rome which is no more, for I have no liking for the new one. The Campo Vaccino, the Forum, the Colosseum, the Baths of Caracalla, the Palatine ruins, these are my favourite walks. Nothing can give one any idea of the feeling that comes over one in the presence of these remains; I am thoroughly imbued with it, but doubt if I shall ever venture to attempt to express it.

One thing one must always keep in mind, however, is that the French occupation of Rome (1808-14) had seen the first comprehensive clearing and restoration of the classical monuments in modern times.[54] As for antiquarians, no one gives us as complete a list as Jean-François Champollion in 1825:

> I leave the dead in peace and pass to the living. The Dukes of Blacas and Montmorency have put me in contact with everything distinguished here by erudition. I was welcomed

in particular by Signor [Angelo] Mai, a professor [Alessandro] Nibbi, Signor [Domenico] Testa, and the excellent Signor [Francesco] Cancellieri. I have seen Mr [Edward] Dodwell, the famous Hellenic traveller, and Sir [William] Gell, an amateur hieroglyphist, as kind as he is learned. I find everything it is possible to desire in kindness and facilities for my research... The Portuguese ambassador, M. de Funchal, could not be kinder to me, and gives charming soirées.[55]

Mai was Vatican librarian 1819-25, Nibby was professor of archæology at the University 1820-39 and author of the monumental *Roma nell'anno 1838* as well as a guide-book, Cancellieri was superintendant of the Propaganda printery and a leading writer on antiquities, and Funchal had financed vital excavations below the Capitol in 1817.

The nineteenth century was to transform the understanding of the topography of the FORUM, identifying securely all the major remains, most of which were still, when the century opened, misnamed: the temple of Saturn was called that of Concord, the temple of the deified Vespasian that of Jupiter Tonans, the temple of Castor that of Jupiter Stator, the basilica of Maxentius was called the Flavian temple of Peace, and the senate house was usually located under the Palatine. Kotzebue in 1804 or 1805 was dismissive:

> a quarter of an hour is amply sufficient to us for wandering from the ruins of the Colosseum to those of the temple of Harmony. Let no traveller visiting Rome neglect to pass over this unparallelled piece of ground: but in this case I earnestly recommend to him not to forget taking 30 or 40 *bajocchi* in his pocket, that during his interview with the ancient Romans, he may get rid, as fast as possible, of the mendicant Romans of the present day.

Petit-Radel, who was there in December 1811, provides a vivid picture of the Forum at a vital moment of transition, during the French clearances. Old and new were still intermingled. There was 'the unfortunate, nonchalantly wheeling his barrow filled with earth

J. M. W. Turner, Forum Romanum, for Mr Soane's Museum, *1826*

from the monuments being cleared, who finds there a way to have better pasta and a little omelette for supper; the soldier, well paid, comes here to spend his coins in the taverns; the more interested vigorously wields the spade... the washerwomen, anxious to satisfy the needs of travellers who have only a suitcase, always find here the air and sun to dry their linen'. As well there were clerks, shopkeepers and artists who flocked here between five and six. There were also carriages of the upper class, but they were often stopped by cows or horses which had come to drink at the great granite basin in the middle. It was Müller seven years later who recorded the debate over these changes. The guide books, he noted, praised the French clearances, but the Romans themselves and the artists lamented 'the disfiguring of the Forum'. Now pits surrounded the main monuments, and there was danger of falling into them; the white cattle with their brown herdsmen could no longer be seen on the green grass. Shelley in 1818 was more graphic:

> The Forum is a plain in the middle of Rome, a kind of desart
> [*sic*] full of heaps of stones and pits and though so near the

Luigi Rossini, The Forum seen from the base of the Capitol, *c. 1820. In the foreground are the Arch of Severus, cleared in 1802-3, the temple of the deified Vespasian and of Saturn, cleared by the French, in the middle the Column of Phocas cleared by the Duchess of Devonshire 1817-19, and the temple of the Disocuroi, cleared by Fea in 1817. The level of the main part of the Forum began to be cleared from the late 1820s*

habitations of men, is the most desolate place you can conceive. The ruins of temples stand in and around it, shattered columns and ranges of others complete, supporting cornices of exquisite workmanship, and vast vaults of shattered domes (laquearis) distinct with the regular compartments once filled with sculptures of ivory or brass. The temple of Jupiter and Concord, and Peace, and the Sun and the Moon, and Vesta are all within a short distance of this spot. Behold the wrecks of what a great nation once dedicated to the abstractions of the mind.

Theodor Mommsen in 1845 reminds us that the Forum was still a public thoroughfare:

Descending the stairs (the famous Capitol cordonata) I trod the sacred place; the evening was rainy and dark; trees, groups

Domenico Amici, The western end of the Forum, *1845. Enormous changes have occurred since Rossini's view. The pits around the main monuments left at the end of the French period have been replaced by the beginnings of the excavation of the whole area down to the classical level from 1827*

of houses, here and there ancient remains, often mentioned by me, the tall column of Phocas, the three columns half in deep ditches, as well as the eight columns, a Roman coachman with his vehicle behind a fire of dry branches which illuminated the brigand-like Italian face and the red waistcoat of that individual – it was a marvellous scene.

A much more depressed view was taken by George Hillard a few years later:

No one, unless forewarned by books and engravings, can have any conception of the change and desolation which have come over this illustrious spot. An unsightly piece of ground disfeatured with filth and neglect, with a few ruins scattered over it, and two formal rows of trees running through it, is all that we see with the eye of the body. A few peasants wrapped in their mud-colored cloaks, a donkey or two, a yoke of the fine gray oxen of Italy, or, perhaps, a solitary wild eyed buffalo, are the only living forms in a scene once peopled with wisdom, valor, and eloquence. Nothing gives a stronger impression of the shattering blows which have fallen upon the Eternal City than the present condition of the Forum.

He revealed, however, that he was on the side of romance as opposed to knowledge:

> To nine travellers out of ten, of what consequence is it whether a particular ruin is called by the name of the Temple of Fortune or the Temple of Vespasian, the Temple of Peace or the Basilica of Constantine? In all cases, indeed, accurate knowledge is not a gain. There is a solitary column in the Forum, which Byron calls 'the nameless column with a buried base', the history and origin of which were long unknown. Recent excavations [financed by the duchess of Devonshire, 1816-1818] have shown it to have been erected by the exarch Smaragdus to the Emperor Phocas, – the venal offering of a servile courtier to one of the most unmitigated monsters that ever stained the pages of history. Has not the column lost something of its charm? Before, there was a beauty and a mystery around it, – there was room for conjecture and food for fancy, – it was a voice that sounded from a dim and distant past, and therefore all the more impressive. But now the ideal light is vanished, and the column loses half its grace, since it speaks to us of the wickedness of tyrants and the weakness of slaves.

Florence Nightingale showed her greater intelligence by spending a whole day with Nibby in her hand and 'digging about in the excavations just behind the Capitol'. Despite that, she gave all the old names for the main monuments, except the Basilica of Constantine (better, Maxentius) instead of the Flavian Temple of Peace – but that was precisely Nibby's sensational contribution! She was also able to report in January 1848 on the new excavations (of Luigi Canina and Pietro Rosa) which had uncovered the Basilica Julia and thus finally established the southern limits of the Forum, and the clearing of the Tabularium, which she thought was the treasury and where the *Fasti Capitolini* were kept – 'the oldest and least wanted, of course, lowest' (but they came from Augustus' arch in the middle of the Forum)! She knew that only the floor remained of the Temple of Concord (excavated by Carlo Fea in 1817) – 'of which I bring you home a bit'! She finally was given a very special view of the basilica Maxentius:

> From the Forum [Henry Colyer] took us to the top of the Temple of Peace. After letting us look through the cleft into that enormous arch from the garden of the Conservatorio delle Mendicanti, he brought us up a little winding stair, which perhaps there are not 10 people in Rome who know of, to the roof of Peace, from which you look over the whole of Rome. Oh lovely spot, when first you hear of peace, you nestle under its most retired shadows, or walk beneath its broad arches, and feel the profoundest rest and safety – but when you have taken courage and are stronger, you no longer keep within its shades and look out from them upon the blue sky – but you mount upon the heights of peace, and no longer half trembling and still hiding, you examine sans peur and sans reproche from these secure heights the whole world which can no longer harm you, and bask in the bright sun and open air and under the free heaven. Happy they who have reached them. We had a lovely walk up there – a splendid view of the Coliseum through a loop hole of the stair coming down – and the fountain and the artichokes and the nice court and pigeon cotes of the Conservatorio made the foreground. I should not mind being a Mendicante there – there are 80 of them, and they have splendid poultry yards and gardens.[56]

Overlooking the Forum was the PALATINE. Here Hauteville in 1815 visited the Farnese Gardens, now a farm. The 'Baths of Livia' were shown him by a peasant with a torch, who lived there, as his ancestors had done for one and a half centuries. 'The products of the soil and the name of Livia form their revenues; they succeeded each other peacefully, handing down the little they know of the wife of Augustus,

Unknown German artist (Ernst Fries?), View from the Colosseum toward the Palatine,
c. 1825

while the kings of Naples lost their crowns.' The same impression was
conveyed by Pasquin in 1828. 'The Palatine, the most famous of the
Seven hills, at once the cradle and throne of Rome, now offers only
some uncertain ruins, among which grow by chance the green oak,
the laurel, ivy and cypress.' At the villa Mills, however, Charles Mills
was very welcoming. From the rose covered garden, there was a
descent to three rooms of the House of Augustus. On his second visit,
in 1836, Charles Ticknor was rather despondent: 'It is vain to ask for
one monument, or to try to verify one record or recollection; the
house where Augustus lived forty years can be as little marked as that
of Romulus; and all reminiscences of Cicero, who dwelt here in the
midst of his future enemies – Clodius and Catiline – of Mæcenas, of
Agrippa, and of Horace, are vain and fruitless.'[57]

The COLOSSEUM excited in Chateaubriand a variety of reflections.
On his first visit on a July evening in 1803 he mused on the

connections between the classical and Christian worlds. The dogs of the hermit who guarded the ruins barked and then the bell of St Peter's echoed under the porticoes. When he returned in January 1804 the hermit had died and he reflected on human mortality: 'man meditates on the ruins of empires, but forgets that he is a ruin still more tottering'. Earl Montcashell at the same time noted the flora:

> The acanthus spreads its large and polished leaves upon the crumbling masses, and adds an indescribable protection to the ruin which it shades; the flowering Rosemary and yellow blossom'd shrubs flourishing in profusion overtop the broken outline, and the broad Ferns, lilac, Hepaticas, perfumed Wallflowers and a variety of aromatic plants peculiar to this country enamel the advances which lead even to the heights of its circumference.

The building was always apt to excite fantasy, and in no one more so than in Kotzebue, who made a point of going first to the Colosseum before St Peter's. He almost thanked the Jews for letting themselves be taken prisoners in order to build it, claimed that its ancient name was Amphiteatrum Colosseum, had Nero fighting a lion here, and claimed that the metal clamps fell out of the stones in a great fire (presumably that of 64). There could not be more historical nonsense. The Flavian Amphitheatre was built by that dynasty (69-98) precisely to reclaim for the people an area which Nero (54-68) had appropriated for himself and his notorious Golden House. How ironic, then, that the theatre is known by association with one of his monuments! It had been used as a hospital for soldiers during the Jacobin Republic, and in 1804 the foundations were being dug up, according to Kotzebue, by Carluccio. He means Carlo Lucangeli, who was constructing a cork model of the building, to which he later refers, noting that it took him 12 years and measured 13' x 11' and was sold for 3,000 *scudi* to a Venetian nobleman (now in the Ecole des Beaux Arts, Paris).

Following pages: Christoffer Wilhelm Eckersberg, A View through three arches of the Third Storey of the Colosseum, *1815*

Washington Irving stated correctly that the name Colosseum came from the colossal statue of Nero, but thought that it was found in the middle of it. One of the last things Mme de Staël planned to do in Rome in May 1805 was visit the Colosseum at 11 o'clock by moonlight with Don Pedro de Souza, the man to whom she declared that a whole life passed with him would seem shorter than it was. Stendhal, always seeking for effect, declared that the thing that most touched him in all his travels in Italy was the singing of birds in the Colosseum. Petit-Radel issued a rarely heard warning: when walking in the upper galleries, one had to take care, for shrubs could hide openings in the floor, through which one could plunge to the level below! He also added to the standard estimate of spectators: there was room for another 20,000 in the porticoes – presumably with what would now be described as 'limited view'! The vegetation again was what struck Shelley in 1818:

> It has been changed by time into the image of an amphitheatre of rocky hills overgrown by the wild olive the myrtle & the fig tree, & threaded by little paths which wind among its ruined stairs & immeasurable galleries; the copse wood overshadows you as you wander through its labyrinths & the wild weeds of this climate of flowers bloom under your feet. The arena is covered with grass, & pierces like the skirts of a natural plain the chasms of the broken arches around. But a small part of the exterior circumference remains, it is exquisitely light & beautiful, & the effect of the perfection of its architecture adorned with ranges of Corinthian pilasters supporting a bold cornice, is such as to diminish the effect of its greatness. The interior is all ruin. I can scarcely believe that when encrusted with Dorian marble & ornamented by columns of Egyptian granite its effect could have been so sublime & so impressive as in its present state. It is open to the sky, & it was the clear & sunny weather of the end of November in this climate when we visited it day after day.

After noting Fontana's plans for a wool-spinning factory in the ruins, circumvented by Sixtus V's death (1590), Pasquin recorded that in the

Joseph Severn, Posthumous portrait of Shelley composing Prometheus Unbound, 1819, *1845*

late 1820s he heard a sermon there on penitence, a poor performance, given by a monk covered all but for his eyes, and continually traversing his platform in cold agitation. Pasquin recommended moonlight visits, of course. He was accompanied by 'Mlle G.' who recited her poem *The Vestal's Farewell* (was this one of the Vestals convicted of breaking her vows?) The emotional outpourings of the nineteenth-century travellers are truly striking. 'Never in his life perhaps', declared Dickens, 'will [the stranger] be so moved and overcome by any sight, not immediately connected with his own affections and afflictions... It is the most impressive, the most stately, the most solemn, grand, majestic, mournful sight, conceivable. Never, in its bloodiest prime, can the sight of the gigantic Colosseum, full and running over with the lustiest life, have moved one heart, as it must move all who look upon it now, a ruin: God be thanked, a ruin!' He also commented on the fact that the cross in the centre of the arena was constantly being kissed from morning to night, because it conferred one hundred days' indulgence, whereas one on a marble slab, which gave two hundred

Ippolito Caffi, Fireworks inside the Colosseum lit by fireworks, *c. 1844-45*

and forty days, was totally neglected! George Hillard, finally, found that the travertine stone was perfect for a great ruin, because of its warm colour and its porous texture, so that it does not splinter, and holds every grain of dust that falls on it: hence the luxuriant vegetation. He analysed the moonlight visit: 'the great charm of the ruin under this condition is that the imagination is substituted for sight; and the mind for the eye'. The light, furthermore, is hard, shadows are defined, there is no gradation of colour. He therefore recommended a young rather than full moon: the latter 'fills the vast gulf of the building with a flood of spectral light, which falls with a chilling touch on the spirit', while the light of the dimmer moon is 'more indistinct, yet not so mournful; contracting the sphere of sight, but enlarging that of thought'.[58] He himself saw the Colosseum illuminated by German artists with blue, red and green lights, but found it unworthy of the majesty of the building.

Few paid attention to the nearby META SUDANS. For Jules Michelet it was the 'first military boundary of the empire' and the place where the gladiators went to wash their wounds! The ARCH OF CONSTANTINE was much noticed, and that emperor had a hard time of it in the early nineteenth century. Kotzebue was succinct: 'Constantine is no hero and his triumphal arch is no remarkable performance.' It was being cleared in 1805. Irving knew at least that 'the part of it which is stolen from an arch of Trajan is of beautiful Workmanship. The part worked in Constantine's time is vastly inferior.' Shelley referred to the arch of Constantine, 'or rather the arch of Trajan, for the servile and avaricious senate of degraded Rome ordered that the monument of his predecessor should be demolished in order to dedicate one to this Christian reptile who had crept among the blood of his own murdered family to the supreme power. It is exquisitely beautiful and perfect.'[59]

The nearby DOMUS AUREA was now being visited. Hazlitt still called it the Baths of Titus. 'In the vaults below they show you (by the help of a torch) paintings on the ceiling eighteen hundred years old, birds and animals, a figure of a slave, a nymph and a huntsman, fresh and elegantly foreshortened, and also the place where the Laocoön was discovered.' The Laocoön was found, in fact, in what were the Gardens of Mæcenas on the Esquiline.[60] Florence Nightingale was repulsed. The ruins were now 'all blocked up with rubbish, so that you poke

Luigi Rossini, The Arch of Constantine, *showing the arch as cleared in 1805, with the remains of the Meta Sudans fountain to the left. The Cælian Hill lies to the right, and the entrance to the Domus Aurea on the Oppian to the left of the Colosseum, 1827*

about them in the dark, by the light of one torch, and feel almost glad that darkness and the bowels of the earth should shroud the memory of such deeds and such thoughts as those walls have seen and the sun cannot smile upon... And the great shadows which prowl about... and stalk over the ceilings seem like the gigantic ghosts of those supernatural wickednesses, uneasy in their living tomb. It is a ghastly place, I never wish to see it again.'[61]

Continuing south from the Colosseum, one reaches the Aventine, near which are the BATHS OF CARACALLA. Petit-Radel was disappointed: 'one seeks what these cold remains could tell of ancient splendour'. He complained that it was hard to find one's way to the baths, and costly to enter when one did. Shelley declared these to be 'the next most considerable relic of antiquity considered as a ruin' after the Colosseum. It was here, in fact, that he wrote acts 2 and 3 of *Prometheus Unbound*. 'Never was any desolation more sublime and lovely. The perpendicular wall of ruin is cloven into steep ravines filled with flowering shrubs whose thick twisted roots are knotted in the rifts of the stones. At every step the ærial pinnacles of shattered stone group into new combinations of effect...' And in one of the huge buttresses was a staircase, giving access to the roofs:

> In one of the buttresses which supports an immense & lofty arch which 'bridges the very winds of Heaven' are the crumbling remains of an antique winding staircase, whose sides are open in many places to the precipice. This you ascend, & arrive on the summit of these piles. Here grow on every side thick entangled wildernesses of myrtle & the myrtelus & bay & the flowering laurustinus whose white blossoms are just developed, the wild fig & a thousand nameless plants sown by the wandering winds. These woods are intersected on every side by paths, like sheep tracks thro the copse wood of steep mountains, which wind to every part of the immense labyrinths.

In the same direction is TESTACCIO. Elisa von der Recke recorded that thousands of cartloads of broken pottery had been taken away in attempts to drain the Pontine marshes.[62]

Sir Charles Lock Eastlake, The Forum of Trajan, *1821; shown as cleared by the French 1811-13*

Returning to the city one passed the FORUM OF TRAJAN. Pasquin, although French, declared that the place was now very unimposing after the French excavations (1811-13). The circular excavation, revealing broken columns, was surrounded by an iron railing.[63] The COLUMN OF TRAJAN was the subject of the last of the twenty-eight sonnets of Wordsworth's *Memorials of a tour in Italy*. He marvelled that it had survived, 'though the passions of man's fretful race/ Have never ceased to eddy round its base'. The virtuosity of the reliefs was noted: 'Still as he turns, the charmed spectator sees/Group winding after group with dreamlike ease.' There were, however, incongruities: 'high or low,/ None bleed, and none lie prostrate but the foe;/ In every Roman, through all turns of fate,/ Is Roman dignity inviolate'. Worst of all, that the Optimus Princeps, 'One thus disciplined, could toil/ To enslave whole nations or their native soil.'

Behind the Forum of Trajan rises the Quirinal. Again the keen eye of Shelley was drawn to the HORSETAMERS (see ill. Vol. II) in the piazza:

> These figures combine the irresistible energy with the sublime & perfect loveliness supposed to have belonged to the divine nature. The reins no longer exist, but the position of their hands & the sustained & calm command of their regard seem to require no mechanical aid to enforce obedience. The countenances at so great a height are scarcely visible & I have a better idea of that of which we saw the cast together in London than of the other. But the sublime and living majesty of their limbs & mien, (the nervous & fiery animation of the horses they restrain), seen in the blue sky of Italy, & overlooking the City of Rome, surrounded by the light & the music of that chrystalline fountain, no cast can com[m]unicate.[64]

And finally we come to the Campus Martius. Elisa von der Recke declared the PORTICO OF OCTAVIA the dirtiest place in Rome, being a fish market. And the THEATRE OF MARCELLUS was occupied by shops selling various commodities; here also 'uncleanliness reigned'. The MAUSOLEUM OF AUGUSTUS presented a sorry sight to her in 1805: the vaults were used as butchers' coolrooms, and above was a stage for tightrope walkers. Kotzebue described it as 'a theatre for bullfights and fireworks'. Irving decried the bull-baiting, but also recorded a seldom-mentioned feature: 'There is a remarkable echo in this circus and two persons applying their ears to the wall on opposite sides may converse with each other in whispers very distinctly.' Nothing had changed by 1828. Longfellow recreates the summer scene:

> Even in this hot weather, when the shops are shut at noon, and the fat priests waddle about the streets with fans in their hands, the people crowd to the Mausoleum of Augustus, to be choked with the smoke of fireworks, and see deformed and humpback dwarfs tumbled into the dirt by the masked horns of young bullocks. What a refined amusement for the inhabitants of 'pompous and holy Rome'!

Bartolomeo Pinelli, The Mausoleum of Augustus, *c. 1810*

It is hard for us to imagine the Mausoleum of Augustus as a ring for bull-fighting, but the most graphic description of such an occasion is given by Müller in 1818. From the narrow streets he entered the brightly lit rotonda swarming with well dressed men. Chandeliers and coloured lamps competed with the black night which provided the cupola for the glittering circle. Two orchestras alternated, one playing marches on Turkish instruments, the other symphonies and overtures. When the lights were extinguished, everyone took a seat. Tightrope dancers appeared over his head, but he did not notice until the audience broke into applause. Then fireworks were set off in the arena: golden fountains, green and red stars, and the shape of the crown and keys of St Peter, but the audience was unimpressed: it was better last time, when a Chinese city was burned! The *giostra* began at 22 hours, and lasted for two hours. Turkish music again rang out, and four matadors entered – young and strong, in white with a red scarf around the waist and a short dagger. In the middle of the arena were placed high barrels and the stuffed doll of a bullfighter. The trumpet sounded and the fighters took their places. A door opened and out sprang a great white ox of the Campanian type with long horns. He surveyed everything, then attacked the barrels and the doll. The matadors dared to move closer and the bull tilted at their red cloths, but the fighters eluded his horns. Then a fighter stabbed him and ran for the protecting wall. The ox continued to tilt at the red cloths until he tired, and a rope was cast over his horns and he was dragged away. Next came buffalo, which tired even more quickly, then an ox with one horn, which still managed to drive all four fighters from the ring. He could have pierced one of their legs, but seemed too considerate! One of the fighters let himself be thrown in the dust to make it seem more serious. Then came buffalo steer of the Campagna type, which were really wild. Against them the fighters did not emerge. Two great butcher's dogs were let loose, which bit them and were dragged around by the bulls, bellowing fearfully. The audience often booed, but after a courageous stroke handed down wine and refreshments. Müller admitted to being impressed with the gymnastic aspects of it all.[65]

Elisa von der Recke declared that no work of modern architecture equalled the PANTHEON, not even St Peter's, although 'barbarian hands' had altered its beauty; she meant Bernini's *campanili*. At this time, there were still to be seen the busts of many famous people in the Pantheon: the poet Metastasio, the musician Antonio Sacchini, the painter Raphael Mengs, the violinist Arcangelo Corelli, the painter Nicholas Poussin, the archæologist Johannes Winckelmann, the engraver Johann Pickler, and the painters Annibale Carracci and Angelika Kaufmann. Shelley visited it by moonlight. 'It is as it were the visible image of the universe; in the perfection of its proportions, as when you regard the unmeasured dome of Heaven, the idea of magnitude is swallowed up and lost... There is only one defect of this sublime temple; there ought to have been no interval between the commencement of the dome and the cornice supported by the columns.' In other words, he disliked the attic. Pasquin called it 'the most elegant building of ancient Rome' and 'the most beautiful of modern Rome' and reminded his readers of the story of the visit of

Jakob Alt, The Pantheon and the Piazza della Rotonda, *1836*

Charles V to Rome in 1536. He climbed to the oculus accompanied by a young Crescenzi, who later told his father that he had wanted to push him in, in revenge for the sack of Rome nine years earlier, to which his father replied, 'There are things one does but does not speak about.' The anomalies struck Macaulay in 1838, and his misdating of the building to Augustus instead of Hadrian does not destroy his point:

> I was as much struck and affected as if I had not known that there was such a building in Rome. There it was, the work of the age of Augustus; the work of men who lived with Cicero, and Cæsar, and Horace, and Virgil. What would they have said if they had seen it stuck all over with 'Invito Sacro', and 'Indulgenza perpetua'?

Mommsen found the lower wall of the interior too low[66] – but the critics have always been in a minority faced with this supreme example of Roman virtuosity.

Of the COLUMN OF MARCUS AURELIUS, finally, Hauteville was one of the few to remark on 'the most bizarre association of objects sacred and profane', the statues of Peter and Paul on the columns of Trajan and Marcus. Pasquin recorded, indeed, that the latter had been struck by lightning, precisely because of this statue.[67]

One traveller mentions EXCAVATIONS being carried out. In 1830 Leopold von Ranke stated that there were four hundred workers, spread out in various parts of the city, 'bringing ancient pavements to light, revealing the bases of monuments concealed by the enormous rubble, to restore to them the appearance of their proportions, and giving the antiquarian something to do'. It was only Imperial Rome that was being revealed, he complained. Of Republican remains there was only a 'tiny, insignificant temple. To transport oneself to ancient times it was better to climb one of the vine-clad hills and look out over the Palatine, Capitol and Aventine.'[68]

The major collection of antiquities remained the CAPITOLINE MUSEUM. Chateaubriand gives an extensive list of exhibits, but comments on few: the 'admirable' relief of Jupiter as a child on Crete,

J. M. W. Turner, Lecture sketch of the column of Marcus Aurelius, *after Piranesi, c. 1810*

Micromosaic after the mosaic of the Capitoline Doves, c. 1835;
a typical luxury souvenir for the tourist trade

'the most beautiful known' alabaster column, and the relief of Endymion asleep on a rock ('one of the most beautiful reliefs known'). He was mainly interested in the portrait busts, and devoted the longest description to a supposed bust of Cæsar, which is now classified as simply a late Republican portrait. Irving in 1805 noted that the finest pieces had been transported to Paris and replaced by plaster casts. There was only one exhibit which Florence Nightingale noticed, the Dying Gladiator. She was eloquent over the sculptor's depiction not only of the body but also of the spirit. 'You see his abstraction, his complete unconsciousness of pain, of the time and place, and all about him... You see a dying man, the body dying in every sense and power, and yet you see a spirit, not there, but far away.' This was of course a paraphrase of those immortal lines by Byron. George Hillard also gave an extended account, lamenting the 'inferior accommodations' of the art to those provided in the Vatican. The mosaic of the doves was 'the most celebrated in the world' and constantly copied by the mosaic workers in Rome. Two of the most beautiful reliefs to have survived were Perseus rescuing Andromeda and the sleeping Endymion. He also noted the seated Agrippina and the very old woman ('The execution is wonderful. The expression of the face is that of stony despair, and the figure is a wreck battered by time and sorrow.') The work to which he devoted pages, however, was Nightingale's choice. He was prepared to put the Dying Gladiator (or Gaul) at the head of all statues in the world. His description is a very fine one.

What is it that we see before us? A man dying; nothing more. It is that which happens to all men; the only inevitable fact in every life. Nor is it a marked or conspicuous person. He is not a hero or a poet or an orator. The form is not ideal, the head is not intellectual, the lips are not refined. The shadows of great thoughts never darkened that commonplace brow, nor did the touch of beauty ever thrill along those coarse fibres. But the charm and power of the statue consist in the amazing truth with which the two great elements of humanity and mortality are delineated. A vigorous animal life is suddenly stopped by the touch of death, and the 'sensible warm motion' becomes a 'kneaded clod' before our eyes. The artist gives us all the pathos and the tragedy of death without its ghastliness and horror. The dying man is no longer a trivial person, stained with coarse employments and vulgar associations, but an immortal spirit breaking through its walls of clay. The rags of life fall away from him, and he puts on the dignity and grandeur of death. We feel ourselves in the presence of that awful power, before whose icy sceptre all mortal distinctions are levelled. Life and death are all that for a time we can admit into the mind.

As the sentiment and expression of this statue are admirable, so is the mechanical execution of the highest merit. The skill with which the physical effects of death upon the human frame are represented is most strongly felt by those whose professional training and experience make their judgment upon such points the most valuable. The hair short and crisp and matted by the sweat of the death struggle, the wrinkled brow, the drooping lid, the lips distended with pain, and the sinking languor of the whole frame, give proof of a patient eye and a skilful hand. No statue was ever more marked by simplicity, or more free from anything like extravagance or caricature. Such a subject presents many temptations, and, unless an artist's taste and judgment were equal to his genius, he would hardly have escaped falling

Benedetto Boschetti, Reproduction of The Dying Gladiator, *c. 1830*
—another typical product for the souvenir market

into the weakness of overdoing the tragic element, and of laying such a weight upon our sympathies that they would have given away under the pressure. But here nothing has been done for effect. No vulgar applause is courted, and the decency and dignity of truth are scrupulously observed.[69]

Two other collections, apart from the villas, attracted attention. Kotzebue in 1804 listed the collection of LUCIEN BONAPARTE, prince of Canino, Bonaparte's brother: the Giustiniani Minerva, the relief of Bacchus suckled by Amalthea, and an antique altar were the foundations of his collection. He intended to acquire three hundred paintings. The other was the collection of GIAMPIETRO CAMPANA (1808-1880). Florence Nightingale was shown around by Campana himself and singled out a bust of Cicero from the via Salaria, an agate head of Livia to be worn as a badge in a breastplate, masses of Etruscan material (jewellery, mirrors, a funeral bed, cooking equipment), an exquisite relief of Menelaus driving Helen home to Troy (*sic*): she driving four horses, he running alongside, and a bronze statue of Ascanius. Hillard noted glass vessels, reliefs (especially a series representing the labours of Hercules), vases, household instruments and

Lorenzo Scarabello, The Villa
Campana, *c. 1847*

gold jewellery. An irony was not lost on him: 'The whole collection was like a leaf torn out of a lost book of history. An Etruscan bracelet made for an arm that has been dust for thirty centuries, viewed by an American, in a Roman house built, perhaps, before his country was

discovered!'[70] A decade later, while president of the Pontifical Academy of Archæology, Campana was convicted of corruption in the administration of Monte de Pietà, sentenced to perpetual banishment, and his collection sold and dispersed.

Ernst Meyer, A smoke in Rome, *1828-32*

CONTEMPORARY ROME

Of general impressions, Elisa von der Recke was negative: she wrote of the melancholy of the 'dirty huts', deserted streets, the crowds of beggars, and the bad air; relief was provided by the fountains. That basic theme was heightened in 1811 for Alphonse de Lamartine:

> The city was very sad and quite deserted; there was no pope, no cardinals, no clergy. Bonaparte had taken them all away... Rome at that time resembled western Thebes, weeping for its oracles in a prospective desert. The population of this capital in ruins amounted to only fifty thousand souls. Monks could be seen each morning pushing a wheelbarrow at the foot of the adjoining temple, to clear it of dust. The living gods were reviving the dead gods.

Hector Berlioz in 1831 had to be dramatic:

> Neither our noisy artistic gatherings, the brilliant balls at the Academy and the Embassy, nor the freedom of the café, could make me forget that I had left Paris, the centre of civilisation, and that I was suddenly deprived of music, theatres, literature, excitement – in fact, all that made life worth living.
>
> Is it surprising that the shadow of Ancient Rome, which alone casts a glory around Modern Rome, did not compensate me for all I had lost?

Hans Christian Andersen first came to Rome in October 1833; his third visit began in March 1846. He recorded tremendous changes:

> Rome is not the Rome it was thirteen years ago when I first was here. It is as if everything were modernized, the ruins even, grass and bushes are cleared away. Everything is made so neat; the very life of the people seems to have retired; I no longer hear the tambourines in the streets, no longer see the young girls dancing their Saltarella: even in the Campagna intelligence has entered by invisible railroads; the peasant no longer believes as he used to do.

At the Easter festival I saw great numbers of the people from the Campagna standing before St Peter's whilst the Pope distributed his blessing, just as though they had been Protestant strangers.

Jacob Burckhardt at the very same time re-emphasised the negative aspects:

The city, so far as it is now inhabited by the poor, seems to me incomparably poorer and ruined than any Lombard village. They have fought here for centuries against work as against the worst enemy; there is scarcely a trace of the lightest industry; the public shoeshine, for example, is completely absent; carriage and bus services have barely begun; there is no newspaper at all; scarcely one or two restaurants have modified their Roman dishes towards French taste. In any German Swiss village there are more tourist industries than here, where 30,000 foreign-ers live, mostly with only the motive of enjoyment. I take this as a divine blessing, because if one were besieged here by commissionaires and rabble of that kind in the same way as in Strasburg, it would be hell. The Roman waits till he is asked, and the ragged street urchin is content with a *bajocco* for accompanying one the length of the street. This is partly what chains the foreigner to this poor Rome, truly miserable in luxury items; sloth has here brought into bloom an art of courtesy, which is all too attractive to the foreigner.[71]

The centre of Rome was the CORSO. Wilhelm Müller in 1818 declared that it was the only street worthy of a capital in the city, lined with milliners, fancy goods sellers, restorers, butchers with their sausages hanging out the front, coffee shops, art dealers with goods displayed on tables, and *osterie* marked by the sign of green branches hanging outside, with red-bodiced women and men in green seated at the wide tables. Nearly twenty years later Dickens described the Corso as 'a mile long; a street of shops, and palaces, and private houses, sometimes opening into a broad piazza. There are virandas [*sic*] and balconies of all shapes and sizes, to almost every house – not on one story alone, but often to one room or another on every story...'[72]

Ippolito Caffi, Via del Corso, at night, *1835-1860*

Few visitors comment on other streets. Berlioz, staying at the villa Medici in 1831, naturally was well acquainted with the VIA PINCIANA, 'the Champs Elysées of Rome, which is thronged every evening with carriages, equestrians and pedestrians, defiling in a never ending stream along the magnificent plateau. They disperse at the stroke of seven like a swarm of flies in the wind, for the Romans have an invincible, almost superstitious, dread of *l'aria cattiva* (bad [night] air).'[73]

The many grand *piazze* were perhaps the most striking feature of modern Rome. The most talked about was PIAZZA NAVONA. Antoine

Piazza Navona, photographed by Giacomo Caneva in 1850

Pasquin thought it magnificent, but observed that it provided no shelter against sun or rain. He stated that the original circus was the work of Alexander Severus (222-35), instead of Domitian. He retold a story about Bernini and the fountain. When Innocent X asked when the water would arrive, the architect said that he would do his best. The pope was moving away when he heard the rush of water. He declared that the surprise would give him another ten years of life! The fountain was unveiled in 1651; Innocent died in 1655. Henry Wadsworth Longfellow described the scene in 1828:

> Every Saturday afternoon in the sultry month of August, this spacious square is converted into a lake, by stopping the conduit pipes which carry off the water of the fountains [Ill. Vol. II]. Vehicles of every description, axle deep, drive to and fro across the mimic lake; a dense crowd gathers around its margin, and a thousand tricks excite the loud laughter of the

idle populace. Here is a fellow groping with a stick after his seafaring hat; there another splashing in the water in pursuit of a mischievous spaniel, who is swimming away with his shoe; while from a neighboring balcony a noisy burst of military music fills the air, and gives fresh animation to the scene of mirth. This is one of the popular festivals of midsummer in Rome, and the merriest of them all. It is a kind of carnival unmasked, and many a popular bard, many a Poeta di dozzina, invokes this day the plebeian Muse of the market place to sing in high sounding rhyme, 'Il Lago di Piazza Navona.'

Perhaps no one, however, provided a wittier account of the summer flooding of the piazza than Berlioz; it also gave him an irresistible opportunity to score some hits:

The square is at once transformed from a vegetable market to a reeking, filthy pond, with cabbage stalks, lettuce leaves, melon rind, wisps of straw, and almond husks floating on its surface instead of water lilies. On a raised platform on the shores of this enchanted lake stand fifteen musicians, with drums, large and small, a triangle, a Chinese pavilion, and two pairs of cymbals, supported, for the sake of appearance, by some horns or clarinets, and performing music of the same degree of purity as the water at their feet. Meanwhile the most brilliant equipages pace slowly through the pool, while the air resounds with the ironical acclamations of the *sovereign people.*

'*Mirate! mirate!* there is the Austrian ambassador!'

'No; it is the English envoy.'

'Look at his arms – a kind of eagle.'

'Not at all; it is some other animal; and besides, I can see *Dieu et mon droit.*'

'There is the Spanish consul with his trusty Sancho. Rosinante does not seem particularly delighted with this watery promenade.'

'What! the French representative here too?'

'And why not, pray? That old man with the cardinal's hat behind him is Napoleon's maternal uncle.' [Joseph Fesch]

'And that little paunchy man, with the malicious smile, trying to look serious?'

'He is a clever man [Stendhal] who has written about art, and is consul at Civitavecchia; he considers himself forced to come here and loll in his carriage in this slum, because it is the *fashion*; he is now contriving a new chapter for his novel, *Rouge et Noir*.'

'*Mirate! mirate!* here is our great Vittoria, our small- (not so very small) footed Fornarina, reposing from her labours in the Academy studios last week, and showing herself off in her cardinal's dress. There she sits in her chariot, like Venus rising from the waves. Listen! the tritons of the Piazza Navone, who all know her, are going to lift up their voices in a triumphal march. Sauve qui peut! What a hullabaloo! What has happened? A shopkeeper's carriage upset? Yes; I see it is the excellent wife of our tobacconist in the Via Condotti. Bravo! she is whipping her little boy as a compensation for his bath, the horses, not being sea-horses, are plunging about in the muddy water. Hurrah! someone is drowned! Agrippina is tearing her hair. Increasing delight on the part of the audience. They are pelting her with orange peel.'

The summer flooding was frivolous. The piazza was also put to a more unseemly, if necessary, use. Hillard disliked the market:

The Piazza also abounds with shops and stalls for the sale of all sorts of second hand articles; and no where else have I ever seen such quantities of broken pottery, old iron, disabled household utensils, and all conceivable kinds of trash piled together; awakening wonder, at every step, that any one should ever buy such rubbish, or could put it to any use when bought. Here, too, are shops of higher pretensions, though not imposing in their outward appearance, occupied by dealers in pictures, engravings, cameos, intaglios, antique gems, and the like; and it is said that those who have time, patience, and money, will sometimes light upon very good bargains.[74]

Edward Lear, Piazza di Spagna, *after 1837*

The PIAZZA DI SPAGNA was the other centre of Rome for the tourist at this time. Jean George Mallet de Hauteville captured its many changing moods in 1815. It was the foreigners' quarter, with post carriages arriving every hour to the sound of cracking whips; every morning the domestic servants, guides, and calèches assembled there seeking custom; while every evening the 'bad air' brought into the city the flocks pasturing in the environs; a troop of goats often crossed the piazza and twice a day scaled the stairs! The steps, indeed, had other hazards. Berlioz and two friends were returning to the Academy when 'some wretches lurking in the shadow' demanded their money or their lives, whereupon the Frenchmen drew their 'big Roman knives, and catching the gleam of these in the moonlight', the would-be robbers 'relapsed temporarily into the path of virtue'.[75] Strange to say, no one referred to the death of a young English poet here in 1821.

Elisa von der Recke considered the PIAZZA DEL QUIRINALE 'without denial the most beautiful in the city', but in her opinion the impression created by the fine statues of the Horsetamers was broken by the obelisk.[76]

John Ruskin, The Trevi Fountain, *1841*

Few visitors at this time commented on the TIBER. Pasquin declared it a sewer and stated that the steamboat in 1828 took five hours to reach Fiumicino. The bridge which caught visitors' attention was ponte Sant'Angelo. Pasquin was still in a bad mood: nothing, he declared, was more ridiculous than the wind in the angels' clothing and the shape of their wings![77]

Rome was a city of water in a more important sense. 'The first object which strikes the foreigner on entering Rome is the multitude of FOUNTAINS he meets, and the abundance of water which they emit under all sorts of shapes,' stated Petit Radel. He singled out the Trevi fountain, 'one of the most beautiful monuments offered by Rome, considered either with regard to the magnificence of the composition or the abundance of water furnished'. Shelley declared the fountains 'in themselves magnificent combinations of art such as alone it were worth coming to see'. His favourite was the Quirinal, but it was his admiration for the Horsetamers which seems to have most influenced him. The atrabilious Pasquin could indulge his critical faculties: at the Aqua Felice the 'ridiculous and colossal Moses... looks like a standing Silenus'. One is therefore surprised to find him praising the Trevi as 'poetic and clever'. Hans Christian Andersen found the fountains 'superbly crafted'. Apart from those in piazza Navona, the Trevi, the Quirinal, and the Aqua Felice, he listed the 'Barcaccia' in piazza di Spagna, the fountain of the turtles in piazza Mattei, and as proof of his special appreciation the rather hidden 'Facchino' off the lower Corso: 'there is a really splendid one in the Corso, where the stone is in the shape of a man with a keg in his hands; the water is squirting out the open bunghole'. Yet another discordant note, however, was struck by Hillard on the Navona fountain:

> The entire combination is a cold and extravagant allegory, hardly inferior in absurdity to the monument to Dr Arne, where he is represented playing on a harpsichord in the river Thames, with tritons and sea nymphs sporting around him. Nor is there any special merit in the execution of the statues, to awaken a forgiving spirit towards the bad taste and want of simplicity in the design. Modelled by Bernini, and executed under his direction, they have the largest measure of his faults, redeemed by the smallest proportion of his peculiar merits. They are sprawling, grotesque, and monstrous; with as little dignity about them as the giants of a travelling caravan. Nothing, however, can be said against the water which foams, gushes, and leaps from every part of the uncouth structure, in streams which are as pure as they are copious. Its curves of breaking silver and its voice of mellow music plead, and not unsuccessfully, in favour of the absurd caricatures which it embellishes.[78]

The key to the control of Rome was the fort – and notorious prison – CASTEL SANT'ANGELO. In 1805 Elisa von der Recke stated that very few of the cells were occupied. Pasquin in 1828 naturally needed special permission to visit the castle, and found a different situation: 'our descent by torchlight into the underground, with soldiers and jailers, after going through the prisoners and convicts who fill the prison, made our expedition seem like a novel', he stated, with repulsive insensitivity. Not all the prisoners were brigands or criminals, he admitted, because condemnation to the galleys was used for 'simple crimes' such as riot, assault and battery, and even whistling at entertainments. Pasquin visited the excavations which had uncovered the ancient entrance and the spiral staircase.[79]

Napoleon had opened the GHETTO. The restored papacy had re-established it. William Hazlitt was outraged:

> The Jews (I may add while I think of it) are shut up here in a quarter by themselves. I see no reason for it. It is a distinction not worth the making. There was a talk (it being *Anno Santo*) of shutting them up for the whole of the present year. A soldier stands at the gate, to tell you that this is the Jews' quarter, and to take any thing you choose to give him for this piece of Christian information. A Catholic church stands outside their prison, with a Crucifixion painted on it as a frontispiece, where they are obliged to hear a sermon in behalf of the truth of the Christian religion every Good Friday. On the same day they used to make them run races in the Corso, for the amusement of the rabble (high and low) – now they are compelled to provide horses for the same purpose. Owing to the politeness of the age, they no longer burn them as of yore, and that is something. Religious zeal, like all other things, grows old and feeble. They treat the Jews in this manner at Rome (as a local courtesy to St Peter), and yet they compliment *us* on our increasing liberality to the Irish Catholics.

That was in 1825. Three years later Pasquin stated that the population had been counted for the first time, because of fear of cholera, and was found to be 3,500, but this 'dirty, narrow, infected quarter by the Tiber is not at all unhealthy'. He described the ghetto as a barbarous indictment of Christian charity. The one hundred richest families paid 7,000 *scudi* for religion, schools, doctors, and help to the poor. Another repulsive ceremony was witnessed at Carnival in 1830 by Felix Mendelssohn:

> On Saturday all the world went to the Capitol, to witness the form of the Jews' supplications to be suffered to remain in the

Hieronymus Hess, Study for 'The Conversion of the Jews in Rome', *1821*

Sacred City for another year; a request which is refused at the foot of the hill, but after repeated entreaties, granted at the summit, and the Ghetto assigned to them.

Of this place a melancholy description was given by Hillard in 1847:

On entering the enclosure, the aspect of the place and its inhabitants leaves an uniform impression of poverty, desolation, and filth. The streets are narrow, crooked, and dark; the houses, which have a look of mouldy decay, are crowded with life, so that, in fine weather, the occupants swarm out, like bees, and sit on the steps or on the pavement in front of the door, and there pursue their usual avocations. There are many shops, but usually a humble class. The Jewish race is here seen in its saddest and lowest plight, not gilded by even a ray of its old glories...

[A]t this moment there are nearly four thousand of them crowded together in this twisted knot of streets, where of the sun and air they have not enough, and of water only too much;

Giacomo Lenghi, The 'Cinque Scole (Five Synagogues under One Roof)
in the Ghetto, *c. 1839*

being always the first and greatest sufferers in those frequent
inundations by which the Tiber vindicates its old reputation for
turbulence and insubordination. The men, excluded from most
attractive callings, are generally petty shopkeepers, pedlers, and
dealers in old clothes and second hand articles. The women
have great skill in mending and repairing garments, and in this
craft their services are in requisition all over the city. Many of
them give themselves to higher and finer kinds of needle work.

Florence Nightingale located the ceremony to beg permission for
longer residence in Rome by the Jews at the Arch of Titus, a ceremony
which Pius IX abolished – as he did that of the Christian sermons
which the Jews were forced to attend.[80]

Such was the topography of Rome. The first half of the nineteenth
century was the last flourish of the old theocratic GOVERNMENT, and
what a government it was! Macaulay pointed up its peculiarities in
1838:

I can conceive nothing more insupportable than the situation of a layman who should be a subject of the Pope. In this government there is no avenue to distinction for any but priests. Every office of importance, diplomatic, financial, and judicial, is held by the clergy. A prelate, armed with most formidable powers, superintends the police of the streets. The military department is directed by a Commission, over which a Cardinal presides. Some petty magistracy is the highest promotion to which a lawyer can look forward; and the greatest nobles of this singular State can expect nothing better than some place in the Pope's household, which may entitle them to walk in procession on the great festivals. Imagine what England would be if all the members of Parliament, the Ministers, the Judges, the Ambassadors, the Governors of Colonies, the very Commanders in Chief and Lords of the Admiralty, were, without one exception, bishops or priests; and if the highest post open to the noblest, wealthiest, ablest, and most ambitious layman were a Lordship of the Bedchamber! And yet this would not come up to the truth, for our clergy can marry; but here every man who takes a wife cuts himself off for ever from all dignity and power, and puts himself into the same position as a Catholic in England before the Emancipation Bill [1829]. The Church is therefore filled with men who are led into it merely by ambition, and who, though they might have been useful and respectable as laymen, are hypocritical and immoral as churchmen; while on the other hand the State suffers greatly, for you may guess what sort of Secretaries at War and Chancellors of the Exchequer are likely to be found among bishops and canons. Corruption infects all public offices. *Old women above, liars and cheats below* – that is the Papal administration. The States of the Pope are, I suppose, the worst governed in the civilised world; and the imbecility of the police, the venality of the public servants, the desolation of the country, and the wretchedness of the people, force themselves on the observation of the most heedless traveller.

What puts flesh on these bones, however, is a story told by George Ticknor about an episode in *c.* 1830:

I had a long visit from [Domenico] De Crollis this morning, and a long talk with him about Dante, and other matters interesting to me. He is one of the first physicians in Rome, Professor of Medicine in the University here, a learned and, what is more rare, a liberal minded, enlightened man. He told me, among other things, that six or seven years ago he began to hold weekly meetings of three or four persons at his house, to study and interpret Dante, and that they made a good deal of progress in it. Two winters ago Count Ludolf, the Neapolitan Minister, who is a great admirer of Dante, desired to join them, and the result was, that the meetings were transferred to the Farnese Palace, and the number of persons, including the Marchese Gaetano, and one or two other of the Roman nobles of some literary taste, was increased to fourteen or fifteen. The thing, of course, began now to be talked about, and whatever is talked about is unwelcome to a government as weak and as anxious as this. About a year ago they received a very remote, gentle, and indirect hint, as mild as priestly skill could make it, that it was feared the tendency of such meetings was not good. The hint was taken, and the meetings have since been discontinued. Yet Count Ludolf is a legitimist of unquestionable fidelity, and the whole party as far as possible from anything political. I could not help contrasting such a state of things with that in Saxony...[81]

Macaulay, with great insight, had drawn attention to the impotent position of the ARISTOCRACY. A vignette of their life is provided again by Ticknor: the birthday of Prince Mario Gabrielli in 1837:

It was a little dinner given on occasion of the Prince's *birthday,* and it would not be easy to find anything more characteristic of the modes of life here. We were led through three or four large and fine halls, all, however, ill furnished, and were received in another where, round a huge fire place and a small fire, we found our host and hostess; General [Pompeo] Gabrielli, the brother; Monsignor Piccolomini; another Monsignor; a young Count, who, at the age of eighteen or nineteen, is about to be

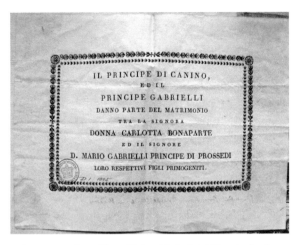

Invitation to the wedding of Prince Mario Gabrielli to the daughter
of Lucien Bonaparte, in 1816

married to a little girl not yet fourteen; and a French lady... Things looked dreary enough, as they always do in these vast palaces; but the conversation was carried on with Italian vivacity and vehemence, and the bonhomie, simplicity, and earnest kindness of the Princess were, as they always are, irresistible. At last dinner was announced, and we were led through the same wide halls by which we had entered, across a magnificent ball room and through a dark passage, to a moderate sized dining room, hung in a careless way with pictures by Perugino, Raphael, Claude, and Andrea del Sarto. The dinner consisted of strange Italian dishes, and was served in the Italian fashion. All the attendants, who were cumbrously numerous, were in shabby liveries, except the major domo, who was in black. Some of them were old; all were easy and familiar, as they always are in these ancient families, and whenever a good joke occurred they laughed, and seemed to enjoy it as much as any of us.

The conversation was lively without any expense of wit. On this point the Italians are not difficult. They content themselves with as little of what is intellectual, in their daily intercourse, as any people well can, but their gaiety is none the less for all that. Monsignor Piccolomini – a great name that has come down from the time of Wallenstein – says his mother was named Jackson, and that her family is connected with that of our President General; a droll circumstance if it is true. His stories, however, are better than his genealogy. We had coffee at table, and then, after freezing a little in the saloon, after the true Roman fashion, we came home in about three hours after we left it.[82]

The state of the government was matched by the ECONOMY. The Swiss naturalist Charles Bonstetten in 1805 listed the only exports of Rome as 'rags, pozzolana, and antiquities'. Half the population, he stated, lived on 'the ruins of past centuries', while the other half 'traded exclusively in the future life'. In 1811 Petit-Radel listed the main income as being taxes on salt, grain and wine. The government set the price of grain and sold its own first, so there was no encouragement for agriculture. He gave the main exports as alum, sulphur, vitriol, silk, oil, wool and art. The enquiring Florence Nightingale, finally, recorded some telling anecdotes in 1847:

> To give you an idea of the state of *commerce* – a splendid silk manufactory, Fabri's at Bologna was ruined, and finally shut up, by the vexatious regulations inflicted, because it undersold the silks of Rome and produced a better article. To give you an idea of the *Agriculture* – there was a corn law, but to make bread cheap – so that, in a bad year, the farmer was ruined, and the land thrown out of cultivation – to remedy this, a cardinal proposed sowing turnips in November.[83]

Travellers noted the many academies and colleges in the city. The UNIVERSITY was the Sapienza (so called from the motto over the door: 'Initium Sapientiæ timor Domini' (the beginning of wisdom is the fear of the Lord) – not the most appropriate legend for a university, some might think – with its five faculties: theology (5 chairs), law (7), medicine (13), philosophy (11) and philology (6). Pasquin heard here a lecture by Alessandro Nibby, professor of archæology, which he declared 'remarkable for its order, precision and solidity'. Hillard was particularly interested in the COLLEGE OF THE PROPAGANDA, where missionaries were trained, because he attended the graduation ceremony in January 1848. Speeches were given in fifty one languages, each one 'rarely exceeding five minutes'. There was a Scottish graduate, Eugene Small, who made clear his wish that Scotland should return to the true church, and two Americans, John Roddan and John Quin from Boston, one of whom spoke in Hebrew and 'Chilean', the other in Paraguayan.

> It has now about sixty pupils at a time, upon an average, within its walls, gathered from all parts of the world. They wear a uniform dress, a long, black robe, or cassock, edged with red, and a red girdle. Two bands, like broad ribbons, depend from the shoulders behind, representing leading strings, and typifying a state of pupilage. The scholars are not obliged to be at any expense; the institution paying the charge of their journey to Rome, of their entire support while there, and of their return to their native country. No one is admitted who is over twenty years old, and each one is obliged to give a pledge that he will devote his life to the dissemination of Catholic doctrines among his own people.

Macaulay visited the ENGLISH COLLEGE:

> We went to the English College, and walked about the cloisters; interesting cloisters to an Englishman. There lie several of our native dignitaries who died at Rome before the Reformation. There lie, too, the bones of many Jacobites, honest martyrs to a worthless cause. We looked into the refectory, much like the halls of the small colleges at Cambridge in my time, – that of Peterhouse, for example, – and smelling strongly of yesterday's supper, which strengthened the resemblance. We found the principal, Dr Wiseman, a young ecclesiastic full of health and vigour.[84]

Nicholas Wiseman was Rector 1828-40, later cardinal and first archbishop of Westminster.

The most celebrated academy of Rome was the ARCADIA. Germaine de Staël was admitted on 14 February 1805, and read her translation of Onofrio Minzoni's sonnet on the death of Jesus. 'After that a down-pour of sonnets fell on my head: ten young people, all declaiming with growing intensity, cast sonnets at me as if they had been Vatican thunderbolts.' The artists' academy was ST LUKE'S. Pasquin reported that they had Raphael's *Virgin and Child*, in front of which was placed his skull, and that the artists used to touch it with their pencil.[85] This mistaken but well meaning respect was to be completely undercut a mere five years later (see p. 168).

On INTELLECTUAL LIFE in general, Petit-Radel in 1811 stated that the only scholars in Rome were the two librarians at the Vatican, those of the Barberini, Corsini and Minerva libraries, as well as some at the Collegio Romano, the Collegio dei Nobili, and the Sapienza (that would seem to make up a fair list: it is a shame that he did not name them: Filippo Aurelio Visconti was keeper at the Vatican 1810-1814; for the Minerva see below). Most of them were writing, he stated, about antiquity, or literature. They nevertheless, in his view, lacked critical power and style. With the enlightened Frenchman agreed the German poet. Wilhelm Müller seven years later devoted a long essay to the intellectual condition of Italy in contrast to northern Europe. In Rome dogma took precedence over knowledge. Müller was horri-fied at what he saw as the castration of classical art, turning the Apollo Belvedere into fallen Adam, and hanging clothing on Raphael's angels and Michelangelo's devils. To live one required private means; official posts were open only to the religious: the scholarly class was the monks. The censorship of books was another problem. No book could be published unless it had the *imprimatur* of the Magister Sacri Palatii, and the Holy Office (Inquisition) could ban any work, 'old or new, native or foreign'. Special permission was required to read Aristo-phanes, Boccaccio and Machiavelli, and absolution was needed to read Voltaire! Some booksellers were allowed to provide foreign editions of the classics for foreigners: de Romanis printed beautiful antiquarian works, for example, for the duchess of Devonshire.[86]

Petit-Radel provided a vital glimpse of LIBRARIES in 1811. Some had not catalogued a new book for half a century. He cited the Minerva, 'so rich in works of theology and natural history, which the worms eat peacefully'. The Lancisiana was for students of medicine at Santo Spirito, but it had had nothing new for thirty years. The Angelica had been enriched by Cardinal Passionei's collection. The Corsini was rich in fifteenth century manuscripts. The most promising from his account seems to be the Barberini, with 60,000 books and more than 9,000 manuscripts, open to the public Monday and Thursday 10-12. This list omits, of course, the Vatican library (see above, palaces). Pasquin was librarian at the Louvre when he came to Rome in 1828, so we would expect him to pay attention. He noted the Casanatense (i.e. the library of the Minerva) with 85,000 volumes and 4,500 manuscripts. This was the largest by that time in Rome for printed books. The librarian was (Giacomo) Magno who had held the post for thirty years. He was, in fact, librarian 1794-1840. The next year another person with special interest in libraries appeared. Leopold von Ranke declared that the libraries were numerous and well equipped. He warned against breaches of protocol, as when he addressed himself to a younger librarian and so slighted his senior. Prince Paluzio Altieri was giving him full access to his manuscript collection, and had put a large room at his disposal. At the Barberini he had a smaller room. He had, however, trouble in the Vatican. Angelo Mai thought it impolitic to give him all the texts which he wanted. He therefore preferred the private libraries, such as the Altieri or the Filippina (Vallicella); the fathers of the last also gave him a small room.[87]

Social life revolved around the CAFÉS and CONVERSAZIONI. Müller in 1818 revealed that German artists gathered at the Caffé Greco (via Condotti, founded 1760) no fewer than three times a day. An attraction seems to be that the coffee was served in cups. High society, on the other hand, frequented the Cafe Nuovo on the ground floor of the palazzo Ruspoli in the Corso, decorated with carpets, chandeliers and imperial busts. Cafés and *osterie* had to close by midnight. Pasquin in 1828 favoured the Cafe Nuovo. It was thought the most beautiful, with its celebrated staircase. Each profession had its own window seats. Cafés in Rome served the same purpose, he suggested, as papers and the opposition in Paris: 'What is printed in Paris is said in Rome'!

Ludwig Pasini, Artists in the Caffè Greco, *1856*

The Caffè Greco was more for artists, the Cafe Montecitorio for professors and savants, and the cafe Trevi was the seat of Carlo Fea and the antiquaries, where the peasants brought the antiquities they had found. The Caffè Greco was also naturally the haunt of the French artists above on the Pincian. No-one could give a more dramatic picture than Berlioz:

> It is a miserable hole – dirty, dark, and damp; and it is impossible to understand why all the artists in Rome should flock there. Its only advantage is its proximity to the Piazza di Spagna and the Lepri Restaurant, which is opposite. You pass your time there in smoking execrable cigars and drinking worse coffee, served on wretched little wooden tables the size of a hat, and

as greasy and filthy as the walls of this delectable resort. Nevertheless, the Caffè Greco is so much frequented by foreign artists that most of them have their letters sent there, and fresh arrivals know they are sure to meet all their countrymen collected there.

As it happens, however, a contemporary whom Berlioz met there confirms this impression. Felix Mendelssohn found the artists detestable, especially for their criticism of the great masters.

> They are most formidable to look at, sitting in their Caffè Greco. I scarcely ever go there, for I dislike both them and their favourite places of resort. It is a small dark room, about eight feet square, where on one side you may smoke, but not on the other; so they sit round on benches, with their broad leaved hats on their heads, and their huge mastiffs beside them; their cheeks and throats, and the whole of their faces covered with hair, puffing forth clouds of smoke (only on one side of the room), and saying rude things to each other, while the mastiffs swarm with vermin.[88]

The most famous Roman social occasion was the CONVERSAZIONE (soirée or salon). The straight-talking Washington Irving was not amused:

> In the evening went to a conversazione at the Marquis of Torlona's [sic] – great number of the nobility there, and foreigners of distinction, particularly two Russian Princes – Assembly most deplorably stupid hardly a handsome woman there the company sat down almost universally to cards and we left them at an early hour. It is a just remark of a traveller in Italy (I believe Dr Moore) that an Italian conversazione is a place where people meet to do any thing else but converse. I have however been to several where they have been more rational.

He clearly did not understand the rules of the game, but Petit-Radel agreed with him. He also found these meetings very boring – except for those of the Duchess Lante and Mme Dionigi (Marianna Candidi,

1756-1826). Ticknor in 1818 described these social groups which met around leading foreigners in their various nationalities:

> These cultivated strangers settle down into coteries of their own, generally determined by their nationality. Thus the Germans, the English, and French have their separate societies, preserving in the forms of their intercourse and in their general tone the national character that marks them at home; except when, perhaps, two or three times in the week all the strangers in Rome, with a few of the best of the Italians, a quantity of cardinals, bishops, and ecclesiastics of all names and ranks, are brought together at a kind of grand rout, called a *conversazione*, or *academia*... Nothing can be more amusing than one of these farrago societies which I have seen at the Duchess of Devonshire's and Count Funchal's, the Portuguese Ambassador, – the east and west, the north and the south... all brought together to be pushed about a couple of hours or more in an endless suite of enormous rooms, and then wait for their carriages in a comfortless antechamber, – all national distinctions half broken down by the universal use of French, even among persons of the same country, and more than half preserved by the bad accent with which it is spoken, – the confusion of the Tower of Babel produced without a miracle or an object... Rome is still as much the capital as it was in the times of Hadrian or Leo X...
>
> Among the Germans there is the family of [Christian] Bunsen, who has married an Englishwoman [Fanny Waddington], and is himself full of good learning and talent; the family of Mad. [Karoline] de Humboldt (in conversation called the Mad. de Staël of Germany), who collects about her every evening the best of her nation, especially the artists [Bertel] Thorwaldsen, [Johann Ludwig] Lund, [Rudolph] Schadow, etc., and to whose society I owe some of the pleasantest hours I have passed in Rome; [Barthold] Niebuhr, the Prussian Minister, who, after all I have heard in Germany of his immense learning and memory, has filled me with admiration and astonishment every time I have seen him;... Baron Eckhardtstein, who has travelled all over Europe with profit, and was distinguished as an officer in

the last war; Baron Ziegenhorn, now in the midst of a course of travels appalling for their length and objects to any but a German. But the person who has excited the most attention among the Germans, and who really deserves it, is the Crown Prince of Bavaria [later Ludwig I], a young man of about thirty, who has been living here in a very simple, unostentatious manner, and enjoying Rome like a cultivated gentleman with much taste and considerable talent... He talks English pretty well, and knows a good deal about general history, and something about America, which he liked well to let me see...

Perhaps the reason for the national congregations was the observations with which Ticknor prefaced his account:

Society in Rome is certainly a remarkable thing, different from society in every other part of the world. Among the Romans themselves the elegant and cultivated class is really so small, the genuine character, civilisation and refinement of the country are so worn out and degraded that, even in their own capital, they are not able, and do not pretend to give a tone to society and intercourse.

Alexander Clemens Wetterling, Domani? Sicuramente!, *1827*

At the same time Müller, while admitting that social life was limited to *conversazioni* and the academies, stressed that an entrée to the aristocracy and the educated middle class was quite easy for foreigners. A letter of introduction, and decent clothing and behaviour – and the fact of being a visitor – were enough to gain admission to the circles of the aristocracy. Introductions by a banker were quite useful, but one could meet young nobles at the coffee houses.[89]

There were, indeed, other social occasions, notably at MUSICAL PERFORMANCES and the THEATRE. We learn much about the programmes at this time. Theatres were open only at Carnival. Kotzebue saw an appalling production at the Argentina of an opera by Pietro Guglielmi (he does not say which of his hundred operas it was!), but the singing, music, orchestra and scenery were all bad. The ballet was 'beneath criticism'. On the other hand, Ferdinando Paer's new opera, *Una in bene ed una in male* was pronounced excellent. Kotzebue also reported that any fraud in selling tickets was punished by three strokes of the cord and anyone keeping a seat for someone else by laying his hat upon it was liable to imprisonment! In 1811 Stendhal was introduced to Duchess Lante, who had been told that he was 'travelling for music'. She asked him to select the pieces to be performed at a concert. The duchess had a theatre in her palace and she performed with her friends, to the amazement of the Frenchmen present. Nicola Zingarelli composed *The Destruction of Jerusalem* for her.

> The Frenchmen had rather a heteroclite look at this concert. What could be further from their manners and morals than a duchess singing with her friends through the love of music, and these friends playing the duet from *The Secret Marriage*, '*Se fiato in corpo avete*', with the gayest kind of buffooneries! The poor Frenchmen were dumfounded at such a thing, notably a chief justice, who with his decorations and dark clothes, remained bolted down to his chair all evening, his legs tight together like an Egyptian statue.
>
> M. Norvins appeared very spiteful and never stopped talking.

Il matrimonio segreto was by Cimarosa. Jacques Norvins, the Minister of Police in French occupied Rome, was also recorded weeping

Jean-Auguste-Dominique Ingres, Jacques Norvins, *1811-12*

during the *Miserere* (see above, p. 62). Petit-Radel at the same time was very interested in the theatres. He noted the strange custom at the Argentina: the members of the orchestra each had a candle to see their music, which they lit and extinguished according to whether they were playing at that moment or not. He judged them good on strings but poor on winds, but he had not heard anywhere in Italy such applause as at Rome. Another problem was that there was no stability in the cast. He saw Giuseppe Farinelli's *I riti d'Efeso* with the ballet *Teseo riconosciuto.* The leading soprano was Marianna Sessi, the prima donna Luisa Velsovani, the bass Luigi Zamballi and the tenor Prospero Pedrezzi. At the Teatro della Valle the clowns were Pellegrini and Zamboni, the tenor Boricelli, and the sopranos Rosa Morandi and Solandri, whom he saw in *Monsieur de Livonie.* Petit Radel merely named the other theatres: the Apollo, via Tordinone; the Clementino, and the Aliberti in via Babuino. There was also a puppet theatre, the Sala Pallacorda; this tended to be indecent, but the French police were forced to be tolerant. The man who was to furnish Schubert with

Dietrich Wilhelm Lindau, A street altar in Rome, hung with votive offerings, attended by itinerant pipers watched by locals, *1835*

immortal verses strangely noted only one of the most popular forms of music in Rome, the *pifferi* (pipers). In the evenings, musicians with shawms, flutes and bagpipes stood before the illuminated street shrines to the Madonna, offering their 'shrill homage'. They were Calabrians, with pointed hats, reddish brown cloaks to the knees, and sandals. At the other end of the spectrum, in May 1825 Champollion attended a mass in S Giovanni Laterano in memory of Henry IV (who obviously was worth a Mass). 'The music was delicious and I would have been enraptured with it, if unfortunately five or six *castrati* had not been constantly in view: this disillusioned everything.'

The most detailed discussion of music at Rome in the first half of the century comes, as one might expect, from Berlioz. He painted a very depressing picture. There is evidence of a striking decline in standards since the eighteenth century. Whereas all the other arts were flourishing, 'music alone is degraded to the level of a poor, hunted slave, singing wretched verses with a threadbare voice to earn a crust of bread'. His first shock was in St Peter's, where he found a 'wretched' organ and expecting a choir of thousands (he would!), discovered that there were eighteen singers on ordinary days and thirty two on solemn festivals. He even heard a *Miserere* in the Sistine Chapel sung by five. If things were bad enough in the greatest basilica, music was even worse in the other churches. His view of theatres was also very poor:

> The music in the *theatres* is in much the same glorious condition, and is about as *dramatic* as that of the churches is *religious*. There is the same amount of invention, the same purity of form, the same charm of style, the same intensity of thought. The singers I heard during the theatrical season had generally good voices, and that facility of execution which is the special characteristic of the Italians; but they were all mediocre except Madam [Karolina] Unger, the German prima donna, who was a great favourite in Paris, and Salvator [the bass Celestino Salvatori?], a fair baritone. The chorus is a shade below that of the Opéra Comique as regards precision, accuracy, and warmth. The orchestra, about as imposing and formidable as the Prince of Monaco's army, has all the qualities which are generally regarded as defects. In the Valle Theatre there is *one* violin cello, a watchmaker by trade – more fortunate in this than one of his colleagues, who has to earn his bread by *mending chairs*.
>
> The words 'symphony' and 'overture' are used in Rome to designate a *certain noise* which the orchestra makes before the curtain rises, and to which no one ever listens. The names of Beethoven and Weber are scarcely known there. A learned abbé, belonging to the Sistine Chapel, told Mendelssohn *that he had heard someone speak of a young man of great promise called Mozart!*
>
> …Instrumental music is a sealed book to the Romans. They have not the most elementary notion of what we call a symphony.

Berlioz's comments might be dismissed as his typical melodrama-tizing, but they were seconded by the other musician who was in Rome at the same time, Mendelssohn. He met the composer and musicologist Giuseppe Baini:

> I think he conceives me to be only a *brutissimo Tedesco*, so that I have a famous opportunity of becoming well acquainted with him. His compositions are certainly of no great value, and the same may be said of the whole music here. The wish is not wanting, but the means do not exist. The orchestra is below contempt. Mlle. [Henriette] Carl (who is engaged as *prima donna assoluta* for the season, at both the principal theatres here,) is now arrived, and begins to make *la pluie et le beau temps*. The Papal singers even are becoming old; they are almost all unmusical, and do not execute even the most estab-lished pieces in tune. The whole choir consists of thirty-two singers, but that number are rarely together. Concerts are given by the so called Philharmonic Society, but only with the piano. There is no orchestra, and when recently they wished to perform Haydn's *Creation*, the instrumentalists declared it was impossible to play it. The sounds they bring out of their wind instruments, are such as in Germany we have no conception of.

Any performances of his works here in Rome was 'quite out of the question'.

> The orchestras are worse than any one could believe; both musicians, and a right feeling for music, are wanting. The two or three violin performers play just as they choose, and join in when they please; the wind instruments are turned either too high or too low; and they execute flourishes like those we are accustomed to hear in farm yards, but hardly so good; in short the whole forms a Dutch concert, and this applies even to compositions with which they are familiar.

Mendelssohn in December 1830 attended at the Apollo theatre a performance of Giovanni Pacini's *Il Corsaro*:

Antoine Thomas, Boxes in a Roman theatre, *1820*

Pacini then appeared at the piano, and was kindly welcomed. He had prepared no overture, so the opera began with a chorus, accompanied by strokes on an anvil tuned in the proper key. The Corsair came forward, sang his *aria*, and was applauded, on which the Corsair above, and the Maestro below, bowed (this pirate is a contralto, and sung by Mademoiselle [Rosa] Mariani); a variety of airs followed, and the piece became very tiresome. This seemed to be also the opinion of the public, for when Pacini's grand *finale* began, the whole pit stood up, talking to each other as loud as they could, laughing and turning their backs on the stage. Madame Samoilow fainted in her box, and was carried out. Pacini glided away from the piano, and at the end of the act, the curtain fell in the midst of a great tumult. Then came the grand ballet of *Barbe Bleue*, followed by the last act of the opera. As the audience were now in a mood for it, they hissed the whole ballet from the very beginning, and accompanied the second act also with hooting and laughter. At the close Torlonia was called for, but he would not appear.

Andersen attended a performance of the *Barber of Seville* at the Alibert in December 1834:

– Went in the evening to the Alibert Theatre, the largest in Rome where they hold the carnival masquerade. It is five balconies high and something like the French Opera. It was jam full, but we were served up a miserable performance of *The Barber of Seville*: the voices sounded as if they had been wrapped in sacking; wretched acting or, rather, none at all. A dreadful count, who looked like a shoemaker's apprentice in disguise – the only time he was convincing was when he played a drunken soldier. Figaro was a boisterous and lewd fellow. Basilio was dressed almost like a Jesuit, but had a Pierrot face. After the first act there was a tightrope walking act; a small young thing went right down from the askew line to the audience, which was wretchedly fearful; and then she sang along with the music – it sounded like when the old father has to sing in *Jean de France* – half-sobbing and half-bawling. The audience clapped for everything. There was also a ballet, balancing acts. A whole nine acts and all for one *paolo* (one Danish mark). At 9:30, when I left, there were still five acts to go. Around the moon there were summer brown clouds. It was freezing.

Things were much better at the Apollo a few days later:

Went to the Apollo Theatre. It belongs to Torlonia; the name of the brothers is in gilt letters on the door in the oval foyer, which is decorated with casts of Canova's *Dancers*. The theatre is the most splendid in Rome – white and gilt, with glass inlaid in the columns. They were doing [Giuseppe Mercadente's] *The Normans in Paris*; and between the acts, the ballet *The Two Queens*. Magnificent costumes, quite good scenic decoration and beautiful dancers. The singer acted especially well; was almost more an actress than a singer.

By 1837 Ticknor could report remarkable improvement:

In the evening there was a great oratorio at the Palazzo di Venezia, given by Count [Rudolph] Lützow, the Austrian Ambassador. [1827-1848] ... It was Haydn's Creation, performed by a chorus of ninety singers and a band of fifty instruments,

Bartolomeo Pinelli, Romans scanning theatre posters, *1832*

with [Violante] Camporesi for the prima donna… Mad. de Lützow herself was in the chorus, and once sung in a trio with a good deal of sweetness; so much does a love and consideration for the arts prevail – at least in Italy and Germany – over the consideration of rank and place. The whole entertainment, indeed, was elegant, and was given in a magnificent room, said to be the finest in Rome, which is opened only at intervals of years. Some notion of its size may be had from the facts that there were eight hundred people in it, nearly all comfortably seated on cushioned chairs, and that, being finished in the style of the Temple of Antoninus and Faustina, it was necessary to make the pilasters taller, and the griffins of the frieze larger, than they are in that beautiful ruin in the Forum, because the proportions of the room required it.[90]

The general impression, however, remains that there had been a severe decline in the standard of music at Rome in the early nineteenth century in comparison with the eighteenth.

Rome had also once been famous for her HOSPITALS. Petit-Radel was somewhat appalled at the largest, Santo Spirito, which had one thousand beds. There was naturally no privacy, and patients might have the spectacle of death in the bed next to them, with often a nun making a list of property in front of the dying. Opposite was the military hospital, founded by Pius VI, praised for its space and air. The Ben Fratelli, founded by Clement XI, had sixty beds. The Consolazione specialised in treating victims of stabbings and had one hundred and fifty beds! The Trinità dei Pellegrini of Filippo Neri had 400 beds. The San Gallicano in Trastevere, founded by Benedict XIII, had fifty beds and was for the treatment of psora and leprosy. There was, finally, S Giacomo, for incurables, which had one hundred-and-twenty beds. Of the mental asylum, however, Pasquin in 1828 painted an appalling picture. At the time it contained 397 inmates (235 men, 162 women), including some English and two Jews. The violent (*folies furieuses*) were chained and beaten, but Bedlam was no different. No-one would have been more interested in this matter than Florence Nightingale. She did a 'course of convents and hospitals'. First was the Buon Pastore. 'Oh the waste of life in this place, the intense cold, the miserable pozza smelling (stagnant water) rooms.' It seemed that any man could have any woman in his family sent here on application to the Vicario on the grounds of 'extravagance or any troublesome conduct'. There were some successes, however, because the women were taught – everything but kitchen work! There were only nine nuns, and very few of them Italian. Santo Spirito, however, received a good shaking up in 1847. Pius IX made a surprise visit and found two attendants for 250 patients and provisions being carried around the brick floors in wheelbarrows 'over the wretched fevered heads of the patients'. The pope tried the soup, and smashed the basin on the floor. Then to S Giacomo: 'I never came out of any place with a heavier heart,' she wrote. All the patients were in the one ward: 'four rows of beds – the stench dreadful, the locale cold, airless, dark – the nuns perfectly over done'; there were only nine of them. At S Gallicano, where scrofulous children were treated, there were 'nice baths and wash houses… but still no gardens, no place for air or exercise or anything to cure the children'.[91]

Bartolomeo Pinelli, Laying out the corpse, *1832*

As Petit-Radel noted, death was ever present in these institutions. Many visitors commented on FUNERALS. Pasquin in 1828 saw that of a young girl in S Maria in Trastevere: she was laid out for a day in nun's habit. He commented on the Roman 'slowness of the last separation, this publicity of death' in contrast to the French 'barbarous and clandestine precipitation of burial'. At the same date Longfellow saw the funeral of a monk:

> I was drawn to the window by the solemn chant, as the procession came from a neighboring street and crossed the square. First came a long train of priests, clad in black, and bearing in their hands large waxen tapers, which flared in every gust of wind, and were now and then extinguished by the rain. The bier followed, borne on the shoulders of four barefooted Carmelites; and upon it, ghastly and grim, lay the body of the dead monk, clad in his long gray kirtle, with the twisted cord about his waist. Not even a shroud was thrown over him. His

Isaac Weld, Funeral procession at Rome, *1818*

head and feet were bare, and his hands were placed upon his bosom, palm to palm, in the attitude of prayer. His face was emaciated, and of a livid hue; his eyes unclosed; and at every movement of the bier, his head nodded to and fro, with an unearthly and hideous aspect. Behind walked the monastic brotherhood, a long and melancholy procession, with their cowls thrown back, and their eyes cast upon the ground; and last of all came a man with a rough, unpainted coffin upon his shoulders, closing the funeral train.

Margaret Fuller Ossoli describes the funeral of Don Carlo Torlonia, who died on 31 December 1848:

Don Carlo was a Knight of Malta; yet with him the celibate life had not hardened the heart, but only left it free on all sides to general love. Not less than half a dozen pompous funerals were given in his honor, by his relatives, the brotherhoods to which he belonged, and the battalion of the Civic Guard of which he was commander-in chief. But in his own house the body lay in no other state than that of a simple Franciscan, the order to which he first belonged, and whose vow he had kept through half a century, by giving all he had for the good of others. He lay on the ground in the plain dark robe and cowl, no unfit subject for a modern picture of little angels descending to shower lilies on a good man's corpse. The long files of armed men, the rich coaches, and liveried retinues of the princes, were little observed, in comparison with more than a hundred orphan girls whom his liberality had sustained, and who followed the bier in mourning robes and long white veils, spirit-like, in the dark night. The trumpet's wail, and soft, melancholy music from the bands, broke at times the roll of the muffled drum; the hymns of the Church were chanted, and volleys of musketry discharged, in honor of the departed; but much more musical was the whisper in which the crowd, as passed his mortal frame, told anecdotes of his good deeds.[92]

For most visitors to Rome there was, of course, one place which they held in special veneration: the so-called PROTESTANT CEMETERY (see ill. p. 299). Shelley's remarks were more prescient than he knew:

The English bur[y]ing place is a green slope near the walls, under the pyramid of Cestius, & is I think the most beautiful & solemn cemetery I ever beheld. To see the sun shining on its bright grass fresh when we visited it with the autumnal dews, & hear the whispering of the wind among the leaves of the trees which have overgrown the tomb of Cestius, & the coil which is stirring in the sunwarm earth & to mark the tombs mostly of women & young people who were buried there, one might, if one were to die, desire the sleep they seem to sleep. Such is the human mind & so it peoples with its wishes vacancy & oblivion.

Hillard noted the restrictions imposed, apart from the old rule about burial at night so as not to excite prejudice from the population:

The papal government, though it defrayed the expenses of the enclosure, will not permit any allusion to hopes beyond the grave to be carved upon the monument to a heretic; and, for this reason, the inscriptions of this cemetery merely set forth the virtues and graces of the deceased, and say nothing of the resurrection and a future life.

The other aspect Hillard commented on was the 'Englishness' of the place, with its lawns and flowers. 'The common monthly rose of our conservatories grows here with great luxury, and is always in bloom, hanging its flowers over the monuments, and filling the air with a delicate and spiritual fragrance.'[93]

We may finally assemble some travellers' notes on the CHARACTER of the Romans in the early nineteenth century. Müller was perhaps most struck by their lack of shame. This was exhibited in the way they relieved themselves in public: in doorways, entrances, and halls and not sparing even churches and chapels. The Swiss Guard, he claimed, could scarcely keep the papal palace undefiled. Crucifixes and holy pictures were put up, with inscriptions such as 'Respect the Holy Cross! Respect the house of the Holy Madonna!' This, he admitted, seemed to be an old Roman problem: he quoted the inscription from the Baths of Titus to the effect that whoever urinated or defecated there risked the anger of the gods. Germaine de Staël looked a little higher, but was critical:

> You must not count on society scarcely at all, not that there is no charm in the character of the men and in the manners of the women, but an Oriental indolence and a flexibility of character which lessens the value of all affections prevent profound links with them. It is however a nation which is interesting to observe and which surely does not deserve the contempt which is heaped upon it.
>
> I have been personally touched by their welcome. The cardinals received me marvellously well, and certainly Rome is a country where there is more freedom in social customs, although there is none at all in the rules. In short, the weak are somewhat good and it is only the strong one must avoid.

Burckhardt, the Swiss art historian, in 1846 was taken with the lower classes:

> The Romans please me, that is the common people, for the middle class is as pitifully foolish as in Milan. The ordinary Roman does not have the malicious repression of the ordinary

Milanese, he is kinder and artistic. Indeed he begs, but he does not annoy the foreigner by offering small services. If anyone offers him nothing, he leaves him completely politely and runs off without any curses. You feel in the largest crowds that you are surrounded so to speak by honest people, especially in the poor and ruined quarters around the Capital and in... Travestere.

Burckhardt's remarks remind us of the famous TRASTEVERINI, whom Longfellow noticed:

Yonder across the square goes a *Minente* of Trastevere, a fellow who boasts the blood of the old Romans in his veins. He is a plebeian exquisite of the western bank of the Tiber, with a swarthy face and the step of an emperor. He wears a slouched hat, and blue velvet jacket and breeches, and has enormous silver buckles in his shoes. As he marches along, he sings a ditty in his own vulgar dialect: -

Bartolomeo Pinelli, Trasteverini and Monticiani in Campo Vaccino, *1823*

Une, due, e tre,
E lo Papa non è Re.

Now he stops to talk with a woman with a pan of coals in her hand. What violent gestures! what expressive attitudes! Head, hands, and feet are all in motion, – not a muscle is still! It must be some interesting subject that excites him so much, and gives such energy to his gestures and his language. No; he only wants to light his pipe!

Pasquin told the amusing tale of the Swiss Guard who moved to eject a Trasteveran from St Peter's because he was disturbing the pope's prayers. He retorted, 'Barbarians, I am of Roman, even Trojan, blood!'[94]

It was the WOMEN of Rome finally who attracted some commentary, from visitors of various nations. First the Englishman Shelley:

> the Romans please me much, especially the women: who though totally devoid of any kind of information or culture of the imagination or affections or understanding, & in this respect a kind of gentle savages yet contrive to be interesting. Their extreme innocence & naivete, the freedom & gentleness of their manners, the total absence of affectation makes an intercourse with them very like an intercourse with uncorrupted children, whom they resemble often in loveliness as well as simplicity. I have seen two women in society here of the highest beauty, their brows & lips and the moulding of the face modelled with sculptural exactness, & the dark luxuriance of their hair floating over their fine complexions – and the lips – you must hear the commonplaces which escape from them before they cease to be dangerous. The only inferior part are the eyes, which though good & gentle, want the mazy depth of colour behind colour with which the intellectual females of England & Germany entangle the heart in soul inwoven labyrinths.

In sum, attractive but shallow; he seems to be talking of the upper classes only. The German poet Müller was impressed with the ease of conversation with Roman women, especially at early mass: S Carlo al

Adolf Carl Senff, Roman Woman, *1820*

Corso and S Silvestro were known as 'gallant churches'! 'Even the richest and foremost women generally disdain no gift from an admirer.' He also claimed that women were easy conquests: attention at a *conversazione* was understood to imply amorous intentions, but frequent gifts were expected. Abbati who acted as guides could find respectable women who lacked pin money. The French painter Jean Baptiste Corot obviously mixed with a different class: he claimed to know the most beautiful women in the world. They were 'not all voluptuous', but physically they were 'superb' and superior in that to French women, but inferior in grace and kindness.[95]

WITNESSED EVENTS

In December 1804 Pius VII went to Paris to crown Napoleon. In August von Kotzebue's words, 'he had left his dominions to refresh the laurel of the French hero by the benificent dew of his blessing, and to assist Bonaparte to bury the recollection of his deeds under a crown'.[96]

Tommaso Minardi and Giovanni Battista Romero, Return of Pius VII, *1814. This is in piazza del Popolo, where two long colonnades have been erected. Orchestras were present. The general direction of the ceremonies was in the hands of Giuseppe Valadier*

Two visitors recorded a very high FLOOD IN 1805. Elisa von der Recke described the terrifying force of the water as seen from the bridges. The worst affected area was the ghetto, and she lamented that no help came from the Christians. She visited the Pantheon where 'the silence was interrupted only by the sound of the waters, which continued to enter'. Mme de Staël was held up at the gates for two days. It was the worst flood for seventy years.[97]

Before leaving Rome, in May 1814 Mme Recamier saw the RETURN FROM EXILE OF PIUS VII. She was standing on the steps of one of the churches in piazza del Popolo. All aristocrats went to meet him at la Storta (about 20 kms to the north). There the horses of his carriage were unharnessed and they drew his coach, in which he knelt. She noted that his hair was quite black, despite his age (in fact, 51). Then she hurried to St Peter's to await his arrival there, where the *Te Deum* resounded. This was, however, a false calm. On 26 February 1815, Napoleon escaped from Elba. The Swiss Jean George Mallet de

Hauteville was there to observe the reaction in Rome. On Good Friday Pius left the Quirinal for the Sistine Chapel, crowded with foreigners and the cardinals, reunited after so many years – but he had gone to Viterbo. Cardinal Fesch was not able to conceal his joy at his nephew's escape, but was sitting a little apart from the bishop of St Malo, the French ambassador, devoted to the Bourbons. The next day the papal rituals were performed by Cardinal Doria (Giuseppe or Anton Maria: they were brothers), who washed the 'apostles' feet. Only six cardinals were now left, and by that evening only one! The administration of the Church was entrusted to Cardinal Giulio della Somaglia. The ambassadors also abandoned the city.[98]

The FUNERAL of a nephew of Pius VI, Cardinal ROMUALDO BRASCHI, took place in May 1817. Byron recorded: 'I have seen the pope alive and a cardinal dead – both of whom looked very well indeed. The latter was in state in the Chiesa Nuova, previous to his interment.'[99]

On 21 June 1818 a new SENATOR WAS INSTALLED, Prince Tommaso Corsini. Wilhelm Müller was there to see. Corsini arrived from Florence with his retinue. At the Quirinal he received the staff of office from the pope, and was then led by the garrison, magistrates and representatives of the cardinals along the Corso to the Capitol. Here the Conservatori gave him the keys to the city. The streets were strewn with sand, the balconies hung with coloured carpets, the pedestal of Marcus' statue was decked with garlands, the columns and arches were hung with lights. The piazzas were crammed with people, who were at every window, every balcony, even on the roofs and statues. The route from the Quirinal was in fact along via Felice to piazza Barberini, then to piazza di Spagna, and via Condotti to the Corso. Military music announced the approaching procession, led by soldiers with their banners emblazoned with 'pax', twenty (*sic*) carriages of the senator with his arms, all the coachmen in white, followed by ten riding horses led by gold laced grooms, and the master of horse on a high stepping mount. The colour then changed, with lawyers and councillors in black, with cloaks and peaked hats, on their patient horses. Everyone was laughing and shouting, trying to make the horses nervous, given that many of the riders were novices. The next group also caused laughter: the cardinals' servants, carrying their red hats;

they jumped from side to side at every step of the horses. Then came the senator, preceded by the papal cavalry in Spanish cloaks and four pages. The senator's horse was tall and strong, but barely able to carry the weight of bridle and trappings. The senator's head was bare, coiffured and powdered, and he carried the staff of office, and wore a broad cloak rich in gold over his new uniform. The people waved their hats and handkerchiefs, and cried 'Viva', and he bowed his head in reply. The end of the procession was formed by the state carriage. At the Capitol, after the consignment of the keys, the senator delivered a long speech in Latin. In the evening naturally there were fireworks, and the museum was opened for *conversazioni*, a concert was given in the council chamber, and the people ran about in the Forum below, where the senator provided wine.[100]

Little did Pius know, but right under his nose a remarkable anniversary was celebrated on 31 October 1817, the TERCENTENARY OF LUTHER'S THESES. George Ticknor was present:

> I had just arrived in Rome, coming from Germany, and was very much among the Germans, – with Niebuhr and Bunsen, [Christian] Brandes and Mad. de Humboldt. Niebuhr thought of getting up the celebration, and at first intended to have it in his own *palazzo*; but he changed the plan, and arranged that it should be held in a large room at Brandes's lodgings, he being connected with the legation [in fact, secretary]. There was nobody present but twenty or thirty Germans, except Thorwaldsen, who, being a Dane, was all one as a German, and myself, who was invited as a kind of German.
>
> Bunsen read something between a speech and a sermon; and there were prayers, that he had translated from the English Prayer Book. Brandes read them, and there was a great sensation produced in the room. What Bunsen said was fine and touching. At the end, Niebuhr – who always reminded me of the Rev. Dr Channing, a small man, with a great deal of soul in his face – went up to Bunsen, meaning to say some words of thanks. He held out both hands to him, and then he was completely overcome; he fell on his neck and wept loud, and I assure you there were not many dry eyes in the room.[101]

The SHORT REIGN OF PIUS VIII ended on 1 December 1830. There were musical aspects, so we are fortunate to have a description by a musician, none other than Mendelssohn:

> I myself saw the corpse lying in state, and the priests standing round incessantly whispering and laughing; and at this moment, when masses are being said for his soul, they are in the very same church hammering away at the scaffolding of the catafalque, so that the strokes of the hammers and the noise of the work-people entirely prevent any one hearing the religious services.
>
> At present a monstrous catafalque has been erected in the nave in this shape. The coffin is placed in the centre under the pillars; the thing is totally devoid of taste, and yet it has a wondrous effect. The upper circle is thickly studded with lights, so are all the ornaments; the lower circle is lighted in the same way, and over the coffin hangs a burning lamp, and innumerable lights are blazing under the statues. The whole structure is more than a hundred feet high, and stands exactly opposite the entrance. The guards of honour, and the Swiss, march about in the quadrangle; in every corner sits a Cardinal in deep mourning, attended by his servants, who hold large burning torches, and then the singing commences with responses, in the simple and monotonous tone you no doubt remember. It is the only occasion when there is any singing in the middle of the church, and the effect is wonderful. Those who place themselves among the singers (as I do) and watch them, are forcibly impressed by the scene; for they all stand round a colossal book from which they sing, and this book is in turn lit up by a colossal torch that burns before it; while the choir are eagerly pressing forward in their vestments, in order to see and to sing properly: and [Giuseppe] Baini with his monk's face, marking time with his hand, and occasionally joining in the chant with a stentorian voice.

On his second visit in 1837, Ticknor was told some details of the subsequent conclave by Cardinal Giacomo Giustiniani, who was one of the *papabili*. His rejection was due to Colomardes, Minister of Justice to Ferdinand VII of Spain, who blamed Giustiniani for Pius VII's recognition of the South American bishops, against the authority of Spain. Colomardes therefore sent in a veto, although Ferdinand may not have known of it. GREGORY XVI WAS ELECTED on 2 February 1831. Mendelssohn was in his room with friends,

> suddenly the report of a cannon was heard, and then another, and the people rushed across the Piazza di Spagna, shouting with all their might. We three started off, Heaven knows how, and ran breathlessly to the Quirinal, where the man was just retreating, who had shouted through a broken window – 'Annuncio vobis gaudium magnum; habemus Papam R. E. dominum Capellari, qui nomen assumsit Gregorius XVI.' [I announce to you a great joy: we have as pope of the church Master Cappelari, who has taken the name Gregory XVI.] All the Cardinals now crowded into the balcony, to breathe fresh air, and laughed, and talked together. It was the first time they had been in the open air for fifty days, and yet they looked so gay, their red caps shining brightly in the sun; the whole Piazza was filled with people, who clambered on the obelisk, and on the horses of Phidias, and the statues projected far above in the air. Carriage after carriage drove up, amid jostling and shouting. Then the new Pope appeared, and before him was borne the golden cross, and he blessed the crowd for the first time, while the people at the same moment prayed, and cried 'Hurrah!' All the bells in Rome were ringing, and there was firing of cannons, and flourishes of trumpets, and military music. This was the *eve* of my birthday.
>
> Next morning I followed the crowd down the long street to the Piazza of St Peter's, which looked finer than I had ever seen it, lit up brightly by the sun, and swarming with carriages; the Cardinals in their red coaches, driving in state to the sacristy, with servants in embroidered liveries, and people innumerable, of every nation, rank, and condition; and high above them the dome and the church seeming to float in blue vapour, for there was considerable mist in the morning air. And I thought that Capellari would probably appropriate all this to himself when

he saw it; but I knew better. It was all to celebrate my birthday; and the election of the Pope, and the homage, a mere spectacle in honour of me; but it was well and naturally performed; and so long as I live, I shall never forget it.

The Church of St Peter's was crowded to the door. The Pope was borne in on his throne, and fans of peacocks' feathers carried before him, and then set down on the High Altar, when the Papal singers intoned, 'Tu es sacerdos magnus.' I only heard two or three chords, but it required no more; the sound was enough. Then one Cardinal succeeded another, kissing the Pope's foot and his hands, when he in turn embraced them. After surveying all this for a time, standing closely pressed by a crowd, and unable to move, to look suddenly aloft to the dome, as far as the lantern, inspires a singular sensation. I was with Diodati, among a throng of Capuchins; these saintly men are far from being devotional on an occasion of this kind, and by no means cleanly.[102]

Ferdinando Cavalleri, Gregory XVI on the feast of Corpus Domini, *1840*

Enjoyment was, however, short lived. CARNIVAL was curtailed for political reasons:

> We return through the Porta del Popolo, amazed to still not see any coaches. I hastily change clothes, buy myself pocketfuls of confetti, with people laughing secretly at me for what reason I don't know; and so I arrive in splendid spirits at the Corso. But it turns out to be filled with dour faced men, no masques, no ladies, no coaches, and made a strange and most disagreeable impression, and finally I found an edict posted at the corner, whose brevity and certitude made for a striking contrast to all of the buffoonery. It began 'La sopra occorenza di gravi circonstanze impone che cessi il Carnevale nei tre giorni che da oggi ne rimangono. – Niuno pertanto si permetterà di andare in maschera, le corse dei cavalli ed i festini non si eseguiranno e taceranno altresì le rappresentazioni teatrali' ['The above grave occurrence requires the suppression of the three remaining days of Carnival. No one therefore is permitted to go about masked, the horse races and festivals will not take place, and theatrical performances likewise will fall silent']. Anyone violating this would be severely punished, and that was the end of it. The news of the unrest in Bologna, Ancona, etc., had arrived, and even in Rome agitators had been discovered, and the militia, instead of keeping watch over the masques, was standing with loaded rifles on the various plazas. In the evening ten to twelve young people really did attack the soldiers at the Piazza Colonna, but were immediately arrested, and since then no further trouble has occurred. Even so, edicts are constantly appearing, with increasing severity and firmness. Saturday evening all foreigners were ordered to report to their embassies, inn-keepers to turn in their names, and the embassies to vouch for their countrymen; most refused to do the latter, and probably rightly so too. Sunday all were called upon to pray for the preservation of the peace, and to this end two miraculous pictures of the Virgin Mary and the chains of Saint Peter were publicly displayed in *Pietro di vincoli*. Yesterday evening an edict appeared calling on all citizens to arm themselves and

Richard Bridgens, Carnival at Rome, *c. 1821*

report to their own sections the moment the cannons were fired and the bells were sounded. The Vatican is closed and the Swiss guards are not even letting anyone into the colonnades of St Peter's. Everything is watchful and calm, and since the lower classes of society are the pope's strongest *supporters*, and have proved it with deputations, *vivati*, and so on, it seems to me that everything is already settled. The middle classes appear to be terribly afraid, though; all of the houses are bolted shut at night, one has to ask three times before they open the door, the stores are closed, with not a soul on the streets. Again there is no lack of humorous touches, but the best of all is that the German painters are cutting off their mustaches out of fear.

To add to the gloom, in April the PLAGUE struck. Berlioz's dramatic eye captured the more macabre realities:

> In the town, a kind of infectious influenza was raging, and people were dying by thousands. Clothed in a long hooded cloak of the sort in which the painters represent Petrarch (a costume which afforded great diversion to the Roman idlers), I accompanied the cartloads of dead to the yawning vault of the Transteverine church. A stone was removed in the inner court, and the bodies were gently lowered by means of an iron hook into this palace of putrefaction. Some of the skulls had been opened by the doctors, with a view to discovering why the sick men had refused to get well, and the brains were scattered about the bottom of the cart.
>
> The man who in Rome replaces the gravedigger of other nations then gathered up these *débris* of the organ of thought with a trowel, and shot them dexterously into the abyss. Shakespeare's immortal gravedigger would assuredly never have dreamt of using a trowel, nor of employing this human mortar.[103]

In 1833, a long standing 'mystery' was solved. For centuries, despite the clearest evidence about the BURIAL OF RAPHAEL in the Pantheon, many had believed that he was buried in S Maria sopra Minerva, and that his head was preserved by the Accademia dei Virtuosi. Gregory finally gave orders in 1833 for the grave in the Pantheon to be opened. The artist's body was authenticated and his head found where it ought to have been. The ceremonial reburial on 18 October was witnessed by Hans Christian Andersen.

> When the grave was opened and the bones brought forth, the painter [Vincenzo] Camuccini had sole permission to paint the whole scene. Horace Vernet, who lived in the French Academy at Rome [he was director! See Portraits] and knew nothing about it, took his pencil and made a sketch. The papal police present forbade it; he looked surprised at them, and said very quietly: 'But at home I can do it from memory?' Nobody could

Francesco Diofebi, The opening of Raphael's tomb in 1833, *1836*

say anything against that, and in the time from twelve o'clock at noon until six o'clock in the evening he painted a beautiful and very truthful picture, and had it engraved afterward; but the plate was immediately seized by the police and confiscated. Thereupon Vernet wrote a violent letter and demanded that they should deliver him the plate within twenty four hours; that art was not a monopoly, like salt and tobacco. They sent it back, and he broke it in pieces and dispatched them with a letter to Camuccini, written in a very fiery style, telling him that he might know by this that he was not going to make use of it to Camuccini's detriment. Camuccini had the plate put together again and sent it, accompanied with a very friendly letter, to Horace Vernet, declaring that he had entirely given up publishing his drawing. After that everybody was allowed to take a drawing of the grave, and in consequence there was a host of pictures.

Our countrymen procured us tickets for the festival, and so our first entrance into Rome was to attend the funeral of Raphael.

Upon a platform, covered with black cloth, stood a coffin of mahogany with cloth of gold. The priests sung a *Miserere*, the coffin was opened, and the reports read were deposited in it.

The singing from an invisible choir sounded strangely beautiful, while the procession was moving around in the church. The most eminent artists and men of rank followed. Here I saw again, for the first time in Rome, Thorwaldsen, who, like the others, marched step by step bearing his taper. The solemn impression was rather disturbed, however, by the carelessness with which they lifted the coffin on end to get it through a small opening, so that we could hear the bones and joints rattle together.[104]

Some groups of visitors maintained their national identity very consciously, as we have seen with the German celebrations for Luther. The Scandinavians were also highly identifiable, as shown by their CHRISTMAS EVE PARTY IN 1833. Again Andersen was present:

Tuesday, December 24. There weren't any locales available to us in the city because it was such a holy day and we wanted to sing. We got one, therefore, outside the city, in the large house on the grounds of Villa Borghese, close to the Amphitheater by the pine forest. Some of us went out there already this morning to set up for the party. Jensen and Christensen, along with me, tied wreaths; mine was the most attractive, and it was intended for the princess. I placed a garland of flowers around the entire table. We ate out there; at 3 o'clock I went home to freshen up and put on my dress suit. – By 6 o'clock we were all gathered; the princess, as a Catholic, didn't dare attend. – Plagemann had painted the coats of arms of the three Nordic nations; they hung decorated with oak leaves and laurel wreaths among large laurel garlands. All around the table I had arranged a flower garland, and on each plate was a wreath of ivy to wear; on the ladies' were roses. We started in by the Christmas tree; it was a magnificent, big laurel tree decorated with oranges

Ditlev Blunck, Danish artists at la Gensola osteria in Trastevere, *1837.*
The figure in the right foreground is Thorwaldsen. Immediately to his right is Ernst Meyer
and then Blunck himself; opposite him Wilhelm Marstrand is eyeing the lobster.
ConstantinHansen enters at the back

and presents. As luck would have it, I got the best and most
expensive present (six and one half *scudi*), a silver cup with the
inscription: 'Christmas Eve in Rome 1833.' In addition to that,
a lovely change purse. My present in all its wrapping paper
was the one that made the biggest hit for being the funniest.
Byström got it, and everyone applauded me. – Hertz got a ring
with an antique inset in it; Zeuthen, Thorvaldsen's medal, given
by Thorvaldsen himself. – When we were eating, Bodtcher
had promised to manage everything to perfection concerning
my song, but he started it three notes too high; didn't want to
admit his mistake, and so no one could sing along. That was
the reason, when the toasts for the kings were proposed, there
was such confusion that they sounded very feeble. – Then they
did a dumb thing and sang it once more and drank toasts with

champagne; the same thing happened with the toast to the princess. Blunck shouted: 'May she live well!' – I thought he said: 'We've got to yell!' Already at 11 o'clock Thorvaldsen and some of the older guests left; I went then along with them. When our first knocks didn't open the gates of Rome, I did some knocking. 'Chi è?' they asked. 'Amici!' we answered, and then a little wicket was opened and we squeezed through.[105]

As the Germans celebrated Luther's anniversary, so they kept up other national occasions. The ninth of December was the BIRTHDAY OF JOHANNES WINKELMANN, the celebrated art historian (1717-68). In 1836 it was celebrated appropriately at the villa Albani. Ticknor was among the guests:

> *December 9.* – To day there was a great fête and dinner in honour of the birthday of Winckelmann, held at the *Villa Albani*, under the auspices and presidency of [Christian] Bunsen [the Prussian minister]. He had invited me to it, when I was still in Florence, and he called to day and took me out in his carriage. The villa is neglected, but its palazzo, a fine building, is well preserved; the collection of antiques, stolen, literally stolen by the French – has been replaced, and the whole is much in the state in which it was when Winckelmann lived there, under the patronage of the well known Cardinal Albani.
>
> Between three and four o'clock about ninety persons were collected, chiefly Germans, with a few English and Italian, and among them were the Russian Chargé d'Affaires; [August] Kestner, the Hanoverian Minister; Thorwaldsen; [Pietro Ercole] Visconti; Dr [John] Carlyle, brother to the obscure writer for the Reviews [Thomas]; [Emil] Wolff; [Ernst] Plattner; all the principal German artists, etc. [Eduard] Gerhard went round with all of us, and lectured on the Gallery and its most interesting monuments, very agreeably; after which we went upstairs, and at five o'clock sat down to an excellent dinner in a truly magnificent hall, all built of brilliant marbles.
>
> Bunsen presided: Thorwaldsen was vice president, at the other end of the table; toasts were drunk, speeches were made, both

in German and Italian, by the president, by Gerhard, Visconti, etc.; and there was a delightful choir of young Germans, who sang with effect several ancient Latin hymns and choruses, a part of the Carmen Seculare of Horace, and some national German airs. There was a good deal of the German enthusiasm about it, and this enthusiasm rose to its height when Bunsen – at nearly the end of the feast – went round to the neighbourhood of Thorwaldsen, and making a speech, and a very happy one, took a wreath of laurel, which was supposed by chance to be near, as one of the ornaments of the occasion, and placed it on Thorwaldsen's head. It was a fine scene. The venerable artist resisted the honour just so far as was graceful, and no further, though taken by surprise entirely, for the speech was so shrewdly adjusted that its full purport was not intelligible till the wreath was on his temples. But everybody felt it was well placed, and a burst of applause followed which must have gratified him.[106]

The Germans also took very seriously ROME'S BIRTHDAY – their archæological institute played a leading role in the uncovering of the Roman past. Ticknor again was present on 21 April 1837:

To day is the accredited anniversary of the foundation of Rome, and the Archæological Society celebrated it with a solemn sitting, and the Prussian Minister [Bunsen] gave a dinner afterwards to about twenty artists, diplomats, and men of letters. I went to both, and enjoyed them in their respective fashions not a little. At the Society a report was made of the doings of the last year, and several papers read, the best being one by Dr [Richard] Lepsius [the famous Egyptologist]... At the dinner were the Bavarian, the Saxon, the Baden Chargés, Kestner, Thorwaldsen, [Emil] Wolff the sculptor; ...in short, the full representation of German intellect and talent now in Rome, with no foreign admixture but myself. The talk, of course, was of a high order.[107]

The occasion, however, seems notably muted in comparison to Winckelmann's birthday!

CHOLERA again broke out in September 1837, to which Nicolai Gogol made only a passing reference, being too occupied with his own hemorrhoidal constipation.[108]

The winter of 1840/1 brought further trials, reported by Andersen: 'The earth quaked, the Tiber rose, flooding the streets, where they rowed in boats; fever snatched numbers away. In a few days Prince Borghese lost his wife and three sons. The weather was sleety and windy; in short, it was dismal.'[109]

Gogol alluded in a line to a VISIT to Rome BY TSAR NICHOLAS I in 1846.[110] His self-involvement again allowed nothing further.

Florence Nightingale is a valuable witness to the prelude to the 1848 REVOLUTION. She waxed lyrical over the institution of the State Council of 24 members set up on 16 November 1847, representing Rome and all her provinces, first chosen by the pope, but thereafter to be popularly elected. She imagined it as a House of Commons; there was but one priest in it. Rome similarly was to have an assembly of one hundred members to replace the ecclesiastical convocations. She observed the procession from the Corso: the banners of the fourteen *rioni* (wards), then the twenty four councillors in carriages lent by the greatest names in the city, each preceded by a band, and followed by fifty or sixty citizens of the province in black, and finally the Civic Guard. She then rushed away to cross the Tiber, risking a ducking in the press, to meet the procession as it entered St Peter's, with all of Rome pouring in behind it.

New Year 1848 opened ominously. The 'Jesuit-Austrian party' excited the people and alarmed the pope. The city was occupied by the army and the Civic Guard on New Year's Eve. On New Year's day the University community went to the Quirinal to greet the pope and found the gates locked. They had been suspected of insurrection! The Jesuit-Austrian party had circulated a rumour that the soldiers would fire on them.

Then came the proclamation of 10 February. Nightingale writes:

> The morning before had come out a proclamation drawn up by Pius's own hand (when the Amnesty came out, which he wrote himself, he had every copy sent up to him, as it was printed off, that he might see that they had not altered the words)

this proclamation, which is beautifully done, has a great hit at Austria, a promise of a laical government, and of improving the military force. There had been a row on the evening of the 8th, paid, there is *no* doubt, by Austrian money. After this proclamation, the people would go up to the Quirinal to see their father – and at 5 o'clock a procession left the Piazza del Popolo. X [Selina] and I, who had only just heard of it, took a carriage, ... and drove up to the Quirinal. There we found every avenue with a mounted guard to prevent the carriages from crushing the people. We got out, and ran between the horses like two winds, and reached the Piazza of the Quirinal. It was quite full already – the great building (the quarters of the Guardia Nobile) had every window full, the whole roof was loaded with people, and even the arms on the top of the roof, was full of legs and heads. The great steps opposite the Quirinal were loaded – the shutters of the Quirinal were still shut – but the round tower was filled with the Pontifical household. Presently the hymn to Pius was heard ascending the steep Colonna Street, and immediately every shutter in the Quirinal was thrown open, and [Tommaso] Corsini, the Senator, [Prince Giulio Cesare] Rospigliosi the Commander of the Civic Guard, [Marcantonio] Borghese, and all the great popular functionaries, appeared at the windows. Such a cheer arose – they all wore the helmets of the Civic Guard.

...The procession arrived – first of all a troop of little children, dressed as Guardie Civiche, and carrying white banners – it was so pretty – then the others – immediately afterwards the sportelli [windows] of the great balcony opened, and without keeping them waiting a moment, the red drapery came out. Oh such a cheer ran from piazza to tower and from tower to roof and along every window in the Piazza, and was echoed from all the side streets, (for I believe the whole population of Rome was there,) when they saw the Pope was coming. The torches glanced past the windows, appeared on the balcony, then the cross, and then Pius himself – there was a great cry, and he, with all his own infinite charm, the charm of kindness and love, received the love of his people. Then he raised his arms to heaven, and there was dead silence, a silence which might be felt – it is really no exaggeration to say that you could have heard a beetle rustle (though had a beetle been there, beetles themselves would have been inclined to kneel), his voice was heard clear and full over all that multitude, 'Sit nomen Domini benedictum,' [Blessed be the name of our Lord] and all that vast crowd made the response with one voice – then 'Nomen Domini in adjutorium nostrum,' [the name of the Lord our aid] and they responded again, 'Qui fecit cælum et terras,' [who created heaven and earth] and one universal Amen seemed to rise from the four quarters of the city. This is what has never been done (these responses made) except for Pius. No, really, it was as if you stood in the presence of a superior being.

But what was the surprise and ecstacy of us all when he began to speak – and with a voice, every word of which was heard to the farthest ends he said, 'Io prego Dio di tutto il cuore Che vi benedica: scenda questa benedizione del cielo su voi tutti, su tutti lo stato, *e su tutta l'Italia,*' [I pray God with all my heart to bless you; may this blessing of heaven be on all of you, on the whole state *and on all of Italy*] and these words he said with that voice which no one who has heard it can ever forget, it has a fervour of love and truth in it, which no one ever doubts – you felt that all Italy *was* in that heart of hearts at that moment. There was a great answer – and then he said, 'Ma, siate *concordi*' [But be of one mind] and the 'Concordi' positively echoed through the night: he said it with such emphasis – the people could not constrain themselves, and they roared, Si, si. Silenzio, cried a voice, which I believe was Ciceruacchio's [Angelo Brunetti: see Portraits] and they were again silent for a moment. 'Ma, le vostre dimande siano confacenti alla santità dello stato.' [But your demands, may they be in conformity with the sanctity of the state.] Si, si, they cried again, and those who were in the side streets and could not see, could hold their tongues no longer. At the first silence he said, 'Alcune gride che non sono del popolo, ma parlino da pochi, io non posso, non debbo, non voglio ammettere.' [Some cries which are not the people's but speak only for a few I cannot, I must not, I will not

Ippolito Caffi, Pius IX blessing the Romans from the Quirinal, *1848*

accept.] – here there ceased all hope of the people remaining quiet. Si, si, they cried and Pius seemed to give up the idea of finishing all that he had to say. There was silence for a minute, while he said, 'A queste condizioni che manteniate le promesse, io vi benedico con *tutta – l'anima – mia.*' [On these conditions that you keep your promises, I bless you with all my heart.] Oh if you had heard the voice with which he said those words – it was as if he were breathing forth his soul for them – and you felt that all that vast people (there were 50,000 there) would have died for him – that they would have gone into the depths of Tartarus, if he had but told them. 'E con queste promesse vi benedica Iddio.' 'A ginocchio,' cried the same voice which had cried Silenzio, and we all sunk on our knees, though there was scarcely room to kneel. And again he raised his hands to heaven and blessed us – and so the beautiful vision disappeared.

By the end of the same month, the national crusade had begun. Nightingale records the enlistment on 23 February and Pius' reactions.

[I]t was an *arruolamento* of the names of the volunteers who would march into Lombardy. Ciceruacchio pressed forward and wrote his name down first. No, no, cried the crowd, You shall not go, you must stay and take care of Rome, and he was obliged to retire – his son went in his stead. [Alessandro] Gravazzi, the monk, went on preaching – a crusade against the *forestiero* [foreigner] – and offered to go with them as their chaplain and he is gone. Then Ciceruacchio spoke, then a Dottor Masi, and lastly a common peasant improvised – there was another arruolamento at St Peter's. Yesterday they left Rome and went up the Tiber by steam as far as Rieti to march from thence.

I went to see Madame Confalonieri – she believed that every Austrian was out of Lombardy – and that Lombardy was going to put herself under the King of Piedmont, making one Kingdom, except Venice, who wished for a republic. She was going to set off for Milan, though [General Joseph] Radetsky was still in the citadel there. Today we hear that the Austrians are bombarding Milan, that 30,000 Piedmontese have marched to her rescue, that 30,000 Neapolitans have sailed for Genoa, and that these are to fight it out with the Austrians. Can there be such a thing as a pitched battle in these days? The Viceroy is certainly gone – and the Duke of Modena has been obliged to fly, and Modena has given herself up to the Pope. Verona, Mantua, Pavia are said to be still in the hands of the Austrians. The constitution granted by the Emperor has been torn down everywhere, è troppo tardi [too late], they said. What of all this is true Heaven only knows – but before 1848 is out, there will not, cannot be an Austrian left on this side the Alps. When the Pope first heard the news, he sat for some time in perfect silence, weighed down with thought, then he started up and cried, Viva Pio Nono. And long live the courage which does not shrink from the consequences of his own great deeds. What days are these. I should like to see the Austrians out of Italy before I go. All the Austrian arms, every thing like an eagle has been torn down here, and burnt in the Piazza del Popolo. This was unwise – still the sympathy for the Lombards would do you good to see. Italy is now all one nation. [Giuseppe] Galletti, the Minister of Finance, said to the Pope yesterday, I shall not see the issue of all this, I have all the dirty work to do, and am too old (he is 70) [he was 50] to see the clearance. 'You will,' said the Pope, 'The people have their rights, the kings have their rights, but the kings have forgotten the rights of the people. If they had listened to my advice six months ago, what has happened would not have happened. They have forgotten the peoples' rights, and they will pay the price, and you will see it, you will live long enough.' He is gay and cheerful, [a] good sign.[III]

The narrative is perfectly resumed by Margaret Fuller Ossoli, who came to Rome in spring 1847 and was an eye witness to the Republic. 1848 was the year of revolutions. All over Italy new constitutions were granted: in Naples and Tuscany in February, in Piedmont and even in Rome in March. A republic was proclaimed in France in February and in Venice the next month. Milan rose in revolt against the Austrians (18-22 March) and forced the garrison to withdraw. Piedmont declared war on Austria, but by August the latter was victorious.

The first shock in Rome came on 29 April, when Pius IX withdrew his support for reform and unity:

A momentary stupefaction followed this astounding performance, succeeded by a passion of indignation, in which the words *traitor* and *imbecile* were associated with the name that had been so dear to his people. This again yielded to a settled grief: they felt that he was betrayed, but no traitor; timid and weak, but still a sovereign whom they had adored, and a man who had brought them much good, which could not be quite destroyed by his wishing to disown it.

The man of tomorrow had redefined himself as the man of yesterday. On 16 September he appointed Pellegrino Rossi Prime Minister. Rossi was murdered on 15 November:

The 15th was a beautiful day, and I had gone out for a long walk. Returning at night, the old Padrona met me with her usual smile a little clouded. 'Do you know', said she, 'that the Minister Rossi has been killed?' No Roman said *murdered*.

'Killed?'

'Yes, – with a thrust in the back. A wicked man, surely; but is that the way to punish even the wicked?'

'I cannot', observed a philosopher, 'sympathize under any circumstances with so immoral a deed; but surely the manner of doing it was great.'

The people at large were not so refined in their comments as either the Padrona or the philosopher; but soldiers and populace alike ran up and down, singing, 'Blessed the hand that rids the earth of a tyrant.'

Certainly, the manner *was* 'great'.

The Chamber was awaiting the entrance of Rossi. Had he lived to enter, he would have found the Assembly, without a single exception, ranged upon the Opposition benches. His carriage approached, attended by a howling, hissing multitude. He smiled, affected unconcern, but must have felt relieved when his horses entered the courtyard gate of the *Cancelleria*. He did not know he was entering the place of his execution. The horses stopped; he alighted in the midst of a crowd; it jostled him, as if for the purpose of insult; he turned abruptly, and received as he did so the fatal blow. It was dealt by a resolute, perhaps experienced, hand; he fell and spoke no word more.

The crowd, as if all previously acquainted with the plan, as no doubt most of them were, issued quietly from the gate, and passed through the outside crowd, – its members, among whom was he who dealt the blow, dispersing in all directions. For two or three minutes this outside crowd did not know that anything special had happened. When they did, the news was at the moment received in silence. The soldiers in whom Rossi had trusted, whom he had hoped to flatter and bribe, stood at their posts and said not a word. Neither they nor any one asked, 'Who did this? Where is he gone?' The sense of the people certainly was that it was an act of summary justice on an offender whom the laws could not reach, but they felt it to be indecent to shout or exult on the spot where he was breathing his last. Rome, so long supposed the capital of Christendom, certainly took a very pagan view of this act, and the piece represented on the occasion at the theatres was 'The Death of Nero'.

Rossi was a reformer, which alienated the conservatives, but also anti-democrat and anti-unification, and a supporter of the temporal power. Nine days later Pius fled from Rome to Gæta near Naples, taking refuge with her tyrannous king.

When I wrote last, the Pope had fled, guided, he says, 'by the hand of Providence', – Italy deems by the hand of Austria, – to Gæta. He had already soiled his white robes, and defamed himself for ever, by heaping benedictions on the king of Naples and the bands of mercenaries whom he employs to murder his subjects on the least sign of restlessness in their most painful position. Most cowardly had been the conduct of his making promises he never meant to keep, stealing away by night in the coach of a foreign diplomatist, protesting that what he had done was null because he had acted under fear, – as if such a protest could avail to one who boasts himself representative of Christ and his Apostles, guardian of the legacy of the martyrs! He selected a band of most incapable men to face the danger he had feared for himself; most of these followed his example and fled. Rome sought an interview with him, to see if reconciliation were possible; he refused to receive her messengers. His wicked advisers calculated upon great confusion and distress as inevitable on the occasion; but, for once, the hope of the bad heart was doomed to immediate disappointment. Rome coolly said, 'If you desert me, – if you will not hear me, – I must act for myself.' She threw herself into the arms of a few men who had courage and calmness for this crisis; they bade her think upon what was to be done, meanwhile avoiding every excess that could give a color to calumny and revenge. The people, with admirable good sense, comprehended and followed up this advice. Never was Rome so truly tranquil, so nearly free from gross ill, as this winter. A few words of brotherly admonition have been more powerful than all the spies, dungeons, and scaffolds of Gregory.

On 29 December the General National Assembly of the Italian States was summoned. Pius excommunicated all concerned:

TO OUR MOST BELOVED SUBJECTS: –

From this pacific abode to which it has pleased Divine Providence to conduct us, and whence we can freely manifest our sentiments and our will, we have waited for testimonies of remorse from our misguided children for the sacrileges and misdeeds committed against persons attached to our service, – among whom some have been slain, others outraged in the most barbarous manner, – as well as for those against our residence and our person. But we have seen nothing except a sterile invitation to return to our capital, unaccompanied by a word of condemnation for those crimes or the least guaranty for our security against the frauds and violences of that same company of furious men which still tyrannizes with a barbarous despotism over Rome and the States of the Church. We also waited, expecting that the protests and orders we have uttered would recall to the duties of fidelity and subjection those who have despised and trampled upon them in the very capital of our States. But, instead of this, a new and more monstrous act of undisguised felony and of actual rebellion by them audaciously committed, has filled the measure of our affliction, and excited at the same time our just indignation, as it will afflict the Church Universal. We speak of that act, in every respect detestable, by which it has been pretended to initiate the convocation of a so called General National Assembly of the Roman States, by a decree of the 29th of last December, in order to establish new political forms for the Pontifical dominion.

The Assembly nevertheless opened in Rome in February 1849.

The opening of the Constitutional Assembly gave occasion for a fine procession. All the troops in Rome defiled from the Campidoglio; among them many bear the marks of suffering from the Lombard war. The banners of Sicily, Venice, and Bologna waved proudly; that of Naples was veiled with crape. I was in a balcony in the Piazza di Venezia; the Palazzo di Venezia, that sternest feudal pile, so long the head-quarters of Austrian machinations, seemed to frown, as the bands each in passing struck up the *Marseillaise*. The nephew of Napoleon [Carlo Luciano, prince of Canino] and Garibaldi, the hero of Montevideo, walked together, as deputies. The deputies, a grave band, mostly advocates or other professional men, walked without other badge of distinction than the tricolored scarf. I remembered the entrance of the deputies to the Council only fourteen months ago, in the magnificent carriages lent by the princes for the occasion; they too were mostly nobles, and their liveried attendants followed, carrying their scutcheons. Princes and councillors have both fled or sunk into nothingness; in those councillors was no counsel. Will it be found in the present? Let us hope so! What we see to day has much more the air of reality than all that parade of scutcheons, or the pomp of dress and retinue with which the Ecclesiastical Court was wont to amuse the people.

A few days after followed the proclamation of a Republic. An immense crowd of people surrounded the Palazzo della Cancelleria, within whose court yard Rossi fell, while the debate was going on within. At one o'clock in the morning of the 9th of February, a Republic was resolved upon, and the crowd rushed away to ring all the bells.

Early next morning I rose and went forth to observe the Republic. Over the Quirinal I went, through the Forum, to the Capitol. There was nothing to be seen except the magnificent calm emperor, the tamers of horses, the fountain, the trophies, the lions, as usual; among the marbles, for living figures, a few dirty, bold women, and Murillo boys in the sun just as usual. I passed into the Corso; there were men in the liberty cap, – of course the lowest and vilest had been the first to assume it; all

Proclamation of the Roman Republic in piazza del Popolo, popular print of 1849

the horrible beggars persecuting as impudently as usual. I met some English; all their comfort was, 'It would not last a month.' 'They hoped to see all these fellows shot yet.' The English clergyman, more mild and legal, only hopes to see them (i.e. the ministry, deputies, &c.) *hung*.

On 9 February 1849 the Roman Republic was declared, and the next month a governing Triumvirate was established of Giuseppe Mazzini, Aurelio Saffi and Carlo Armellini. The French, who had had their own revolution sixty years earlier, but were under their second Napoleonic tyranny, sent an expedition to crush the Roman Republic which landed in Italy on 24 April. Garibaldi and the youth of Italy came to Rome's defence. Margaret Fuller Ossoli denounced the attitude of the other nations, particularly England and the United States, which gave no aid. Their visitors to Rome fled the city and spread reactionary rumours.

Garibaldi's force repulsed the French under General Charles Oudinot, 29-30 March, but at great cost. Princess Belgioso organised the hospitals:

She published an invitation to the Roman women to make lint and bandages, and offer their services to the wounded; she put the hospitals in order; in the central one, Trinità dei Pellegrini, once the abode where the pilgrims were received during holy week, and where foreigners were entertained by seeing their feet washed by the noble dames and dignitaries of Rome, she has remained day and night since the 30th April, when the wounded were first there. Some money she procured at first by going through Rome, accompanied by two other ladies veiled, to beg it. Afterward the voluntary contributions were generous; among the rest, I am proud to say, the Americans in Rome gave $250, of which a handsome portion came from Mr Brown, the Consul.

When the French had tried to search his house for refugees, Nicholas Brown, from Rhode Island, after whose family's philanthropy Brown University is named, American ambassador 1845-1849, met them on the stairs, sword in one hand, the American flag in the other.

Rome was also changing physically owing to the pressures of the siege:

And the ruin that ensues, how terrible! Let those who have ever passed happy days in Rome grieve to hear that the beautiful plantations of the Villa Borghese – that chief delight and refreshment of citizens, foreigners, and little children – are laid low, as far as the obelisk. The fountain, singing alone amid the fallen groves, cannot be seen and heard without tears; it seems like some innocent infant calling and crowing amid dead bodies on a field which battle has strewn with the bodies of those who once cherished it. The plantations of Villa Salvage on the Tiber, also, the beautiful trees on the way from St John Lateran to La Maria Maggiore, the trees of the Forum, are fallen. Rome is shorn of the locks which lent grace to her venerable brow. She looks desolate, profaned. I feel what I never expected to, – as if I might by and by be willing to leave Rome.

Then in May Ferdinand de Lesseps was sent out as an envoy of the

French government, to compound French treachery. Oudinot had declared himself the friend and protector of the Italians on landing at Città Vecchia – and promptly seized the city. Although it was clearly French policy to occupy Rome as well, de Lesseps declared that 'friendship and violence are incompatible', and that the French would never bombard Rome. The bombardment began precisely on Sunday 3 June.

The attack began before sunrise, and lasted all day. I saw it from my window, which, though distant, commands the gate of St Pancrazio. Why the whole force was bent on that part, I do not know. If they could take it, the town would be cannonaded, and the barricades useless; but it is the same with the Pincian Gate. Small parties made feints in two other directions, but they were at once repelled. The French fought with great bravery, and this time it is said with beautiful skill and order, sheltering themselves in their advance by movable barricades. The Italians fought like lions, and no inch of ground was gained by the assailants. The loss of the French is said to be very great: it could not be otherwise. Six or seven hundred Italians are dead or wounded. Among them are many officers, those of Garibaldi especially, who are much exposed by their daring bravery, and whose red tunic makes them the natural mark of the enemy.

Yes! the French, who pretend to be the advanced guard of civilization, are bombarding Rome. They dare take the risk of destroying the richest bequests made to man by the great Past. Nay, they seem to do it in an especially barbarous manner. It was thought they would avoid, as much as possible, the hospitals for the wounded, marked to their view by the black banner, and the places where are the most precious monuments; but several bombs have fallen on the chief hospital, and the Capitol evidently is especially aimed at. They made a breach in the wall, but it was immediately filled up with a barricade, and all the week they have been repulsed in every attempt they made to gain ground, though with considerable loss of life on our side; on theirs it must be great, but how great we cannot know.

…When the bombs began to come, one of the Trasteverini, those noble images of the old Roman race, redeemed her claim to that descent by seizing a bomb and extinguishing the match. She received a medal and a reward in money. A soldier did the same thing at Palazza Spada, where is the statue of Pompey, at whose base great Cæsar fell. He was promoted. Immediately the people were seized with emulation; armed with pans of wet clay, they ran wherever the bombs fell, to extinguish them. Women collect the balls from the hostile cannon, and carry them to ours. As thus very little injury has been done to life in this way, the people cry, 'Madonna protects us against the bombs; she wills not for Rome to be destroyed.'

The fatal hour came on 22 June, when the French broke into Rome at San Pancrazio on the Janiculum and at villa Poniatowski by Porta del Popolo.

The night of the 21st-22nd, we were all alarmed about two o'clock, A.M. by a tremendous cannonade. It was the moment when the breach was finally made by which the French entered. They rushed in, and I grieve to say, that, by the only instance of defection known in the course of the siege, those companies of the regiment Union which had in charge a position on that point yielded to panic and abandoned it. The French immediately entered and intrenched themselves. That was the fatal hour for the city. Every day afterward, though obstinately resisted, the enemy gained, till at last, their cannon being well placed, the city was entirely commanded from the Janiculum, and all thought of further resistance was idle.

It was true policy to avoid a street fight, in which the Italian, an unpractised soldier, but full of feeling and sustained from the houses, would have been a match even for their disciplined troops. After the 22d of June, the slaughter of the Romans became every day more fearful. Their defences were knocked down by the heavy cannon of the French, and, entirely exposed in their valorous onsets, great numbers perished on the spot. Those who were brought into the hospitals were generally grievously wounded, very commonly subjects for amputation.

With Austrians advancing from the north and Neapolitans from the south as well, there was only one option:

> [O]n the morning of the 30th, in a contest at the foot of the Janiculum, the line, old Papal troops, naturally not in earnest like the free corps, refused to fight against odds so terrible. The heroic Ma[s]ina fell, with hundreds of his devoted Lombards. Garibaldi saw his best officers perish, and himself went in the afternoon to say to the Assembly that further resistance was unavailing.

> The Assembly sent to Oudinot, but he refused any conditions, – refused even to guarantee a safe departure to Garibaldi, his brave foe. Notwithstanding, a great number of men left the other regiments to follow the leader whose courage had captivated them, and whose superiority over difficulties commanded their entire confidence. Toward the evening of Monday, 2d of July, it was known that the French were preparing to cross the river and take possession of all the city. I went into the Corso with some friends; it was filled with citizens and military. The carriage was stopped by the crowd near the Doria palace; the lancers of Garibaldi galloped in full career... all are light, athletic, resolute figures, many of the forms of the finest manly beauty of the South, all sparkling with its genius and ennobled by the resolute spirit, ready to dare, to do, to die. We followed them to the piazza of St John Lateran. Never have I seen a sight so beautiful, so romantic, and so sad... The sun was setting, the crescent moon rising, the flower of the Italian youth were marshalling in that solemn place. They had been driven from every other spot where they had offered their hearts as bulwarks of Italian independence; in this last strong hold they had sacrificed hecatombs of their best and bravest in that cause; they must now go or remain prisoners and slaves. *Where* to go, they knew not; for except distant Hungary there is not now a spot which would receive them, or where they can act as honor commands. They had all put on the beautiful dress of the Garibaldi legion, the tunic of bright red cloth, the Greek cap, or else round hat with Puritan plume. Their long hair

was blown back from resolute faces; all looked full of courage. They had counted the cost before they entered on this perilous struggle; they had weighed life and all its material advantages against liberty, and made their election; they turned not back, nor flinched, at this bitter crisis. I saw the wounded, all that could go, laden upon their baggage cars; some were already pale and fainting, still they wished to go. I saw many youths, born to rich inheritance, carrying in a handkerchief all their worldly goods. The women were ready; their eyes too were resolved, if sad. The wife of Garibaldi followed him on horseback. He himself was distinguished by the white tunic; his look was entirely that of a hero of the Middle Ages, – his face still young, for the excitements of his life, though so many, have all been youthful, and there is no fatigue upon his brow or cheek. Fall or stand, one sees in him a man engaged in the career for which he is adapted by nature. He went upon the parapet, and looked upon the road with a spy glass, and, no obstruction being in sight, he turned his face for a moment back upon Rome, then led the way through the gate.[112]

Carl Friedrich Heinrich, Battle of the Casino dei Quattro Venti, *1849*

PORTRAITS

We begin as always with the popes. PIUS VII Chiaramonti (1800-23;
was seen by Chateaubriand in 1803 in St Peter's: 'the pope has an
admirable face: pale, sad, religious, all the tribulations of the Church
are on his brow'. Elisa von der Recke at the same time was relying on
report not observation, but recorded that he dined alone, attended
only by his doctor-cum-foodtaster, and when the pope drank all present had to kneel. George Ticknor had an audience in 1818:

> We were presented by Abbé Taylor, an Irish Catholic, who is
> appointed by the Pope to present the English; but as we were
> Americans we had a kind of national privilege to have a private
> audience at a time when it is not commonly given, and no one
> went with us except Prof. [John] Bell of Edinburgh, the famous
> anatomist. There was very little ceremony or parade about it,
> and in all respects it pleased me extremely. On entering we
> knelt and kissed his hand.
>
> He is, you know, very old, but he received us standing, and
> was dressed with characteristic simplicity and humility as a
> friar, without the slightest ornament to distinguish his rank.
> Bell spoke no Italian, and therefore the conversation was chiefly
> with us, and, as we were Americans, entirely on America. The
> Pope talked a good deal about our universal toleration, and
> praised it as much as if it were a doctrine of his own religion,
> adding that he thanked God continually for having at last
> driven all thoughts of persecution from the world, since persua-
> sion was the only possible means of promoting piety, though
> violence might promote hypocrisy. He inquired respecting the
> prodigious increase of our population in a manner that showed
> he had more definite notions about it than we commonly find
> in Europe; and when I explained a little its progress to him, he
> added that the time would soon come when we should be able
> to dictate to the Old World.
>
> He had heard, too, of the superiority of our merchant vessels
> over those of all other nations, and spoke of our successes in

Thomas Lawrence, Pius VII, *1819*

the last war against the English with so much freedom that I suspect he had forgotten two British subjects stood at his elbow. The Abbé, however, reminded him of it by saying, as a half joke, that we had done very well, to be sure, but it was because we had always had the English for masters. 'Yes,' said the Pope, not willing to lose either his argument or his jest, – 'yes, M. Abbé, that is very true; but I would advise you to take care that the scholars do not learn too much for the masters.'

In the whole conversation he showed great good nature and

kindness, and a gaiety of temper very remarkable in one so old and infirm. When it was over we left him with the same ceremonies with which we had entered...[113]

GREGORY XVI Capellari (1831-46) gave an audience to Julia Howe in 1843:

> Papal etiquette was not rigorous in those days. It only required that we should make three genuflections, simply bows, as we approached the spot where the Pope stood, and three more in retiring, as from a royal presence, without turning our backs. Monsignore Baggs, after presenting my husband, said to him, 'Dr Howe, you should tell his Holiness about the little blind girl [Laura Bridgman] whom you educated.' The Pope remarked that he had been assured that the blind were able to distinguish colors by the touch. Dr Howe said that he did not believe this. His opinion was that if a blind person could distinguish a stuff of any particular color, it must be through some effect of the dye upon the texture of the cloth.
>
> The Pope said that he had heard there had been few Americans in Europe during the past season, and had been told that they had been kept at home by the want of money, for which he made the familiar sign with his thumb and forefinger. Apropos of I forget what, he remarked, 'Chi mi sente dare la benedizione del balcone di san Pietro intende ch'io non sono un giovinotto,' 'Whoever hears me give the benediction from the balcony of St Peter's will understand that I am not a youth.' [He was 78.] The audience concluded, the Pope obligingly turned his back upon us, as if to examine something lying on the table which stood behind him, and thus spared us the inconvenience of bowing, curtsying, and retiring backward.[114]

Perhaps no pope received such approval from a visitor as PIUS IX Mastai (1846-78) from Florence Nightingale, who was in Rome immediately before the 1848 revolution, when liberal hopes were still attached to the pontiff. She saw him in St Peter's on New Year's eve:

The Pope looked beautiful, as he always does, without any physical beauty at all – and his Blessing did one good. As a much
less ardent admirer than I said, 'There is Dignity and Peace
and Humility all in one in his expression – his countenance
is so calm, now calmness generally means indifference, but in
his calmness there is real Christian peace.' And really that is
the only way I could describe it – he turned his head round,
as he passed us, and looked up into the church, and seemed to
say, Nothing can disturb me now. Really, do you know, that
countenance will go down with me to the grave.

A few days later she had an audience:

The Santo Padre stood in a small oblong room by a table with
a crucifix upon it, with his face to the light. Vengano, vengano,
vengano pure avanti, he said, We kissed his hand. Then he
talked a little in Italian about the bankruptcies in England, the
distress, the Statistical returns of deaths being increased, etc.
and gave us his blessing. His voice is one of the most charming
I have ever heard, and his manner easy, courteous, benevolent,
is quite that of a man of the world, with the grace besides of
his own good heart. It is a very pretty picture, the reception
room, that beautiful old man (for his hair is very grey, and
his face wrinkled, though he is but 55, and walks so fast, he
outstrips all his court) entirely in white, with his little white
cap, standing by the table.

At the end of January she saw him investing a cardinal; 'I cannot
conceive a voice which touches so much, or which has such a sovereign
effect as that of Pio Nono. But he did look so different from what he
had when we first saw him – so subdued and worn out... he looked
ten years older... No one can mistake the overflowing milk of human
kindness in that man.'[115]

George Ticknor provides a most detailed account in 1818 of a whole
dynasty in exile at Rome, the BONAPARTES:

I have reserved the Bonapartes to the last, because I really do not know where to class them; for they belong, now at least, to no nation, and live at home as among strangers. Their acquaintance, however, is more sought than that of any persons in Rome; and as for myself, I found no societies so pleasant, though I found others more cultivated and more fashionable.

To begin, then, with Mad. Mère, as she is still called [Letizia Romolino, 1750-1836]. She lives in the same palace with her brother, Cardinal [Joseph] Fesch, – the Cardinal in the upper part, and Madame in the principal story, but both with princely state, in a magnificent suite of apartments. The Cardinal has the finest private gallery of pictures I have seen, and shows them with great liberality and kindness; generally receiving in person those who come to see it. In the evening he goes down to 'Madame', and they form their coterie together, to which I sometimes went; but it was rather dull, though everything wealth could do to make it splendid was done...

Louis, the former King of Holland [1778-1846], who now passes under the title of the Count de St Leu, lives more simply than any of the family, and preserves the character for good nature and honesty which he did not lose even in Holland when acting under the orders of a cruel despotism. He has one son, a promising boy of fourteen, to whom he is devoted, and occupies himself with his education [he had, in fact, three sons, the youngest of whom became Napoleon III]. The rest of the time, it is said, he passes in reading Latin and in writing poetry. In the evening he has his coterie, which is pleasanter than his mother's, because his own conversation is more amusing; and, on the whole, from the nature of his pursuits, the simplicity of his manners, and the kindness of his disposition, I think he lives more happily than any of his family.

The Princess Borghese [1780-1825] is the most consummate coquette I ever saw. At the age of forty two she has an uncommonly beautiful form, and a face still striking, if not beautiful. When to this is added the preservation of youthful gaiety, uncommon talent, and a practical address, it will be apparent she is, if not a Ninon de l'Enclos, a most uncommon woman. At Lucien's, where a grave tone prevails, she is as demure as a nun;

Antonio Canova, Pauline Bonaparte, Princess Borghese, *c. 1805-8*

but in her own palace, where she lives in great luxury, she comes out in her true character, and plays herself off, in a manner that makes her as great a curiosity as a raree show. On her birthnight she gave a supper to seventy people, and the whole service was in gilt silver. But, notwithstanding the Eastern splendour of everything, united to European taste and refinement, I am persuaded the strangers there, like myself, were more struck with her manœuvres, seated between the old Cardinal [Giuseppe] Albani and the Cardinal Vicar, than by all the magnificence and luxury about them. On another evening she showed her jewels to four young men of us who happened to call on her, and I am sure I shall never forget the tricks and manœuvres she played off. It is, after all, but coquetry, and it is possible to have but one opinion of her character; but it is not a vulgar coquetry, and it is the talent and skill about it which redeem it from ridicule, and make her a curiosity, – like Napoleon himself, – not respectable, to be sure, but perfect in its kind.

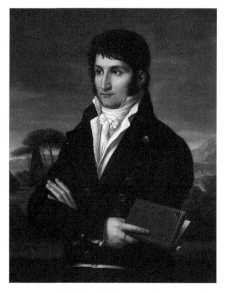

François-Xavier Fabre (studio), Lucien Bonaparte, *after 1800*

At Lucien's, now Prince of Canino [1775-1840], all is different, and I have been there so much, and so familiarly, that I know his family better than any other in Europe. In all respects it is an interesting one, and in many it is amiable and attracting. He has been married twice; and besides the two children by his first wife [Catherine Boyer, d. 1800], and seven by the second [Alessandrine de Bleschamp, widow Jouberthou], his second wife herself has a daughter by a first husband; and all three sets live happily together, and the present Princess is a kind and good mother to them all. They live retired, and since I have been in Rome have not made a single visit, except to their daughter, the Princess Prossedi. They are at home in the evening to a few persons, who, finding no house in Rome so pleasant, generally avail themselves every evening of the privilege. The Prince is about fifty, of a most immovable character, – always the same, always untouched by changes. If this has produced no other good effect, it has certainly given him the entire confidence of his family; who thus always know where to find him. In conversation he is barren, partly from diffidence, but more from secretness and reserve of character. During the day he employs himself with mathematics, and particularly astronomy; and, except a little while after dinner, is not with his family until eight in the evening, when he comes from his study and remains with them till midnight. The pleasure I have often seen kindle in their countenances as he entered at this hour is a proof how he is beloved by them; and the kiss he always gave the Princess Prossedi, when she came and went, proved, too, how dear his children are to him.

The Princess is about forty, with a good deal of talent, uncommon beauty, and considerable culture and accomplishment… The Princess Prossedi [Carlotta, 1796-1865], Lucien's oldest daughter by his first wife, is not beautiful, though not ugly, – a simple, kind, and affectionate woman, looking up to her father as to a superior being, loving her husband with unreserved confidence, and doting on her child to extravagance. She is pious and actively benevolent, and in talents, manners, and character such a person as would be loved and respected in any country. Christine, the next oldest, and now about eighteen, is a very different character. She has more talent than her sister, an unquenchable *gaieté de cœur*, sings, plays, and dances well, says a thousand witty things, and laughs without ceasing at everything and everybody. Loving admiration to a fault, she is something of a coquette, though her better qualities, her talents, her good nature and wit, keep both under some restraint. She always sits in a corner of the *salon*, and keeps her little court to herself, for she chooses to have an exclusive empire; but this is soon to be over, for she is to be married directly to Count Possé, a Swede…

The daughter of Madame by her first husband, Anna, is a most beautiful creature, about seventeen; just going to be married to Prince Hercolani of Bologna, – a love match which promises much happiness. She has not much talent, and no showy accomplishments, but has a sweet disposition and affectionate ways. This is all the family I meet. Two other daughters are at the convent, and a son at college.

Nearly twenty years later, in 1836, everything had changed.

I went this morning to see the Princess Gabrielli [previously Princess Prassedi]. In personal appearance she is less changed than I expected to find her. In the extremely winning frankness and sincerity of her character she is not changed at all. During an hour that I sat with her she told me the most extraordinary succession of facts about her own family that I ever listened to. Her father, Lucien Bonaparte, is now in England, poor; ... the Prince Musignano – Charles [son of Lucien] – is suing his father and mother for his wife's [his cousin Zenaïde] dowry; Queen Caroline is quarrelling with Joseph and Jerome for the inheritance she claims from Madame Mère; the Princess of Canino is in Tuscany, furiously jealous of her husband, and yet refusing to join him in England. One of her daughters is Mrs Wyse, who threw herself into the Serpentine River in St James's Park, a few years ago [she did not drown]; ... one son is exiled to America for having been concerned in a murder; another is now in the castle of St Angelo, under sentence of death, as the principal who committed it; and so on, and so on.

Of the whole Bonaparte family, the Princess Gabrielli is, in short, the only one who can now be said to be in an eligible position in society, or personally happy, and she owes the whole of this to her good sense, to freedom from all ambition, and to her truly simple, kind, and religious character. *Au reste*, she lives perfectly retired in her palace, with her husband and her little boy; her daughters are in a convent for their education; she receives no society and goes nowhere, but is made happy, I doubt not, as she assured me she is, by her domestic relations and her religious duties. Certainly, nobody could be more cheerful, bright, and agreeable than she was this morning; but though the Gabrielli family is rich, and her husband is now the head of it, and possesses the estates of his house, everything in her noble and beautiful palace looked neglected and comfortless. I was sorry to see it, for though this is the way in which almost all ladies of her rank in Rome live, yet one educated as she has been should not have sunk into it.

Antonio Canova, Bozzetto for bust of Cardinal Fesch, *1807*

Ticknor also visited Napoleon's uncle, Cardinal JOSEPH FESCH (1763-1839):

> I went to see Cardinal Fesch this morning, and sat an hour
> with him. He is now seventy four years old, and is somewhat,
> though not much, changed since I saw him nineteen years
> ago. Indeed, he is uncommonly hale and well preserved for his
> years; dresses with ecclesiastical precision and niceness, and has
> the most downright good natured ways with him, as he always
> had. He talked a vast deal of nonsense about the cholera and
> cordons; undertook to be learned about the plagues of ancient
> and modern times, but succeeded only in making a clumsy and
> awkward display of scraps of knowledge which... he knew not
> how to put together; and finally he told me of a plan he has
> now in progress, for establishing an academy of sculpture and
> design in Ajaccio, in Corsica; but I could not find out that he
> had any further present purpose in relation to the matter than
> to erect a building, and fill it with casts and the refuse pictures
> of his own admirable gallery. However, if his vanity gets excited,
> his legacies may be worth something.[116]

Alphonse de Lamartine has left us a striking recollection of a young female painter, BIANCA BONI. She made him a copy of Reni's Virgin, and then he decided to have her paint his portrait for his mother. She was 'young, sweet and attractive' and he fell for her and let her know. 'She became angry, angrily destroyed my portrait and sent me packing with the money she had received.' No pleas by the poet would reconcile her and he was forced to give to the poor the money she would not take.[117]

One of the most famous aristocratic families was the BORGHESE. Camillo had died in 1832, and his wife Pauline in 1825. Again Ticknor describes the new prince, his brother Francesco (1776-1839):

> The evening I passed at the Princess Borghese's, who receives every evening, but has *grande réception* only once a week. Guards of honour were stationed at the gates of her palazzo, the court was splendidly lighted, and a row of thirty or forty servants was arranged in the antechamber, while within was opened a noble suite of rooms richly furnished, and a company collected just as it is in one of the great salons of Paris. The Princess, indeed, is a French woman [Adelaïde de la Rochefoucauld], granddaughter of the Duke de la Rochefoucauld, who wrote travels in the United States; and the Prince, though of Italian blood, lived at Paris for thirty years and until about two years ago, when he came to the title and estates and removed to Rome. I brought them letters, but I knew them formerly, both at Florence and Paris... and they received me most kindly.
>
> The Prince Borghese is now, I suppose, fifty five years old [he was 60], very simple, direct, and, as we should say, hearty in his manners; the Princess about forty five, with the remains of much beauty, with a good deal of grace and elegance, and that sort of good breeding which puts a stranger immediately at his ease. She presented me to her eldest son [Marcantonio], the Prince of Sulmona, and to his wife, [Gwendolyn Talbot] a daughter of Lord Shrewsbury, one of the most beautiful creatures I ever looked upon; to her second son, who has the title of Don Camillo Borghese; and to her only daughter [Maria], the

Viscountess Mortemart, who with her husband, an intellectual Frenchman, is passing the winter in Rome.[118]

In the mid-nineteenth century one of the most famous figures in Rome was the democrat ANGELO BRUNETTI (1800-1849), known as CICERUACCHIO ('old Cicero'), who has already been seen in 1848 (see above, p. 176). Florence Nightingale provides the most important portrait of him:

> I dare say you know who Ciceruacchio is. He can hardly read or write, sells wood to all the English, has not genius, but a commonsense almost amounting to genius, and can turn the whole Roman people round his fingers. He is a sincere, good man, and means well both by the people and the pope – a sort of honest tribune. The princes send for him, court him and invite him, but he will not go – he keeps to his fustian jacket – but he has enemies, and never walks without one of his men, because he says, he has not eyes at the back of his head. He is about 50. In the procession of Wednesday, when the hundred [the municipal council] drove from the Quirinal to the Campodoglio, he carried the white flag of the city, and walked first. He has the most incomprehensible power, and in the conspiracy and insurrection of July, was really the efficient cause of restoring quiet, The people, under his direction, behaved miraculously well, demanded and obtained the Guardia Civica, and went home to bed. If I were not afraid of telling you what you know already, the whole history of that insurrection is a most curious one.[119]

He joined Garibaldi in 1848, was captured by the Austrians the next year and shot along with his son. The monument to the two of them stands in Passeggiata di Ripetta.

There seemed not a leading figure at Rome in this generation whom Ticknor did not meet. CHRISTIAN BUNSEN (1791-1860), Prussian minister 1818-38 and scholar, had enormous influence over two decades:

> He lives very agreeably, but not showily, in the Caffarelli Palace,

J. H. Robinson after G. Richmond, Christian Bunsen, *1859*

which stands on one of the summits of the ancient Capitol, and has, on two sides, the Tarpeian Rock for the limits of its gardens and territories. In his neighbourhood he has erected one building for the Archæological Academy, which has existed at Rome, through his means, since 1829; and another building for the sick Protestants, who are not received into the hospitals of the city, and whom he formerly used to have treated in a wing of his own palace; while, within the palace itself, he has made arrangements for Protestant worship in German, French, and Italian.

Besides all this, he is the most active person in whatever of literary enterprise there is in Rome, and a truly learned man in the wide German sense of the word. I went with him this morning over his academy and hospital, and received a sort of regular learned lecture from him on whatever can be seen from the windows of his palace, or from the roof of his hospital, which comprehends a view of all the seven hills, and nearly the whole neighbourhood of the city. It was very interesting, the more so from the place where it was given; and the explanations of the Tarpeian Rock, and some portions of the Capitol itself, were extremely curious and satisfactory…

There was virtually no subject which did not interest him, including archæology, on which he was a leading authority (with Ernst Plattner, *Beschreibung der Stadt Rom*, 1830). What a privilege Ticknor enjoyed!

> After the lecture Mr Bunsen went, with old Mr Elphinstone and myself, through all the Forums, beginning with the Forum Romanum, and ending with that of Trajan; descending into all the excavations, and visiting every trace and relic of each of them, whether in cellars, barns, or churches, or in the open air. It took about three hours, and was quite curious; for Bunsen is familiar with every stone in the whole of it. He showed us, among other things, that it was possible, when these forums were in their palmiest state, to have walked from the Tabularium, or Ærarium, on the declivity of the Capitol, round by the Coliseum, and up to the farther end of the Forum of Trajan, – which he supposed to have ended near the Piazza di Venezia, on the Corso, – and yet have been the whole time sheltered by grand porticos and in the presence of magnificent buildings. This gives an idea of what Rome once was. What it now is our senses too faithfully informed us, as we passed through almost every possible variety of filth, wretchedness, and squalid misery, while we made our researches.

The last glimpse of Bunsen vouchsafed us is poignant:

> I had a long and interesting talk with Mr Bunsen on matters relating to the Roman government and society, about which he feels all the interest of one who has lived here twenty very active and happy years, where he was married, and where his nine children were born to him; but though he loves Rome as few Romans do, no man sees more clearly its present degraded state and its coming disasters.[120]

The next year he was recalled.

The acknowledged master of European sculptors was ANTONIO CANOVA (1757-1822). Washington Irving visited his studio in 1805, where he had just finished *Cupid and Psyche*, and was busy with the Bonaparte

Antonio d'Este, Portrait bust of Antonio Canova, *1808-10*

family: a colossal naked one of Napoleon (now in Milan), and another colossal one, this time as an ancient warrior, of Joachim Murat. Stendhal described the studio and his methods. He found him of remarkable simplicity in his manners. His studio was five or six rooms. 'He has removed all physical pain. A mass of clay is prepared for him, and he makes the statue he has conceived. His workers plaster this clay to make a mould, and reproduce the statue in plaster. Canova perfects it, and his workers make an exact copy in marble. This is taken to the special workroom of Canova, who finishes it.' Jeanne Récamier visited Canova in 1813, who henceforth spent every evening at her salon and sent her a card every morning. His studio was on the second floor on the Corso, and the walls were decorated with engravings of his masterpieces. His servants were not liveried, his carriage nothing special, but his table was very hospitable and he was famous for his generosity. She remarked that he did not speak French very well. She spent that summer with him at Albano. By Easter 1814 he was finishing *Hercules and Lycas*, and had made two busts of Récamier.[121]

John Hoppner, Elizabeth, Duchess of Devonshire,*c. 1799*

Elizabeth Cavendish, DUCHESS OF DEVONSHIRE (1758-1824), second wife of the fifth duke, was one of the leading semi-permanent English émigrés. Ticknor describes her in 1818:

> I went to the Duchess of Devonshire's *conversaziones*, as to a great exchange, to see who was in Rome, and to meet what is called the world... The Duchess is a good, respectable woman in her way. She attempts to play the Mæcenas a little too much, it is true; but, after all, she does a good deal that should be praised, and will not, I hope, be forgotten. Her excavations in the Forum, if neither so judicious nor so fortunate as Count Funchal's, are satisfactory, and a fair beginning... Her 'Horace's Journey to Brundisium'... is a beautiful book, and her 'Virgil', with the best plates she can get of the present condition of Latium, will be a monument of her taste and generosity.[122]

She was most famous for financing the clearing of the Column of Phocas in the Forum in 1816-8, superintended by David Akerblad.

It is extraordinary that no full portrait is provided by any visitor of one of the most striking figures of the papal administration, Cardinal ERCOLE CONSALVI (1757-1824), Secretary of State 1800-06, 1815-23. Even Ticknor says only that at the duchess of Devonshire's reception: 'the most important and interesting man who went there was undoubtedly Cardinal Consalvi, the pope's prime minister, and certainly a thorough gentleman and a man of elegant conversation... He has talent and efficiency in business, and deserves, I am persuaded, the character of a liberal and faithful minister.'[123]

Another leading figure in archæology was COUNT FUNCHAL (Domingos Antonio de Sousa Coutinho, 1760-1823), the Portuguese ambassador 1814-7.

> Count Funchal... is now, at the age of sixty, a dignified representative of his government. As he is ambassador, and therefore the very sovereign present, besides being rich, there is a state and magnificence in his house such as I have not seen anywhere else... Where it is not necessary for him to play the king, he is simple and unaffected; and his literary dinners, if not so pleasant as those of the Russian minister [Italinski, see below], because he has not the personal means to make them so, are still much sought after, ... and it is thought no small distinction to be invited to them.[124]

Few British in Rome cut such an eccentric figure, however, as FREDERICK AUGUSTUS HERVEY, earl of Bristol and bishop of Derry (1730-1803), father of the duchess of Devonshire. Earl Montcashell saw him just before he died. He was 'the patron of all modern artists, whose wives he not only associates with as his only female company, but has their pictures drawn as Venuses all over the house'. It was the figure he cut riding or driving which was most extraordinary:

> His figure is little and his face very sharp and wicked; on his head he wore a velvet nightcap, with a tassle of gold dangling over his shoulder and a sort of mitre to the front; silk stockings and slippers of the same colour, and a short round petticoat such as bishops wear, fringed with gold above his knees. A loose

Hugh Hamilton, Frederick Augustus Hervey, 4th Earl of Bristol and Bishop of Derry, in the Borghese Gardens, *1790*

dressing gown of silk was then thrown over his shoulders. In this Merry Andrew trim he rode on horseback to the never ending amazement of all beholders.[125]

The Prussian minister in Rome 1801-8 was WILHELM HUMBOLDT (1767-1835), brother of the better known Alexander, the naturalist. Lamartine slightingly labelled the latter 'le roi de savoir faire', but he found Wilhelm 'a very honest man, very modest and very statesman-like. He flattered no one for the sake of being flattered, but when one knew him, he grew in one's esteem.'[126]

Ticknor preserves a portrait of the Russian ambassador, ANDREI ITALINSKI (1743-1827), ambassador 1817-27, in 1818:

the Russian Ambassador, whom I know more, because I am in the habit of going frequently to see him. He is the author of the Explanations to the three volumes of Tischbein's Etrus-can Vases, and a man of Eastern learning, particularly in the modern languages of Asia… He is now infirm, though not very old; gentle and kind in his manners; living rather retired for a public minister, though with a kind of hospitality that in his hands takes the form of Eastern luxury. At his dinners, when I was there, there was either fashion or splendour, which he did not seem much to enjoy… or else a simply learned meeting of a few friends he knew well… such as [Carlo] Fea, the head of the Roman antiquaries, [David] Ackerbladt the Swede, Wiegel from Dresden, etc., which was more pleasant than any society of the sort in Rome.[127]

Although most portraits of ANGELIKA KAUFFMANN (1741-1807) (see Vol. II) are given by eighteenth century visitors, she was also recalled in the last decade of her life. Montcashell often visited her in the morning in 1804, because her delicate health meant that she was unable to go out. He described 'her delightful mildness of manners and sweetness of voice' and 'the pale transparency of her complexion'. By 1805 Elisa von der Recke found her bowed with age.[128]

One of the most famous of the Vatican librarians was ANGELO MAI (1782-1854), keeper 1819-1833.

I went this morning to see Monsignor Mai, the famous discov-erer of the Palimpsest manuscripts. It was not my first visit to him… He is now Secretary of the Propaganda, and likely before long to be made a Cardinal; an easy, round, but still intellectual looking man, very kind in his manner, and with more the air of a scholar in his looks, conversation, and the arrangement of his rooms, than any Italian I have seen in Rome.[129]

The most famous palimpsest Mai discovered was the remains of Cicero's *de re publica*; he ruined many others trying reagents to bring up the original script. He was then (1837) editing the Vatican Greek Bible, already partly in proof, which he expected to be out in the course of the year. It was not to appear until 1850. He was made cardinal the next year.

Carlo Maria Viganoni, Angelo Mai, *1820*

It was Ticknor again who provides us with an intimate picture of one of the most famous Roman aristocratic families 'at home', the Massimo. The current prince was CAMILLO MASSIMILIANO (1770-1840), married to Cristina of Saxony, and the palace is Peruzzi's masterpiece with the gently curving facade now on the Corso Vittorio Emmanuele. The family are famous for their hospitality.

> In the evening we went for a short time to the Princess Massimo's. We brought letters to her, but did not deliver them until lately, because they have been in great affliction, on account of the dangerous illness of one of the family. She is a Princess of Saxony, own cousin to the unfortunate Louis XVI, and married to the head of that ancient house which has sometimes claimed to be descended from Fabius Maximus. When she is well, and her family happy, she receives the world one or two evenings every week, but now her doors are shut. She is old enough to

have a good many grandchildren, and we found her living quite in the Roman style.

We passed up the grand, cold, stone staircases, always found in their palaces, through a long suite of ill-lighted, cheerless apartments, and at last found the Princess, with two rather fine looking daughters, sitting round a table, the old Prince playing cards with some friends at another, with Italian perseverance, while one of her sons, attached to the personal service of the Pope, was standing with two or three other ecclesiastics near a moderate fire, whose little heat was carefully cut off from the company by screens; for the Italians look upon a direct radiation of warmth from the fireplace as something quite disagreeable. The whole appearance of the room was certainly not princely; still less did it speak of the grandeur of ancient Rome.

But we were very kindly and pleasantly received, and passed an hour agreeably…

We dined today at Prince Massimo's, and met there the Prince, his son; Monsignor; several other Italians; three or four English, whom we are in the habit of meeting everywhere in society… a party of thirteen or fourteen. Some rooms in their magnificent palace were opened which we had not seen before, which are worthy of the oldest of the Roman families; particularly a large saloon painted in fresco by Giulio Romano, in one corner of which is the famous ancient statue of the Discobolus, for which the Prince was offered twelve thousand of our dollars, and was able – which few Roman princes would be – to refuse it [it was sold by Ciano to Hitler in 1938, but is now in the Museo Nazionale]. He is, too, more enlightened, I am told, than most of his caste, and the family is of such influence, that the Prussian Minister [Bunsen] told me the other day that he knows no individual so likely, in his turn, to become Pope, as Monsignor. I talked with the Prince to day for the first time; for, whenever I have been there before, he has been diligent at the card table. He talked very well, sometimes with scholarship. He said, among other things, that the strangers who come to Rome occupy themselves too much with the arts and antiquities, to the exclusion of all consideration of Rome itself as a city, which, under all its governments and through all its changes, has so much influenced and continues still so much to influence the condition of the world. It was a remark worthy of a Roman Prince who felt the relations and power of his great name and family, which very few of them feel at all.

The dinner was an elegant one, in the Roman style, with sundry unaccountable dishes, all served on silver or beautiful porcelain, and with a great retinue of servants, all ostentatiously out of livery. It was, throughout, a curious and agreeable entertainment to us, for I am not aware that there is any other great Roman house where strangers are invited to dinner, or where they can see so much of Roman manners.[130]

An intellectual phenomenon of the time was GIUSEPPE MEZZOFANTI (1774-1849), keeper of the Vatican library, 1833-8.

Mezzofanti came to see us to day, the famous linguist, who talks some forty languages without having ever been out of Italy. He is a small, lively little gentleman, with something partly nervous and partly modest in his manner, but great apparent simplicity and good nature. As head of the Vatican Library he is quite in his place; besides which, he enjoys a good deal of consideration, is a Monsignor and a Canon of St Peter's, and may probably become a Cardinal. His English is idiomatic, but not spoken with a good accent, though with great fluency. The only striking fact he mentioned about himself was that he learnt to talk modern Greek, easily, in eight days.[131]

Mezzofanti did indeed become a cardinal in 1838, and forty-three professors at the Propaganda congratulated him, to all of whom he replied in their own languages.

One of the leading figures of the French occupation (1808-14) had been the governor of Rome, General ALEXANDRE MIOLLIS (1759-1828). Petit-Radel noted that he lived in the palazzo Doria. Mme Récamier must have seen him in 1814 just before the French capitulation. He had always been kind to her. Now he was living alone in his villa with one servant.[132]

Felix Mendelssohn knew the musicologist abbé FORTUNATO SANTINI (1778-1862):

> Santini is a genuine collector, in the best sense of the word, caring little whether his collection be of much value in a pecuniary point of view. He therefore gives everything away indiscriminately, and is only anxious to procure something new, for his chief object is the diffusion and universal knowledge of ancient music. I have not seen him lately, as every morning now he figures, *ex officio*, in his violet gown at St Peter's; but if he has made use of some ancient text, he will say so without scruple, as he has no wish to be thought the first discoverer. He is, in fact, a man of limited capacity; and this I consider great praise in a certain sense, for though he is neither a musical nor any other luminary, and even bears some resemblance to Lessing's inquisitive friar, still he knows how to confine himself within his own sphere. Music itself does not interest him much, if he can only have it on his shelves; and he is, and esteems himself to be, simply a quiet, zealous collector. I must admit that he is fatiguing, and not altogether free from irritability; still I love any one who adopts and perseveres in some particular pursuit, prosecuting it to the best of his ability, and endeavouring to perfect it for the benefit of mankind, and I think every one ought to esteem him just the same, whether he chance to be tiresome or agreeable.[133]

The indefatigable Swiss historian JEAN SIMONDE DE SISMONDI (1773-1842), friend of Mme de Staël and the duchess of Albany, was in Rome in 1837, where Ticknor found him:

> In the evening the Sismondis, with Miss Allen [Mrs Sismondi's sister?], made us a long and very agreeable visit, uninvited. He is growing old, and has given up his 'Histoire des Français' from weariness [it was published in 31 vols, 1821-44], and seems disposed to seek, hereafter, chiefly for comfort and rest. He cares, he says, nothing about the arts, and therefore looks, even in Rome, to social intercourse for his chief pleasures;

and having an excellent and sensible wife [Jessie Allen], enjoys himself with his plain common sense not a little. Their fortune is moderate, but equal to their moderate wants; and, indeed, he has lately been able to spare enough to make happy a favourite niece in a love match, to which her friends would not consent on account of the want of means between the parties. It was a beautiful and characteristic piece of kindness on the part of Sismondi, and made a good deal of talk when we were in Florence.[134]

In 1811 Lamartine came across an amazing survivor from past upheavals: GIUNTO TARDI (*sic*), professor of languages. 'He was a very handsome man, whom a Russian woman had married. He had been named consul of Rome during the recent Roman Republic. This Republic did not last long: the French soldiers helped cut it short. Tardi returned to the rank of Roman citizen, but his moderation and justice while he was in power preserved the esteem and respect for him. He was living poor but honoured in the city which he had governed, on the salary which rich foreigners paid for his lessons.' His brother, also called Giunto, was a painter.[135] The only problem is that there is no one of this name among the consuls.

On Canova's death, his place as the leading European sculptor was taken by BERTEL THORWALDSEN, the Dane (1770-1844). Pasquin described him in *c.* 1828, while he was working on Christ and the Apostles for the Copenhagen cathedral. 'Despite his twenty years in Rome, [he] had remained totally a Northerner, and his harsh aspect, which detracts in no way from his politeness and kindness, forms a real contrast with his works, imitating and inspired by Greek art, and the Italian physiognomies which people his studio.' Mendelssohn in 1830 was also deeply impressed:

> He looks like a lion, and the very sight of his face is invigorating. You feel at once that he must be a noble artist; his eyes look so clear, as if with him every object must assume a definite form and image. Moreover he is very gentle, and kind, and mild, because his nature is so superior; and yet he seems to be able to enjoy every trifle. It is a real source of pleasure

to see a great man, and to know that the creator of works that will endure for ever stands before you in person; a living being with all his attributes, and individuality, and genius, and yet a man like others.

His relationship with the sculptor was very special:

You know how Thorwaldsen loves music, and I sometimes play to him in the morning while he is at work. He has an excellent instrument in his studio, and when I look at the old gentleman and see him kneading his brown clay, and delicately fining off an arm, or a fold of drapery, – in short, when he is creating what we must all admire when completed, as an enduring work, – then I do indeed rejoice that I have the means of bestowing any enjoyment on him.

Ticknor, finally, in 1837 saw him in his mid 60s:

We went to see Thorwaldsen in his own house [in via Gregoriana]. He received us in a slovenly dishabille, too neglected to be quite fit to see ladies: but this is the only way he is ever found, and we forgot his appearance in his good nature and his kindness. He showed us everything; his collection of pictures, chiefly of living German artists, with one or two ancient ones, and a pencil sketch by Raffaelle over the head of his bed, and a few things of his own in progress, especially the fresh model in clay of a statue of Conradin – mentioned by Dante – which he is making for the Crown Prince of Bavaria, who intends it for the grave of that unfortunate Prince at Naples...

Thorwaldsen has for some years refused to receive any fresh orders, and I think for a good while he has ceased to do more than to model, and to touch the marble enough to call it his work. His skill with the chisel was, I suppose, always small, and a statue modelled by him, and executed by such artists as he could easily procure in Rome, would probably be finer than anything entirely by his own hand. The poetry of his bas-reliefs seems to me to exceed anything in modern sculpture.

Horace Vernet, Bertel Thorwaldsen, with the bust of
Horace Vernet, *1833 or later*

He showed us one today containing, first, Apollo in his car, followed by the Muses and the Graces, and then a procession to consist of all the great poets, artists, etc., of all ages. He has modelled it as far as Homer, and if it is ever finished it will be a magnificent work indeed.[136]

The *Procession to Parnassus* is in the Thorwaldsen Museum, in Copenhagen.

HORACE VERNET (1789-1863) was Director of the French Academy 1829-34. Mendelssohn knew the whole family. Vernet told Mendelssohn that his favourite music was *Don Giovanni,* and the musician delighted him by playing a prelude to Weber's *Konzertstück* and gliding into improvisations on the Mozart. For this, Vernet insisted on painting his portrait. Mendelssohn saw Louisa Vernet dance the saltarella with her father. The final impression is of Vernet as a painter again:

He produces with incredible facility and freshness. When a form meets his eye which touches his feelings, he instantly adopts it, and while others are deliberating whether it can be called beautiful, and praising or censuring, he has long completed his work, entirely deranging our æsthetical standard. Though this facility cannot be acquired, still its principle is admirable, and the serenity which springs from it, and the energy it calls forth in working, nothing else can replace.

Among the alleys of evergreen trees, where at this season of blossoms the fragrance is so charming, in the midst of the shrubberies and gardens of the Villa Medicis, stands a small house, in which as you approach you invariably hear a tumult, – shouting and wrangling, or a piece executed on a trumpet, or the barking of dogs; this is Vernet's *atelier*. The most picturesque disorder everywhere prevails; guns, a hunting horn, a monkey, palettes, a couple of dead hares or rabbits; the walls covered with pictures, finished and unfinished. 'The Investiture of the National Cockade' (an eccentric picture which does not please me), portraits recently begun of Thorwaldsen, Eynard, Latour-Maubourg, some horses, a sketch of Judith, and studies for it; the portrait of the Pope, a couple of Moorish heads, bagpipers, Papal soldiers, my unworthy self, Cain and Abel, and last of all a drawing of the interior of the place itself, all hang up in his studio.[137]

SOURCE NOTES

1. Kotzebue, 4.136; Petit-Radel, 2.524f.; Müller, 285; Emerson, 3.96.
2. Burckhardt, 3.15; Nightingale, 146; Emerson, 3.97; Burckhardt, 3.15; Emerson, 3.84; Burckhardt, 3.15; Balzac, 110; Longfellow, 238.
3. Hillard, 130.
4. Thackeray, 2.185.
5. von Ranke, *Briefwerke*, 194.
6. Wordsworth, *Letters*, 6.400; Hauteville, 145.
7. Ticknor, 1.148-9; Macaulay, 461; Dickens, 177-8; Fuller Ossoli, 359-60.
8. Hillard, 270.
9. Chateaubriand, 1457; Ticknor, 1.140-1; Burckhardt, 3.18; Mommsen, 130; Howe, 129.
10. Hazlitt, 232-3; Staël, 5.490; Dickens, 201.
11. Chateaubriand, 1481-2; Staël, 5.545, 527; Shelley, 2.59; Burckhardt, 3.15; Pasquin, 429; Balzac, 5.111; Byron, 5.221; Mommsen, 106.
12. Recke, 2.292f; Kotzebue, 3.167; Stendhal, *Journal*, 1144; Hauteville, 142; Byron, 5.221; Shelley, 2.87, 93; Hazlitt, 235-6; Pasquin, 381f; Berlioz, 139-40; Emerson, 3.87, 94; Wordsworth, *Letters*, 6.394; Macaulay, 457; Liszt (1), 101; Gregorovius, *Tombs*, 147; Mommsen, 109; Dickens, 163 and 165-8; Hillard, 141; Nightingale, 254-7.
13. Recke, 2.151; Pasquin, 407; Nightingale, 44; Hauteville, 113.
14. Recke, 2.202; Pasquin, 418.
15. Nightingale, 142.
16. Pasquin, 409, 403; Irving, 3.46. 'Two pictures once extravagantly admired', Bædeker's *Central Italy*, 1909, 336. Nightingale, 241-2; Pasquin, 402; Longfellow, 246; Dickens, 181-2; Nightingale, 148; Montcashell, 186; Kotzebue, 3.257; Nightingale, 224-5; Recke, 2.265, 2.120; Pasquin, 410; Liszt (1), 101; Nightingale, 143-4; Dickens, 185.
17. Kotzebue, 3.198; Dickens, 183-4.
18. Nightingale, 203-4.
19. Staël, 5.536; Recamier, 1.222; Dickens, 202; Balzac, 110.
20. Mommsen, 129-30; Dickens, 205-7.
21. Recke, 2.387; Recamier, 1.222; Dickens,

202; Balzac, 111.
22. Emerson, 88-89; Dickens, 211-3.
23. Recke, 2.181.
24. Howe, 128-9; Dickens, 187-8; Nightingale, 187-8; 245-8.
25. Kotzebue, 3.262; Pasquin, 422; Hillard, 228; Cooper, 163-4.
26. Irving, 3.4-2; Pasquin, 427; Mommsen, 110-11; Dickens, 197; similar reactions in Hillard 232; 233.
27. Hazlitt, 23; Pasquin, 430. Rubens' Visitation: examples are known in Strasbourg, London and Prague, but none via the Borghese collection. There are two paintings of David in the collection, one by Caravaggio, the other a copy. *The Return of the Prodigal Son* is now attributed to Antonio Palma.
28. Hillard, 229f.
29. Pasquin, 423.
30. Kotzebue, 4.71; Nightingale, 205.
31. Recke, 2.361; Hazlitt, 239; Pasquin, 433. Titian's *Philip II*: there is one in Cincinatti, but it was previously in Venice and Padova. Raphael's *Julius II*: the famous one is in the Uffizi, but did not come via Corsini. Rubens' *Tiger Hunt*: part of the famous hunt cycle, but that was painted for Maximilian I of Bavaria.
32. Chateaubriand, 1455-6; Hazlitt, 238; Pasquin, 425; Andersen, *Diary*, 59.
33. Recke, 2.168-9; Irving, 3.34-6; Pasquin, 435; Mommsen, 134.
34. Kotzebue, 4.29f.
35. Recke, 2.223; Hazlitt, 237-8; Nightingale, 122. Poussin's *Infant Cupid* or *Bacchus*: there is a painting of this subject in London National Gallery, and another in the Louvre, another in Chantilly, but none came via the Rospigliosi.
36. Pasquin, 425.
37. Guercino's *David with the head of Goliath*: there are versions in London and Kansas, but neither via the palazzo Spada.
38. Recke, 2.171; Pasquin, 435; Dickens, 198; Nightingale, 195.
39. Chateaubriand, 1451; Petit-Radel, 2.189.
40. Recke, 2.341; Petit-Radel, 2.174f; Byron, 5.227; Hazlitt, 240; Pasquin, 392; Emerson, 3.77; Mommsen, 117;

Nightingale, 60-1 and 192; Müller, 297-8.
41. Recke, 2.316; Hazlitt, 241; Michelet, 1.67; Dickens, 195; Nightingale, 109-115, 240.
42. Recke, 2.324; Petit-Radel, 2.158, 161; Hazlitt, 240; Pasquin, 386; Emerson, 3.77; Nightingale, 193.
43. Stendhal, *Corr.*, 328; Hazlitt, 240; Nightingale, 226.
44. Hazlitt, 240; Pasquin, 393; Ticknor, 2.66.
45. Ticknor, 2.68-9; Macaulay, 459.
46. Pasquin, 444f; Ticknor, 2.48.
47. Kotzebue, 4.69; Petit-Radel, 2.304; Pasquin, 443; Hillard, 245.
48. Hazlitt, 239.
49. Recke, 2.262f; Kotzebue, 3.251; Irving, 3.67; Petit-Radel, 2.299f; Pasquin, 425-6; Mommsen, 128; Nightingale, 219-222.
50. Recke, 2.357; Petit-Radel, 393; Pasquin, 443.
51. Petit-Radel, 2.309; Berlioz, 122.
52. Recke, 2.235.
53. Kotzebue, 3.189; Petit-Radel, 2.313-5; Pasquin, 443.
54. Recke, 2.209-11; Liszt (1), 101. – For the French work 1809-1814, see my *Eagle and the spade*, Cambridge 1992.
55. Champollion, 204.
56. Kotzebue, 1.200; Petit-Radel, 2.317-8; Müller, 289f; Shelley, 2.59; Mommsen, 107-8; Hillard, 186-9; Nightingale, 81-2, 92, 217-8, 252-3; Ridley, 'Monuments'.
57. Hauteville, 110-11; Pasquin, 397; Ticknor, 2.51.
58. Chateaubriand, 1483-4; Montcashell, 173; Kotzebue, 1.180-9, 3.198; Irving, 3.45; Staël, 5.549; Stendhal, *Corr.*, 328; Petit-Radel, 2.342f; Shelley, 2.59; Pasquin, 395-6; Dickens, 163-4, 184-5; Hillard, 194-5. On the vegetation of the Colosseum, see Deakin.
59. Michelet, 1.62; Kotzebue, 1.191; Irving, 3.44; Shelley, 2.59. At this time all the pre-Constantine reliefs, Trajanic, Hadrianic and Aurelianic, were regarded as Trajanic (Petit-Radel, 2.337-8).
60. Paris, Antonella, and Rita Volpe: 'Alla ricerca di una scoperta: Felice de Fredis e il luogo di ritrovamento del Laocoonte', *Bull. Comm. Arch. Rom.* 110 (2009), 81-109.
61. Hazlitt, 234; Nightingale, 140.
62. Petit-Radel, 2.355; Shelley, 2.84-5;

Mommsen and friends also made this ascent, Mommsen, 112; Recke, 2.198.
63. Pasquin, 439.
64. Shelley, 89.
65. Recke, 2.128-9; Kotzebue, 4.8; Irving, 3.49; Longfellow, 246-7; Müller, 192f.
66. Recke, 2.287; Petit-Radel, 2.116; Shelley, 2.87-8; Pasquin, 414; Macaulay, 457; Mommsen, 109.
67. Hauteville, 108; Pasquin, 424.
68. von Ranke, *Briefwerke*, 189-90.
69. Chateaubriand, 1453-5; Irving, 3.67; Nightingale, 93-4; Hillard, 181-2.
70. Kotzebue, 4.81; Nightingale, 98-9; Hillard, 266-7.
71. Recke, 2.5; Lamartine, *Memoires*, 433; Berlioz, 139; Andersen, *Autob.*, 258; Burckhardt, 3.16-7.
72. Müller, 286f; Dickens, 169.
73. Berlioz, 121.
74. Pasquin, 430; Longfellow, 240-1; Berlioz, 143-3; Hillard, 302.
75. Hauteville, 81; Berlioz, 141.
76. Recke, 2.74.
77. Pasquin, 433, 435-6.
78. Petit-Radel, 259f, 263; Shelley, 2.88; Pasquin, 426, 427; Andersen, *Diary*, 60-1; Hillard, 301-2.
79. Recke, 2.123; Pasquin, 436.
80. Hazlitt, 233; Pasquin, 443; Mendelssohn, 2.112; Hillard, 303-4; Nightingale, 259.
81. Macaulay, 461-2; Ticknor, 2.57.
82. Ticknor, 2.55-6.
83. Bonstetten, 26; Petit-Radel, 2.521f; Nightingale, 65.
84. Pasquin, 436; Hillard, 267-70; Macaulay, 458-9.
85. Staël, 501-2; Pasquin, 404.
86. Petit-Radel, 2.500; Müller, 173f.
87. Petit-Radel, 2.249f; Pasquin, 416; von Ranke, *Briefwerke*, 189, 192.
88. Müller, 285; Pasquin, 423; Berlioz, 124; Mendelssohn, 2.81-2.
89. Irving, 3.48; Petit-Radel, 498f; Ticknor, 1.146-7; Müller, 277f.
90. Kotzebue, 4.85f; Stendhal, *Journal*, 1145; Petit-Radel, 2.477f; Müller, 292; Champollion, 1.205; Berlioz, 153-60; Mendelssohn, 2.71, 98, 100; Andersen, *Diary*, 66, 68; Ticknor, 2.62. – Those musical persons not fully identified elude such standard works as C. Parsons,

Mellen opera reference index; the *New Grove dictionary of opera*, Loewenberg, *Annals of opera*, or K. Kutsch and L. Riemens, *Grosses Sänger Lexikon*.

91. Petit-Radel, 2.226f; Pasquin, 421; Nightingale, 175, 183f, 190.
92. Pasquin, 420; Longfellow, 249-50; Fuller Ossoli, 293.
93. Shelley, 2.59-60; Hillard, 271.
94. Müller, 205; Staël, 543; Burckhardt, 3.16; Longfellow, 250-1; Pasquin, 420.
95. Shelley, 2.92-3; Müller, 235f; Corot, 184.
96. Kotzebue, 4.3.
97. Recke, 2.342; Staël, 5.490.
98. Recamier, 1.256f; Hauteville, 87f.
99. Byron, 5.227.
100. Müller, 147f.
101. Ticknor, 1.147-8.
102. Mendelssohn, 2.73, 86-7; Ticknor, 2.60; Mendelssohn, 2.109-11.
103. Mendelssohn, (2) 157-9; Berlioz, 176-7.
104. Andersen, *Autob.*, 108-9.
105. Andersen, *Diaries*, 63.
106. Ticknor, 2.48-9. Perhaps Ticknor here shows animus against Carlyle, but in fact it was only after the publication of his *French Revolution* the very next year that his reputation was made.
107. Ticknor, 2.69.
108. Gogol, *Letters*, 71.
109. Andersen, *Autob.*, 160.
110. Gogol, *Letters*, 161.
111. Nightingale, 46-51; 156-7; 235-8; 282-3. The Italian has been translated. Galletti (1798-1873) had been sentenced to life imprisonment as a liberal in 1845, but was pardoned by Pius and became his minister of police in 1848.
112. Fuller Ossoli, 323-4; 338-9; 348-9; 351; 357-8; 385; 383; 390, 405, 406; 411; and 412-3.
113. Chateaubriand, 1438; Recke, 2.75; Ticknor, 1.144.
114. Howe, 125-6.
115. Nightingale, 154, 163, 202.
116. Ticknor 1.150-2; 2.49; 2.52-3.
117. Lamartine, *Memoires*, 138-9. Bianca Boni is unknown to the *Diz. biog. ital.*, *Indice biografico italiano* (fiche), and standard dictionaries of arts and artists such as Benezit, Thieme-Becker, and Groves.

118. Ticknor, 2.49-50.
119. Nightingale, 67.
120. Ticknor, 2.50-1; 2.57-8; 2.70.
121. Irving, 3.49; Stendhal, *Journal*, 1146; Récamier, 1.222f, 253.
122. Ticknor, 1.149.
123. Ticknor, 1.149.
124. Ticknor, 1.149.
125. Montcashell, 178.
126. Lamartine, *Memoires*, 137.
127. Ticknor, 1.148-9.
128. Montcashell, 177; Recke, 2.371.
129. Ticknor, 2.67.
130. Ticknor, 2.53-4, 56-7.
131. Ticknor, 2.64.
132. Petit-Radel, 2.224; Recamier, 1.258.
133. Mendelssohn, 2.80-1.
134. Ticknor, 2.63.
135. Lamartine, *Memoires*, 136. – The consuls are given in A. Cretoni, *Roma giacobina*, Rome 1971, 47, 59f, 118. – There is a Pietro Giuntotardi (*sic*) who composed a funeral hymn for General Duphot (ibid., 81).
136. Pasquin, 428; Mendelssohn, 2.77, 92; Ticknor, 2.64.
137. Mendelssohn, 2.102-4, 121-2.

Samuel Palmer, The Golden City: Rome from the Janiculum, *1873*

N.º 1195. Roma—Tempietto di Villa Albani.

THE NINETEENTH CENTURY:
THE SECOND HALF

INTRODUCTION

If the Republic of 1848 constitutes the most important cæsura in the first half of the nineteenth century at Rome, an even more lasting and defining gulf was created by 'La Breccia', 20 September 1870, when Piedmontese troops broke through the Aurelianic walls to the west of Porta Pia and overthrew the temporal power of the papacy. Italy became a monarchy, with Rome once again its capital and the power of the popes confined within the walls of the Vatican. The most momentous transformation of the city in almost two thousand years was the result, a transformation mostly to be regretted, as the continuum linking classical Rome and the city of the Middle Ages, Renaissance and Baroque was brutally broken. So much of what had made Rome so special was swept away as the city was transformed to accommodate the bureaucracy of the new capital and the aristocracy saw the possibilities for acquiring undreamed of riches through speculation, and most of their villas were sold and demolished.*

What we may call, in a large sense, the area around piazza di Spagna (east of the upper Corso from del Tritone to piazza del Popolo) remained the preferred RESIDENCE for visitors: Julia Howe had an apartment in via Capo le Case (1850), Ferdinand Gregorovius stayed at 107 via Felice (Sistina) (1852) and 63 via della Purificazione (1854), William Thackeray was at the Hotel Franz in via Condotti, then the palazzo Poniatowski in via della Croce (1853), the Brownings stayed at 43 via Bocca di Leone (1853-4, 1859), then moved to 28 via del

---

* The travellers in this century are introduced at the beginning of the previous section.

Opposite: Roberto Rive; The Tempietto of the Villa Albani, 1860-89

Tritone (1860), the Goncourt brothers were at 24 via di S Andrea delle Frate (1856), Pauline de la Ferronays (Mme Augustus Craven) in via della Croce (1858), Nathaniel Hawthorne stayed at the palazzo Larazani in via porta Pinciana, George Eliot was first at the Hôtel l'Amérique in via Babuino (1858), Franz Liszt was first at 113 via Felice (1863) and returned to 43 vicolo dei Greci (1873), Henrik Ibsen stayed at 55 and 75 via Capo le Case and at 46 via Gregoriana (1865 and 1878-85), Harriet Hosmer lodged at the palazzo Barberini from 1865, Henry James stayed at the Hôtel de l'Angleterre (via Bocca di Leone), then the Hôtel de Rome (1869), as did Henryk Sienkiewicz (1893), after Hotel Oriente (v. del Tritone), Thomas Hardy was at the Hotel d'Allemagna (18 via Condotti) (1877), and Piotr Ilych Tchaikovsky stayed first at the Hôtel de Russie (piazza del Popolo), then Hotel Costanzi (via San Niccolo di Tolentino) (1879) and Hotel Molaro (via Gregoriana). The Corso had been a favorite location in the eighteenth century: now only George Ticknor (1857) and George Eliot, at no. 117 (1860) stayed there. A few travellers lodged in the Campo Marzio: Ernest Renan at the Albergo della Minerva in the homonymous piazza (1850), Herman Melville (1857) and Sienkiewicz (1890), and Ibsen at the palazzo Correa (the Mausoleum of Augustus!) (1864-5). Ludwig Pastor lodged at the German College, S Maria dell'Anima. Liszt, finally, in his many removals, stayed at the Vatican, Madonna del Rosario, and S Francesca Romana (1865-6).

There are few comments on these lodgings. Tchaikovsky, however, alluded to a perennial danger:

> I cannot get rid of my inexplicable antipathy to this city. But what is becoming quite impossible are the dinners in the hotel restaurant. Up to now Modest [his brother] and I managed to ignore our neighbours but two or three days ago *la glace a été rompue*. The ladies and gentlemen sitting next to us made conversational openings which could not go without acknowledgment, and now we have to keep up an impossibly banal chatter, and all the time put up with the most awful ideas about Russia and the Russians.[1]

Few visitors speak of EXPENSES. Ibsen averred in the 1860s that

Piazza di Spagna in 1868 by an unknown photographer

'everything is extraordinarily cheap', but in 1873 Liszt stated that 'nowadays the Italian capital offers no economic advantages whatever to foreigners'. He was obviously referring to Rome post-1870. For particulars, Renan recorded that he had a hotel with pension for 160 francs per month at the Minerva in 1850. In 1869 James was paying much more:

> I made a rapid and feverish excursion into a *pensione* of good repute – but what with high terms, poor room and a vicious *table d'hôte* concluded I had not changed for the better and backed out. I should have paid seventy-five francs a week; here (the Hotel de Rome) I live for about eighty – dining to suit myself at a very good restaurant. It's not cheap – but for Rome, apparently (and for comfort) it's not dear.

Apartments were much cheaper. George Eliot had a 'second floor of three good rooms comfortably furnished' at 117 San Carlo al Corso for 25 *scudi* per month, one-third of the hotel prices, in 1860. Liszt undoubtedly had the best of all arrangements in 1868:

I for my part remain hidden away at *Santa Francesca Romana*, in the ruins of the Forum. It is the very opposite of the Boulevard Haussmann and of the *Venusberg*, even though from my windows can be seen a row of trees planted as though along a boulevard, and the ancient remains of the Temple of Venus and Rome frame my dwelling place. Visitors to the city are amazed at the panorama which from the Capitol to the Colosseum takes in a prodigious mass of monuments and ruins, the Palace of the Cæsars, the Arch of Titus, the Basilica of Constantine, etc., etc. – of which the daily usufruct costs me a rent of only 1,500 francs a year.[2]

As for food, prices varied enormously. The Brownings found game the cheapest meat: 'it is a fact that we have lived for the last three weeks on nothing else – woodcocks and snipes being the cheapest – two woodcocks cost 14d – a hare 18d.' Melville in 1857 dined at Lepri's in via Condotti for 19 cents – but it was a notoriously bohemian restaurant. He breakfasted similarly for 16 pennies at Café Nuovo in the palazzo Ruspoli but that was much more elegant. Five years later, Liszt with friends, including Pietro Visconti, dined at the Baths of Titus, at Véfours, and the total bill for six people, was 3 *scudi*![3]

No one mentions the cost of hiring transport in Rome, but Hawthorne records the important information that the hire of a coach to take him and his family to Florence, a journey of eight days, with a contract 'in which everything is set down, even to milk, butter, bread, eggs and coffee, which we are to have for breakfast, the vetturino being to pay every expense for himself, his horses, and his passengers', cost 95 *scudi*.[4]

To make sense of these varying currencies, it is enough to know that the *scudo* of 100 *bajocchi* or 10 *paoli* was worth 4/3d English and $1 American, or 5.3 francs, so that the sou (5 centimes) was about 1 *bajoccho*. And Hippolyte Taine provided in 1864 some idea of Roman values when he revealed that a poor worker on the railways was paid 4 *paoli* per day, and could not marry, because that would require 100 *scudi* to set up house (250 days' pay).[5]

Previous page: Hans Jørgen Hamme, A view of Rome seen from the artist's dwelling, *1858*

Giovanni Battista de Rossi, 1866, by an unkonwn photographer

A number of travellers name their GUIDES in Rome, and they had the privilege of the expertise of the leading scholars, especially archæologists. The greatest expert on Christian Rome was Giovanni Battista de Rossi (1822-94), discoverer of the catacombs of S Callisto; the leading classical archæologist was Pietro Ercole Visconti (1802-80), the last Commissario delle Antichità, 1836-70. These guided George Ticknor in 1857, Pauline Ferronays in 1858, and Liszt in 1862. The last also had the services of Pietro Rosa (1815-91), who succeeded Visconti as director of excavations in the Forum and Palatine. The leading classical Roman topographer in the later nineteenth and early twentieth centuries was Rodolfo Lanciani (1846-1929); he guided George Trevelyan in 1897.

The city still made an indelible, if varied, IMPRESSION ON THE TRAVELLER. Perhaps the most amazing was on Robert Browning, who, having arrived in Rome on 23 November 1853, admitted to his friend William Story in April 1854:

Meanwhile, of course I 'don't boast of having seen Rome'...
no indeed. I am properly humiliated for all my disadvantages
& defects, & confess meekly in writing to England that I am
the most ignorant of travellers & have seen just nothing. After
this Easter hubbub however, we are going to visit galleries,
villas, ruins, & crowd as much sightseeing as possible into a
little space. We heard the wrong *Miserere* I believe, on Friday –
but it was very fine, wrong or right, & very overcoming in its
ejaculating pathos. I sat that day in the *Sistine Chapel* for the
first time.

If Browning is disappointing, Melville was disappointed. On his
first day, 25 February, 1857: 'Walked to Capitol. Took view from tower.
Whether it is having come from the East, or chafed mood, or what,
but Rome fell flat on me. Oppressively flat. – Didn't sleep any last
night, though.' His compatriot Hawthorne arrived a year later, on 20
January 1858, with similar grumbles:

> Cold, narrow lanes, between tall, ugly, mean looking white-
> washed houses, sour bread, pavements most uncomfortable to
> the feet, enormous prices for poor living; beggars, pick pockets,
> ancient temples and broken monuments, and clothes hanging
> to dry about them; French soldiers, monks, and priests of every
> degree; a shabby population, smoking bad cigars – these would
> have been some of the points of my description. Of course there
> are better and truer things to be said...

Pauline de la Ferronays berated the railways for allowing one
hundred travellers to arrive 'tumultuously all together in a station
exactly like that of the most obscure place on earth'. That was at Easter
1858. The Rome-Frascati line was opened in 1856, and for tourists, the
more important Civitavecchia line in 1859. George Eliot on 1 April
1860 had a similar experience to that of Hawthorne:

> Since our arrival in the middle of Sunday, I have been gradually
> rising from the depth of disappointment to an intoxication
> of delight; and that makes me wish to do for you what no

Albert Bierstadt, Roman Fishmarket, *1858*

one ever did for me – warn you that you must expect no grand impression on your first entrance into Rome, at least if you enter it from Civita Vecchia. My heart sank, as it would if you behaved shabbily to me, when I looked through the windows of the omnibus as it passed through street after street of ugly modern Rome, and in that mood the dome of St Peter's and the Castle of St Angelo – the only grand objects on our way – could only look disappointing to me. I believe the impression on entering from the Naples side is quite different: there, one must get a glimpse of the broken grandeur and Renaissance splendour that one associates with the word 'Rome'.

She also arrived by train. She caught the omnibus from the station. Taine in March 1864 described Rome as

only a large bric à brac shop: what can one do except study art, archæology and history? I know very well for my own part that,

if I were not working there, the disorder and filth of the bric
à brac, the spiders' webs, the smell of mould, the sight of so
many precious things, once living and complete, now tarnished,
mutilated, spoiled would cast gloom over my mind.

Night was worse:

The small lights seem swallowed up in the gloomy shadow like
a shroud, and the fountain faintly whispers in the silence with
a ghostly sound. One cannot describe this aspect of Rome at
night: by day it smells of death, but at night there is all the
horror and grandeur of the tomb.

Tchaikovsky's first impressions in May 1874 were mixed. He saw

Aleksandr Gierymski, Street in Rome at night, *c. 1890*

'such marvellous things as the Colosseum, the Thermæ of Caracalla, the Capitol, the Vatican, the Pantheon, and lastly the summit of human genius – the Cathedral of St Peter'. He distinguished these famous buildings from the city itself: 'Except for the historical and artistic sights of Rome, the town itself with its narrow and dirty streets, lacks interest, and I do not understand how one can live all one's life here (after our vast and free countryside), as some Russians do.' Thomas Hardy in March 1887 also contrasted ancient and modern: 'I am so overpowered by the presence of *decay* in Ancient Rome that I feel it like a nightmare in my sleep. Modern Rome is full of building energy – but how any community can go on building in the face of the Vanitas Vanitatum reiterated by the ruins is quite marvellous.' He repeated this theme in his poem, 'Building a new street in the ancient quarter':

> And yet within these ruins' very shade
> The singing workmen shape and set and join
> Their frail new mansion's stuccoed cove and quoin
> With no apparent sense that years abrade,
> Though each rent wall their feeble works invade
> Once shamed all such in power of pier and groin.

It seems that the later nineteenth century travellers lacked the romance and excitement of their predecessors: they arrived at the wrong end of the city, and were now brought up against the old being superseded by the new. There were those, however, who fortunately still experienced the old emotions. For Ibsen, 'Rome is beautiful, wonderful, magical.' James is the most expansive, having arrived on 30 October 1869:

> *Que vous en dirai je?* At last – for the first time – I live! It beats everything: it leaves the Rome of your fancy – your education – nowhere. It makes Venice – Florence – Oxford – London – seem like little cities of pasteboard. I went reeling and moaning thro' the streets, in a fever of enjoyment. In the course of four or five hours I traversed almost the whole of Rome and got a glimpse of everything – the Forum, the Coliseum (stupendissimo!), the Pantheon, the Capitol, St Peter's, the Column of Trajan, the Castle of St Angelo – all the Piazzas and ruins and monuments.

Pius IX and members of the papal court, including Cardinal Antonelli (third from left) and Monsignor Talbot (behind the pope's left shoulder), 1868, by an unknown photographer

The effect is something indescribable. For the first time I know what the picturesque is. – In St Peter's I stayed some time. It's even beyond its reputation. It was filled with foreign ecclesiastics – great armies encamped in prayer on the marble plains of its pavement – an inexhaustible physiognomical study. To crown my day, on my way home, I met his Holiness in person – driving in prodigious purple state – sitting dim within the shadows of his coach with two uplifted benedictory fingers – like some dusky Hindoo idol in the depths of its shrine. Even if I should leave Rome tonight I should feel that I have caught the keynote of its operation on the senses. I have looked along the grassy vista of the Appian Way and seen the topmost stone work of the Coliseum sitting shrouded in the light of heaven, like the edge of an Alpine chain. I've trod the Forum and I have scaled the Capitol. I've seen the Tiber hurrying along, as swift

NINETEENTH CENTURY: THE SECOND HALF

and dirty as history! From the high tribune of a great chapel of St Peter's I have heard in the papal choir a strange old man sing in a shrill unpleasant soprano. I've seen troops of little tonsured neophytes clad in scarlet, marching and countermarching and ducking and flopping, like poor little raw recruits for the heavenly host. In fine I've seen Rome, and I shall go to bed a wiser man than I last rose – yesterday morning. –

Notwithstanding arrival at the station, Pastor on 18 March 1876 declared: 'I would willingly have thrown myself on the ground and kissed it.'[6]

Depictions of NATIONAL TYPES of visitors are now rare. Frances Elliot describes the English:

Wherever they go – our delightful countrymen – they take their manners like their clothes, carefully packed up, and preserved quite unaltered or improved; and they drink their burning wines in tropical heats, and import 'papers', which they read all day seated in stifling rooms in glorious weather, and cultivate their *morgue* and pride, and their long purses, their unquenchable curiosity, their iron prejudices on all subjects, and their utter inability to speak any tongue but their own; and, last of all, they take their horses, and their dogs, and their grooms, and the whole paraphernalia of their hunt. Although I am a born Englishwoman, I never knew to what a singularly remarkable and obstinate nation I belonged until I came into Italy. A wonderfully national nation are we, and therefore it is quite astonishing why people so satisfied and delighted with their own habits and customs should ever leave that all perfect country they will insist on forcing everywhere.

But I have done – leaving the sturdy English squires with their ill dressed wives and daughters to strut about the Piazza di Spagna, peering into the shops of ready witted Italians, who, calculating on their folly and ignorance, levy a heavy black mail in the way of dollars; or to parade up and down the Pincian with their *noli me tangere* look, so becoming in fellow sinners and Christian brethren.

She provided more detail some pages further on:

> that awful amalgamation of dissipation, riches, scandal, and exclusiveness, the English set, who have appropriated to themselves an entire quarter of the city, comprising the beautiful Pincian, where they have their English shops, English prices, books, papers, servants, and *cuisine*. They live much together, sharing only in the grand festivities of the Roman nobles and the diplomatic corps. They are a powerful faction, and are constantly endeavouring to Anglicise Rome by dint of money and overbearing arrogance. They picnic in solemn temples, and underground in dim and dreary baths; drink champagne among moss grown tombs; ride donkeys to Hannibal's camp; get up horse and hurdle races over the consecrated soil of the classic Campagna; light up the Coliseum with blue and red lights; sit on camp stools in St Peter's; and invade every gallery, palace, or monument with the Saxon tongue and Saxon ill breeding. Those who wish fairly to judge of Rome proper should 'stay over the season', and see the English all out, in order to understand how much they have spoilt it. They give no end of balls and suppers, dance in Lent when they dare, turn their backs on the Pope, ridicule the Catholics, talk shocking scandal – which the Italians *never* do, left to themselves – and spend oceans of money, causing Rome, at this moment, to be the dearest residence on the Continent.[7]

BASILICAS, CHURCHES AND CATACOMBS

Ernest Renan was disappointed with ST PETER's for reasons as individual as one would expect: 'The impression one experiences on coming out of St Peter's is that of fatigue. It is too big, too many details. The view of the whole does not offer a beautiful unity as does the Gothic. Coming out of a church one should be lighter, sweeter… It is large mathematically, not æsthetically.' William Thackeray had other criticisms:

We went to St Peters yesterday and Miss Anny & I agreed Pisa is the best: the other is a huge Heathen parade: all the Statues represent lies almost: & the founder of the religion utterly disappears under the enormous pile of fiction and ceremony that has been built round him. I'm not quite sure that I think St Peters handsome: – yes as handsome as one of those splendid strumpets I saw at the ball at Paris. The front is positively ugly that's certain.

Herman Melville also made comparisons: 'Front view disappointing. But grand approach. Interior comes up to expectations. But dome not so wonderful as St Sophia's.' Henry James, for his part, had come from the Pantheon:

St Peter's beside it, is absurdly vulgar. Taken absolutely however St Peter's is extremely interesting – not quite so much so as it pretends to be – but quite enough so to give you a first class sensation. Its pretention, I take it, is to be the very synthesis and summit of all sensations and emotions. I can't dispose of it in three words. As a whole it's immensely picturesque. As you journey thro' its various latitudes, moreover, you really feel that you stand at the heart and centre of modern ecclesiasticism: you are watching the heart beats of the church.

George Eliot's reactions, finally, were subdued:

Of Christian Rome, St Peter's is of course the supreme wonder. The piazza, with Bernini's colonnades, and the gradual slope upward to the mighty temple, gave me always a sense of having entered some millennial New Jerusalem, where all small and shabby things were unknown. But the exterior of the cathedral itself is even ugly: it causes a constant irritation by its partial concealment of the dome. The first impression from the interior was perhaps at a higher pitch, than any subsequent impression either of its beauty or vastness; but then, on later visits, the lovely marble, which has a tone at once subdued and warm, was half covered with hideous red drapery.

There is hardly any detail one cares to dwell on in St Peter's. It is interesting, for once, to look at the mosaic altar pieces, some of which render with marvellous success, such famous pictures as the Transfiguration, the Communion of St Jerome, and the Entombment, or Disentombment of St Petronilla. And some of the monuments are worth looking at more than once, the chief glory of that kind being Canova's lions [the tomb of Clement XIII]. I was pleased one day to watch a group of poor people looking with an admiration that had a half childish terror in it at the sleeping lion, and with a sort of daring air, thrusting their fingers against the teeth of the waking 'mane bearer'.[8]

At the basilica of s GIOVANNI IN LATERANO in 1858 Nathaniel Hawthorne was still shown relics:

The most interesting thing which we saw in this church (and, admitting its authenticity, there can scarcely be a more interesting one anywhere) was the table at which the Last Supper was eaten. It is preserved in a corridor, on one side of the tribune or chancel, and is shown by torch light suspended upon the wall beneath a covering of glass. Only the top of the table is shown, presenting a broad, flat surface of wood, evidently very old, and showing traces of dry rot in one or two places. There are nails in it, and the attendant said that it had formerly been covered with bronze. As well as I can remember, it may be five or six feet square, and I suppose would accommodate twelve persons, though not if they reclined in the Roman fashion, nor if they sat as they do in Leonardo da Vinci's picture.

And in 1860 George Eliot saw something much more extraordinary: the excommunication of the king of Sardinia (Victor Emmanuel) posted up at this basilica, 'out of everybody's way, and yet there are police to guard it'. Hippolyte Taine found the basilica in 'the unfortunate taste of the seventeenth century, neither pagan nor Christian, or rather, both with each spoiling the other'. The twelve colossal statues of the apostles seemed to him to say: 'Look how remarkable we are!' The Torlonia chapel was 'a charming boudoir to take the air', with statues like 'fashionable dolls'. A young priest told him that at the altar St Peter had said mass.[9]

The novelty of the new ST PAUL's seems to have worn off. For George Eliot, 'the reconstructed San Paolo fuori le Mura is a wonder of wealth and beauty with its lines of white marble columns – if one could possibly look with pleasure at such a perverted appliance of money and labour as a church built in an unhealthy solitude'. Franz Liszt, on the other hand, declared that 'The columns of St Paul's are magnificent, and, taken as a whole, of a serene and majestic harmony.' He knew of the common view: 'Notwithstanding the widely accepted criticism leveled against the reconstruction of this church, it harmonizes more with my own personal feelings of worship than any other in Rome excepting Santa Maria degli Angeli.'[10]

In S MARIA MAGGIORE Taine admired the simplicity of the fifth century basilica, the plan of which had been preserved, to his delight. The classical columns made it like a Greek temple. 'Everything which was built since is barbarous' especially the chapels of Sixtus V and Paul V: so many famous names of painters and sculptors, such vast expense, 'but while with slender means the antique makes a great effect, the modern makes little effect with large means – the multicoloured marbles, pedestals of agate, columns of Oriental jasper: one hastens to come away as if leaving a shop or bonbonnière'.[11]

The criticisms of Bernini were dying away. Hawthorne was rightly struck with the virtuosity of S ANDREA AL QUIRINALE. 'I have not seen, nor expect to see, anything so entirely and satisfactorily finished as this small oval church; and I only wish I could pack it up in a large box, and send it home.' At S ANDREA DELLA VALLE, Renan was appalled when he attended the saint's feast day: 'Nothing religious. Everyone turned towards the orchestra, no one towards the altar, standing, cloak over the shoulder, coming in, going out.' Taine came especially to S Andrea to see the frescoes of Lanfranco and Domenichino. The latter's evangelists were 'very handsome, but quite pagan'; S Andrea was 'an old Hercules'. The allegorical women were superb, and the spectator came here only to see 'bold gestures and powerful bodies'.

Of smaller churches, Eliot remembered especially, alongside S Maria degli Angeli, that of SAN CLEMENTE, for its frescoes by Masaccio and the perfect example of an ancient enclosure near the tribune. James in 1869 was an early visitor to the excavations revealing that the Romanesque church had two earlier levels beneath it:

> A few days since I went to see the strange old church of *San Clementi*, which has long passed for one of the most curious and interesting of the early Roman basilicas. You may judge whether its reputation was increased by the recent discovery of a complete subterranean church, upon whose walls as on a foundation, the later edifice was reared. Thro' the now wholly excavated labyrinth of this primitive tabernacle, taper in hand, I was *promené* by an old Irish monk, who told me stories of all the blessed saints whose adventures you may yet decipher in the most rudimentary frescoes on the walls. But he ended by conducting me down into a still deeper and darker and narrower compartment and in this triply buried sanctuary laid my hand upon an enormous block of granite (or what not) and pronounced in a magnificent brogue the name of Servius Tullius. [!] To the non antiquarian mind these are quite first class sensations.

Hawthorne had a most unsettling revelation after his visit to DOMINE QUO VADIS along the via Appia. He was shown the imprints of Christ's feet, but

> on looking into Murray, I am mortified to find that they are merely facsimiles of the original impressions, which are treasured up among the relics of the neighbouring basilica of St Sebastiano. The marks of sculpture seemed to me, indeed, very evident in these prints, nor did they indicate such beautiful feet as should have belonged to the bearer of the best of glad tidings.

Taine was shocked at the GESÙ. 'This church resembles a magnificent banqueting hall, some royal town hall which adorns itself with all its silverware, its crystal, its damask linen, its embroidered curtains, to receive a monarch and honour the city.' It makes a proclamation: 'Ancient Rome united the world in an empire; I renew it and I am its successor.' Hawthorne was highly critical of s LUIGI DEI FRANCESI: 'a most shamefully dirty place of worship, the beautiful marble columns looking dingy, for the want of loving and pious care'.[12] His judgement, however, is somewhat undercut by claims that it was so 'dusky' within the church that he did not know that there were any pictures there worth looking at. He redeemed himself in s MARIA DEGLI ANGELI. He noted the unprepossessing facade, the brickwork of Diocletian's baths, but within, 'the space is so lofty, broad, and airy, that the soul forthwith swells out and magnifies itself, for the sake of filling it… There is a grand simplicity about the church, more satisfactory than grand ornament'. He was shown Domenichino's *Saint Sebastian*, the fresco removed from St Peter's, and now replaced by a mosaic. For Taine the church reinforced a rule: 'Always the same impression returns in Rome, that of a Christianity poorly plastered onto the old paganism.' The cloister, however, delighted him: 'I believe that there are few things in the world as grand and as simple.' Renan's views of religious history found fertile stimulus in the erroneous siting of s MARIA D'ARACŒLI on the temple of Jupiter Capitolinus:

Church of the Ara Cœli, marbles of Jupiter Capitolinus, which the Romans had taken from the temple of Olympian Jupiter (in Athens). Holy columns which for 2,500 years carry to heaven the religious thought of humanity! There is religion, creating itself out of ruins. A Greek column under Roman skies, and with less delicate taste overall, then all this mixed in a hotchpotch of bad taste, paved with pieces of mosaic, which is the Christian church. In bad taste, but touching and popular…

Ara Cœli, Christmas Day. The wholly popular crib. Shepherds, poor, simple, wholly engaged. It is the simple ones who look and well understand. The women hold up the children in their arms to show them the Madonna and the Bambino…

Nothing, nothing equals Christmas at Ara Cœli. Totally popular, only the people. A children's holiday. Preaching, recitals, dialogues by children [see ill. p. 53]. The little girls climb up on stage, a charming ease of gesture. A little one pauses, bursts of laughter, she opens her large eyes, also laughs and comes down. Charming, divine. Ah, the little creature, the poor little one. Charming girl, a wise face, frowning. The bambino [see ill. p. 51]: O what a bambino, how handsome, say the children. It is their holiday. They talk that day in the church, they shout as they want. A delightful disorder, groups, chatting, coming in, going out.

In 1850 Julia Howe heard a military mass there performed by the band of a French regiment, during the occupation. S MARIA DELLA CONCEZIONE, famous for the Capuchin cemetery, made a major impression on Taine. At the entrance he passed a funeral, with two rows of monks, the first in white, the second the capuchins. 'We see something similar at the Opera, where it makes us laugh. Here the seriousness of death takes you by the throat.' In the cemetery, along with a stylish description of the famous arabesque decoration, Taine was shown the recent dead still in their habits: one a friend of his monkish guide, dead six years earlier; he was told that two monks were sick and the graves were already made: 'this poor man, with his grey beard and old sunken eyes, was quite lively as he gave this explanation; he laughed. It is impossible to convey the effect of this gaiety in such a place on such a subject.' The same church was remembered by Thomas Hardy, who, as a result of 'the sly humour' of some Roman monks, was sent alone into the vaults – but he was prepared and 'therefore not startled at the ghastly scene'. It was, however, Hawthorne who left the most memorable account, in his *Marble Faun*:

> The arrangement of the unearthed skeleton is what makes the special interest of the cemetery. The arched and vaulted walls of the burial recesses are supported by massive pillars and pilasters made of thigh bones and skulls; the whole material of the structure appears to be of a similar kind; and the knobs and embossed ornaments of this strange architecture are represented by the joints of the spine, and the more delicate tracery by the smaller bones of the human frame. The summits of the arches are adorned with entire skeletons, looking as if they were wrought most skilfully in bas relief. There is no possibility of describing

Santa Maria della Concezione, with the skulls and skeletons of the friars arranged in arches and columns around the walls of the Convento dei Cappuccini; by unknown photographer, c. 1900

how ugly and grotesque is the effect, combined with a certain artistic merit, nor how much perverted ingenuity has been shown in this queer way, nor what a multitude of dead monks, through how many hundred years, must have contributed their bony framework to build up these great arches of mortality. On some of the skulls there are inscriptions, purporting that such a monk, who formerly made use of that particular headpiece, died on such a day and year; but vastly the greater number are piled up indistinguishably into the architectural design, like the many deaths that make up the one glory of a victory.

In the side walls of the vaults are niches where skeleton monks sit or stand, clad in the brown habits that they wore in life, and labelled with their names and the dates of their decease. Their skulls (some quite bare, and others still covered with yellow skin, and hair that has known the earth damps) look out from beneath their hoods, grinning hideously repulsive. One reverend father has his mouth wide open, as if he had died in the midst of a howl of terror and remorse, which perhaps is even now screeching through eternity. As a general thing, however, these frocked and hooded skeletons seem to take a more cheerful view of their position, and try with ghastly smiles to turn it into a jest. But the cemetery of the Capuchins is no place to nourish celestial hopes: the soul sinks forlorn and wretched under all this burden of dusty death; the holy earth from Jerusalem, so imbued is it with mortality, has grown as barren of the flowers of Paradise as it is of earthly weeds and grass. Thank Heaven for its blue sky; it needs a long, upward gaze to give us back our faith. Not here can we feel ourselves immortal, where the very altars in these chapels of horrible consecration are heaps of human bones.

Yet let us give the cemetery the praise that it deserves. There is no disagreeable scent, such as might have been expected from the decay of so many holy persons, in whatever odor of sanctity they may have taken their departure. The same number of living monks would not smell half so unexceptionally.

The beautiful round church of s MARIA DELLA PACE enriched Taine's understanding of Raphael's conceptions in the Sibyls (see ill. p. 54).

They are standing, leaning or seated, to suit the curve of the vault, and little angels, offering them parchment for writing, complete the group. Silent, peaceful, they are superhuman creatures, placed, like ancient goddesses, above the action; one calm gesture suffices for them to appear complete, their being is not dispersed or transitory; they exist unchanging in an eternal present. A man such as he has put all the nobility of his heart, all his lonely concepts of charming and sublime happiness in their shapes and attitudes, in the fraternal entwining of the beautiful, peaceful arms, which, extended in search of one another, form a garland.

The same church brought James to a terrible conclusion:

It was worth the trouble going, afterwards, as we did this morning, to San Agostino and Sta. Maria della Pace to look upon Raphael's two wretchedly decayed frescoes of Isaiah and the Sybils, in which *il a voulu faire du Michel Ange*. There was in him none but the very smallest Michel Angelesque elements. – I fancy that I have found after much fumbling and worrying – much of the deepest enjoyment and of equal dissatisfaction – the secret of his incontestable thinness and weakness. He was incapable of energy of statement.

It was s MARIA DEL POPOLO which impressed on Taine the prominence of tombs in Roman churches:

The church is populated: twenty cardinals have their monuments there. Their statues sleep on the stone; others dream half-lying or pray; often there is only a bust, sometimes only a head of the deceased over an inscription or a memorial; several graves are in the floor, and the feet of the faithful have worn away the reliefs. Everywhere death is present and palpable; under the funerary slabs, one realises that there are bones, miserable remains of a man; these cold forms of immobile marble which rest eternally in the corner of a chapel, raising a thin finger, are all that remains of a warm, trembling life which burned with flames and flashes in the world's view, to leave only a little heap of ashes. Our French churches do not have this mortuary pomp.

At s MARIA DELLA VITTORIA the same art historian gave one of the most sensuous descriptions of one of the most sensuous sculptures in the city, *Santa Teresa* by Bernini (see ill. Vol. II):

She is adorable: lying, fainting with love, her naked hands and feet hanging, her eyes half-closed, she has collapsed from happiness and ecstasy. Her face is thinned, but how noble! She is the true lady pining in fire and tears, awaiting her lover. Even the twisted drapery, the languour of her fatigued hands, the sigh which murmurs on her half opened lips – there is nothing in her or around her which does not express the voluptuous anguish and the divine transport. One cannot describe in words such an intoxicated and touching attitude. Turned on her back, she swoons, her whole being dissolves; the poignant moment arrives, she groans; it is her last groan, the sensation is too strong. The angel, however, a young page of fourteen, in a light tunic, his breast uncovered, arrives gracious and kind; he is the most handsome page of the great lord who has come to make a too tender vassal happy. A half complaisant, half wicked smile creases the dimples of his fresh, shining cheeks; his golden arrow in his hand indicates the delightful and terrible shudder with which he will shake all the nerves of this charming, eager body which is exposed before his hand.[13]

Melville provides a depressing picture of s ONOFRIO, where Torquato Tasso died. 'On the Janiculum, fine view of Rome. Sad corridors, cloisters, and no grass. Doleful old chamber – Wax cast. – Sad little garden, mouldering gateways – Quaint church – damp and doleful – New monument in wretched taste.' The monument to Tasso by Giuseppe de Fabris was dedicated in 1857. At s PIETRO IN VINCOLI Michelangelo's *Moses* (see ill. Vol. II) was always the focus of interest. Hawthorne found it 'grand and sublime, with a beard flowing down like a cataract; a truly majestic figure, but not so benign as it were desirable that such strength should be.' George Eliot was critical: 'The Moses did not affect me agreeably: both the attitude and the expression of the face seemed to me, in that one visit, to have an exaggeration that strained after effect without reaching it. The failure seemed to me of this kind: Moses was an angry man trying to frighten the people by his mien, instead of being rapt by his anger and terrible without self consciousness.' James, on the other hand, made a special point of revisiting the *Moses* on the day before his departure, and came to the conclusion that Michelangelo was the greatest of artists.

So far from perfection, so finite, so full of errors, so broadly a target for criticism as it sits there, the *Moses* nevertheless by the vigor with which it utters its idea, the eloquence with which it tells the tale of the author's passionate abjuration of the inaction of fancy and contemplation – his willingness to let it stand, in the interest of life and health and movement as his best and his only possible – by this high transcendent spirit, it redeems itself from subjection to its details, and appeals most forcibly to the generosity and sympathy of the mind.

It is surprising to find Renan so unemotional confronted with the ghastly frescoes of s stefano rotondo on the Cælian. 'Admirable poem. Heroic gallery. Beauty of this legend of the martyrs. I love the martyrs. Slightly critical, absolute. It is a creation of Christianity.'[14]

It is obvious that, despite the high literary and artistic skills of the later nineteenth century visitors, they provide far less than their predecessors by way of appreciation and criticism of the art and architecture of the many basilicas and churches.

There were still ecclesiastical festivals to describe. The ritual of the blessing of horses on st anthony's day near S Maria Maggiore had always attracted visitors' attention. Norton saw it in 1856:

At the side door, just out of the rain, stood a good natured, dirty looking priest, with a brush in his hand and an earthen jug full of water at his side, who, when a carriage or a wagon drove up or passed by, shook his brush, dipped in the holy water, at the horses, and muttered some words of benediction. A good many of the country carts came along and stopped at the door; their drivers gave the priest a little fee for shaking his brush, and then went on. Many of the carriages came, apparently, to bring persons who wanted to see the show, if by chance there were any; but others were brought up with the express purpose of getting a blessing for the horses, which was paid for according to the wealth of the owner, or perhaps according to his superstition or his love of display. It is a rule here, that those blessings which we are accustomed to consider the free gifts of God must be paid for in some way, either in hard money or in harder penance. Heaven is not given away in Rome. The Pope himself, the cardinals, and the nobles, all send their horses, during the course of the feast, to be blessed. [Alessandro] Torlonia sends his best carriage drawn by eighteen horses. The coachmen are in their best liveries, and the footmen splendid in powder and lace. It is said he pays a thousand dollars for the benediction.

Beside the wagons and carriages that came this afternoon, (the air was so gray and thick that one could not see the Alban Hills,) there were a good many horses and donkeys ridden up one by one, or sometimes two or three together. Some of them had ribbons braided in their tails and manes, and hanging about them in streamers, and their riders looked as fine as the horses; while others were such rough, uncared for, bare boned, worn looking creatures, that one could not but wish that the blessing would turn into a good supper and shelter for them.[15]

He also records a much more disturbing celebration about the same time at S Andrea delle Fratte by piazza di Spagna, to commemorate the CONVERSION IN 1842 OF A JEW, Alfonso Ratisbonne, of Strasbourg, who became a Jesuit. The Dominican who preached the sermon on this occasion described Ratisbonne before his conversion as 'rich and scornful'.[16] In 1858 in Bologna, Edgardo Mortara was kidnapped by papal police from his Jewish parents, on the grounds that he had been baptised.

On PALM SUNDAY 1856 the Goncourt brothers were in St Peter's, listening to the music of the Passion:

The voice of the tenor giving the solemn recitative. The voice of Christ (bass): like a voice rolling from echo to echo in the faraway mountains: a broad, balanced chant, similar to the sad lullaby for a sick child; notes plaintively floating above the earth; a tremulous melody, where the last syllables of the words of pain, hanging long on the singer's lips, breathe forth in murmuring sighs; anguished vocalisation representing the human failing of a god. The voice of the Gentile, of the Pharisee the voice of the counter tenor: a voice of caricature, an over sharpened falsetto, an organ comically breaking, the song of a broken cock – which the ample voice of Christ buried under his deep bass. And the voices of the Jewish crowd, the voices of the mob, rendered by the angry voices, the murdered voices of the castrati.

The choir of the Sistine Chapel in 1898. The castrati are numbered in red.
The practice was brought to an end in 1903

The centre piece of Easter seems to have remained the performance of ALLEGRI'S MISERERE – and Frances Elliot in 1870 captured the human pageant:

> The Sistine Chapel, where the 'Tenebræ' and 'Miserere' are performed on the two days preceding Good Friday, is besieged by thousands of infatuated females for hours before the services begin, all struggling to obtain a front position on the forms placed behind the screen in the lower half of the chapel, which (as this, the private oratory of the Pope, is supposed to be inaccessible to women) are pushed back as far as possible.
>
> The ascent was beset with Swiss guards, their brilliant uniforms and glancing steel accoutrements looking exceedingly picturesque and mediæval; hundreds of ladies in black, gentlemen in evening dress, and militia and military heroes in full uniform trooped up this truly magnificent and regal entrance to the countless splendours of the Vatican, all laughing, talking, and joking with quite praiseworthy forgetfulness of the solemn nature of the anniversary. Some ladies tried to smuggle in camp stools under their petticoats – a *ruse* instantly detected and ruthlessly exposed by the all-seeing officials; while

others, coming in greater numbers than their tickets allowed, were remorselessly sent back, in spite of lamentations and reproaches in unmistakably Anglican Italian.

Thousands of men and women, gathered from the four quarters of the globe, are rushing about, crowding every space, treading on each other's heels, talking, wondering, pushing; every face turned towards the open door, with its ample drapery of crimson, leading into the Sistine Chapel, which they are all firmly resolved to enter at all risks. And though that door is guarded by military – obstinate Swiss guards, who, if Venus herself fresh from Olympus, or all the Circes and Armidas that ever existed in fact or fable, tried to cajole, would not budge one single inch – still, so vast is the crowd, its own weight carrying it irresistibly onward, that all slowly disappear under the overhanging curtain.

Every one knows that the Sistine Chapel is not large. Imagine, then, what it must be when, in the space assigned to the public – in which five hundred might commodiously sit – ten thousand persons are, by some miracle of crushing, collected. Imagine the heat, the squeezing, the elbows poked into one's sides, the furious glances, the hatred, malice, and uncharitableness of all those living beings, each wanting to see and to hear; and all, save a few in the front, effectually prevented from doing either, and furiously incensed in consequence.

The EASTER BENEDICTION was recorded by Pauline de la Ferronays in 1858.

In the immense space, and as far as the eye could see, not an empty place could be discerned. The steps of the obelisk are entirely occupied by peasants, men, women and children from all the surrounding districts, and by the Trasteverans in their holiday costume. The sun makes the gold pins, the white veils of the women, the striking red of their skirts, and the men's belts sparkle. Troops are drawn up to right and left. The colonnade is two thirds covered with people, and the confused murmur of the animated and innumerable crowd is heard everywhere.

Soon on the loggia appears a priest who exhibits the mitres designed to recall that all the dignities of the bishopric are possessed by the bishop of bishops. The people pay attention: all eyes are directed to the same place, but no one is silent until the moment when on the same loggia a white handkerchief is seen to flutter. Then happens what never happens anywhere except Rome in this unique minute, namely the instantaneous and universal silence of an immense crowd gathered in the open air. The effect is indescribable. The whinnying of the horses which alone disturbs it only renders the complete absence of any sound of a human voice more remarkable. Little children even are silent in their mother's arms. A unanimous feeling passes like electricity through the whole crowd. The pope, tiara on head and carried in his pontifical chair has appeared in the loggia... Everyone kneels. Then in the silence which is so profound that one would hear a bird flying in the air, in the

Benediction of the Pope on Easter Sunday, 1880s, by an unknown photographer; by this stage people had been replaced by carriages

immensity of the square his accentuated and sonorous voice
rings out:

Sit nomen domini benedictum.

Everyone replies: *Ex hoc nunc, et usque in sæcula.*

Adiutorium nostrum in nomine Domini.

The reply is: *Qui fecit cælum et terram.*

The pope extends his arms; no one ever could give to this
gesture its sublime meaning better than Pius IX. Every head
is bowed, while, right hand raised, he pronounces on the city
and the world the solemn words of blessing. The amen issues
from every breast, and is repeated, and reaches the edges of the
square, and the canon of l'Angelo announce to the Eternal City
that the pope's blessing has descended on it and the world.[17]

Charles Norton recorded at length another striking feature of the
Church even in the second half of the nineteenth century: indulgences. These were enough, he declared, 'to afford ample room for
the starting point of a new Reformation'. He had obtained a copy of
*Raccolta di Orazioni e Pie Opere per le quali sono state concedute dai
Sommi Pontefici le S Indulgenze*, 12th edition, 1849. This list of only
perpetual indulgences occupied 527 pages. It was sanctioned expressly
by the cardinal prefect of the Congregation of Indulgences. Norton
noted that many churches in Rome displayed a sign: 'Plenary indulgences every day'; S Giovanni in Laterano was an example. Its altars,
paradoxically, were less frequented, however, than the Santa Scala, the
ascent of which on one's knees, earned remission of only two-and-a-
half centuries in Purgatory.[18]

Léon Bonnat, Interior of the Sistine Chapel, *c. 1880*

PALACES

The main object of every visitor to the Vatican palace was the SISTINE CHAPEL. Nathaniel Hawthorne was, of course, querulous. 'Methinks I have hardly seen anything else so forlorn and depressing as it is now, all dusky and dim, even the very lights having passed into shadows, and shadows into utter blackness, so that it needs a sunshiny day, under the bright Italian heavens to make the designs perceptible at all...' The depiction of Christ unnerved him:

> It would be a very terrible picture to one who should really see Jesus, the Saviour, in that inexorable judge; but it seems to me very undesirable that he should ever be represented in that aspect, when it is so essential to our religion to believe him infinitely kinder and better towards us than we deserve.

He concluded, however, with an admission:

> I am not unwilling to believe, with faith beyond what I can actually see, that the greatest pictorial miracles ever yet achieved have been wrought upon the walls and ceiling of the Sistine Chapel.

Tchaikovsky at first found the frescoes 'incomprehensible' but finally was 'full of astonishment at their original and powerful beauty'. George Eliot very carefully specified: 'I care for the chapel solely for the sake of its ceiling... the most wonderful fresco in the world.' Hippolyte Taine provided some direct comparisons:

> Superhuman personages as unfortunate as ourselves, the bodies of the gods taut with earthly passions, an Olympus where human tragedies collide, this is the thought which descends from all the vaults of the Sistine Chapel. What an injustice to compare these with Raphael's Sibyls and Isaiah! They are strong and beautiful, I admit; they exhibit an art as profound, but what one sees at the first glance is that they do not have the same soul; they were never set up like these by an impetuous and irresistable will; they have never experienced like these the thrill and tension of the nervous being who gathers himself up and charges forward completely at the risk of destruction.

What pleased Taine most in the chapel, however, were the Ignudi:

> the twenty young men seated on the cornices in the four corners of each painting, truly painted sculptures which represent a higher, unknown world. They are all adolescent heroes, of the time of Achilles and Ajax, as fine a type, but more passionate, or a ruder energy... One did not think that the human frame, curved or erect, could touch the heart with such a diversity of emotions. The thighs support, the chest breathes, the whole clothing of flesh is taut and trembles, the trunk is bent over the haunches, the shoulder furrowed with muscles impetuously raises the arm.[19]

Next came the RAPHAEL STANZE. If we are to believe Hawthorne, they were in a sorry state, 'so faded as they are, so battered by the mischance of years... They have been scrubbed, I suppose – brushed at least – a thousand times over, till the surface, brilliant or soft, as Raphael left it, must have been quite rubbed off, and, with it, all the consummate finish.' After some very strong criticisms of the *Fire in*

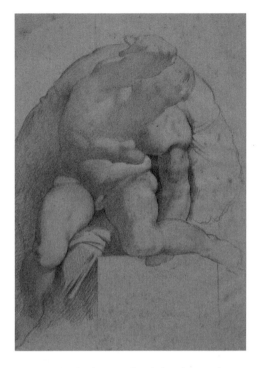

Léon Bonnat, Study after one of Michelangelo's ignudi, *c. 1860*

the Borgo (it was not a real fire, since the buildings were all of stone, and no one was in any danger), Taine saw the essentials of Raphael in the *School of Athens*:

> These groups on the stairs, below and around the two philoso-phers, never existed, never could have existed, and it is precisely because of this that they are so beautiful. The scene is in a higher world, never seen by mortal eyes, completely the product of the artist's mind. All these people are of the same family as the goddesses of the ceiling. One must stay looking at them for a whole afternoon.

James was disappointed on another count: he compared the paint-ings unfavourably to Raphael's portraits which he had seen in Florence.

The frescoes of the RAPHAEL LOGGIE were, according again to Hawthorne, 'so defaced as to be untraceable and unintelligible along the side wall of the gallery'. In the ceiling alone were still some bright paintings. When Taine came to recall Raphael, however, the first thing was the loggie: for example, 'the bent back of Eve picking the apple, her charming head, the vigorous muscles of this young body twisted on her haunches, all these people so strongly built and so free in movement'.[20]

It is Charles Norton who had the taste to pay special attention to the CHAPEL OF NICHOLAS V (1446), decorated by Fra Angelico. 'The saints that he painted have more the air and likeness of saints than those of anyone else.' Norton singled out *The preaching of St Stephen* and *The distribution of Alms by St Lawrence*, of which he gave extensive and most sensitive analysis of their composition.[21]

The PINACOTECA was now an established gallery in the Vatican. Henry James, however, came with too many established preferences – the great Venetian school, the early Italians (especially Giotto and Orcagna), and Leonardo and Raphael for their portraits. This explains his dullness when confronted with the *Transfiguration* (see ill. Vol. I).

> Without going into metaphysics, it is easy to say that the great works of Rafael are vitiated by their affected classicism – their elegance and coldness. I sat staring stupidly at the *Transfiguration* and actually *surprised* at its thinness – asking myself whether *this* was the pretended greatest of pictures.

Taine's saw the genius: 'Is there in the world the subject of any painting more mystical?' It was a vision like that of Dante. He observed Raphael's quintessential grace: the arms of the kneeling young woman, the foot of the reading man, and the apostles who fall to create a symmetrical group. Ludwig Pastor put it in one sentence: 'Raphael's *Transfiguration* alone is worth a journey to Rome.'[22]

We may now turn to antiquities. The original heart of the collection was the BELVEDERE. Hawthorne recorded that he saw it on a Monday when the public was admitted for three hours.

I saw the Apollo Belvedere [see ill. Vol. II] as something ethereal

View of the display of classical statues in the Vatican, photographed by James Anderson in 1859

and godlike; only for a flitting moment, however, and as if he had alighted from heaven, or shone suddenly out of the sunlight, and then had withdrawn himself again. I felt the Laocoön [see ill. Vol. II] very powerfully, though very quietly; an immortal agony, with a strange calmness diffused through it, so that it resembles the vast rage of the sea, calm on account of its immensity; or the tumult of Niagara, which does not seem to be tumult, because it keeps pouring on for ever and ever.

George Eliot mentioned only the Apollo in a very evocative recalling of a visit by torchlight:

Perhaps the greatest treat we had at the Vatican was the sight of a few statues, including the Apollo, by torchlight – all the more impressive because it was our first sight of the Vatican. Even the mere hurrying along the vast halls with the fitful torchlight falling on the innumerable statues and busts and bas reliefs and sarcophagi, would have left a sense of awe at these crowded silent forms which have the solemnity of suddenly arrested life. Wonderfully grand these halls of the Vatican are, and there is but one complaint to be made against the home provided for this richest collection of antiquities: it is, that there is no historical arrangement of them and no catalogue. The system of classification is based on the history of their collection by the different Popes, so that for every other purpose but that of securing to each Pope his share of glory, it is a system of helter skelter.

James' reaction was mixed: 'The Apollo is really a magnificent youth – with far more of solid dignity than I fancied. The Laocoön, on the other hand, strikes me as a decidedly made up affair and much less complete and successful embodiment of human anguish than that sublime Niobe at Florence...'[23] Florence again!

The opposite comparison occurred to the Goncourts. After mentioning the animals in the museum at Florence:

> But what are these alongside the marble panther in the Vatican, the body quite flat, the head raised and roaring, and all the muscles, represented in this hard stone, like a sketch in clay, and yet with a nervosity, a strength, an anger beyond that of the best animal artists – and also the eagle phoenix, with wings extended, its two talons on a brazier, the flames of which lick its belly, its eye both mournful and ferocious, the beak half open and the tongue beating furiously the inside of this beak.

In the Room of the Muses, the statue which most impressed Henrik Ibsen was, naturally, that of Melpomene, the muse of tragedy, which he understood to be a true revelation of the meaning of that dramatic form. The Aldobrandini Wedding (see ill. Vol. II), finally, caught the Goncourts' attention: 'the most astonishing revelation of ancient painting, the most skilled and felictous exposition of female poses...'[24]

The MOSAIC SCHOOL at the Vatican was still famous. When Hawthorne visited it in 1858, the workers were chiefly employed with medallions of heads of the saints for the new St Paul's. No large painting was being reproduced; rather 'small and delicate subjects': a *Holy Family* by Raphael, and the *Sibyls* of Guercino and Domenichino.[25]

The gardens of the Vatican were then, as now, rarely open to visitors. One who made the most of it was Oscar Wilde in April 1900:

> I found that the Vatican Gardens were open to the Bohemian and the Portuguese pilgrims. I at once spoke both languages fluently, explained that my English dress was a form of penance, and entered that waste, desolate park, with its faded Louis XIV gardens, its sombre avenues, its sad woodland. The peacocks screamed, and I understood why tragedy dogged the gilt feet of each pontiff. But I wandered in exquisite melancholy for an hour. One Philippo, a student, whom I culled in the Borgia room, was with me: not for many years has Love walked in the Pope's pleasaunce.[26]

Taine provides an introduction to conditions awaiting the later nineteenth century visitor to the ARISTOCRATIC PALACES:

> The ex-king of Naples inhabits the palazzo Farnese, so that it is difficult to see the paintings; the others are open on fixed days. The owners have the good sense and the good taste to make their private galleries into public museums. Placards serving as booklets are lying on the tables at the visitors' disposition; the concierges and attendants gravely receive their two *paoli*: they are in fact the functionaries who serve the public and must be paid by the public. There is the transition from aristocratic life to the democratic regime.

And Hawthorne made the same criticism of the aristocratic palaces as we have seen in previous centuries, but more concisely and wittily:

> There was never an idea of domestic comfort, or of what we include in the name of home, at all implicated in such structures; they being generally built by wifeless and childless churchmen for the display of pictures and statuary, in galleries and long suites of rooms.[27]

We turn now to the individual palaces. The custom will again be observed of signalling with an asterisk works still in the named collection, and of indicating, where known, the present location, if it is elsewhere. Herman Melville seems to have gone to the PALAZZO BARBERINI to see a very select number of paintings: Reni's *Beatrice Cenci* (in fact Elizabetta Silvani's *Sibyl*) ('appealing look of innocence'), Albani's 'lovely little painting of Galatea in car – two swimmers in dark blue shadowed water – gleam of limbs', and Holbein's (in fact Dürer's) *Christ disputing with the doctors* (Thyssen collection). Hawthorne was similarly overwhelmed by the *Beatrice Cenci*:

> as regards Beatrice Cenci, I might as well not try to say anything; for its spell is indefinable, and the painter has wrought it in a way more like magic than anything else…
>
> It is the most profoundly wrought picture in the world; no artist did it, nor could do it again. Guido may have held the brush, but he painted better than he knew. I wish, however, it were possible for some spectator, of deep sensibility, to see the picture without knowing anything of its subject or history; for, no doubt, we bring all our knowledge of the Cenci tragedy to the interpretation of it.

Enrico Fanfani, Guido Reni paints Beatrice Cenci in prison, *1855-60*

Hawthorne declared the central hall of the palace 'the most splendid domestic hall I have seen, eighty feet in length at least, and of proportionate breadth and height', with a ceiling fresco 'indescribably gorgeous'. The palace, he noted, was inhabited by a cardinal, a prince and a duke, 'all belonging to the Barberini family, and each having his separate portion of the palace, while their servants have a common territory and meeting ground in this noble hall'. Taine gave an earthy description of the *Fornarina*: 'a vigorous woman of the people… strong limbed'. Reni's *Cenci*, on the other hand, is a 'delicate and pretty pale young woman… all the curves of her face are graceful', but without the pallor, she is 'an agreeable young woman'.[28] This illustrated Taine's theory of the loss of vitality between the eras of the two artists.

Hawthorne found the BORGHESE PALACE had 'a kind of splendid shabbiness thrown over it' and was 'very comfortless – indeed, I suppose nobody ever thought of being comfortable there, since the house was built – but especially uncomfortable on a chill, damp day like this'. As for the picture gallery, it was 'one of the most celebrated in the world', containing eight or nine hundred paintings.

> I was glad, in the very last of the twelve rooms, to come upon some Dutch and Flemish pictures, very few, but very welcome; Rubens, Rembrandt, Vandyke, Paul Potter, Teniers, and others – men of flesh and blood, and warm fists and human hearts. As compared with them, these mighty Italian masters seem men of polished steel; not human, nor addressing themselves so much to human sympathies as to a formed, intellectual taste.

The prince's generosity was noted:

> The Prince Borghese [Marcantonio, 1814-1886] certainly demeans himself like a kind and liberal gentleman, in throwing open this invaluable collection to the public to see, and for artists to carry away with them, and diffuse all over the world, so far as their own power and skill will permit. It is open every day of the week, except Saturday and Sunday, without any irksome restriction or supervision; and the fee, which custom requires the visitor to pay to the custode, has the good effect of making us feel that we are

not intruders, nor received in an exactly eleemosynary way. The
thing could not be better managed.

Taine mused on the way the needs of Christianity had been super-
imposed on the naturalness of earlier Italian art: 'what occupied men
about the year 1500 was the human animal and his accompaniment'.
Del Sarto's Madonnas and Venus were related, del Piombo's *Visitation*
could be called simply 'a young woman standing next to an old bent
woman', *Titian's *Sacred and Profane Love* is simply a beautiful clothed
woman alongside a naked one, but the painting he remembered best
was *Domenichino's *Diana's Hunt* (see ill. Vol. II): the artist dared
interpret nature in his own way, and he was punished for it. James
recorded breathlessly that 'in the Borghese collection is a Correggio
of heavenly merit [the Danaë?] – and a Titian of earthly'. Pastor, not
unexpectedly, declared that everything there had to give way to
*Raphael's *Entombment*.[29]

In the complex of palaces on the CAPITOL the museums contained
both antiquities and a pinacoteca. William Thackeray was dismissive:
'I declare that the *Dying Gladiator* is very well, but it is no such
wonder. As for the *Domenichino [the *Cumæan Sibyl*] (it is at the
Capitol, you know over the way) Pish! it is a great clumsy woman
affected ogling and in a great turban.' This was certainly a minority
view. Melville noted the antiquities: 'Hall of Emperors. "That Tiberius?
he don't look so bad at all" – It was he. A look of sickly evil, – intellect
without manliness and sadness without goodness. Great brain over-
refinements. Solitude. – Dying gladiator. Shows that humanity existed
amid the barbarians of the Roman time, as it now among the Christian
barbarians. Antinoüs beautiful.' Hawthorne was shocked at what was
then thought to be the bust of Cæsar: 'a very ugly old man indeed –
wrinkled, puckered, shrunken, lacking breadth and substance;
careworn, grim, as if he had fought hard with life, and had suffered
in the conflict; a man of schemes, and of eager effort to bring his
schemes to pass'. As for the *Dying Gladiator*, he did not believe that
'so much pathos is wrought in any other block of stone', although it
made great demands on the viewer. On a subsequent visit, he asked
some French soldiers the way to the picture gallery, but it was his

Unknown artist, British Tourists and the Dying Gladiator, *1872*

experience that they did not ever know even the place they were guarding. After complaining about the lack of cleaning and varnishing and good framing in Italian galleries, he singled out *Veronese's *Rape of Europa* as one that would benefit from such attention. When he visited the sculptures, the Faun of Praxiteles caught his eye: it was to inspire the *Marble Faun*. George Eliot listed her favourite paintings:

> This last week of our stay we went for the first time to the Picture gallery of the Capitol, where we saw the famous Guercino – the *Entombment of Saint Petronilla* [see ill. Vol. II] – which we had already seen in mosaic at St Peter's. It is a stupendous piece of painting, about which one's only feeling is that it might as well have been left undone. More interesting is the portrait of Michael Angelo by himself – a deeply melancholy face. And there is also a picture of a Bishop by Gian Bellini which arrested us a long while. After these I remember most distinctly *Veronese's *Europa*, superior to that we afterwards saw at Venice; a delicious mythological Poussin, all light and joy; and a *Sebastian* by Guido, exceptionally beautiful among the many detestable things of his in this gallery.

Taine cast an art historian's eye on a few masterpieces: *Guercino's *Saint Petronilla*, with its contrasts of light and shade, of the saint being

buried and the saint in heaven, and the realism of elements such as the
boy with the candle ('you have met him in the street'); Fra Bartolomeo's
Presentation in the temple ('nothing is more noble, simple, calm, pure');
and *Tintoretto's *Magdalene*. James simply yielded himself up to the
masterpieces:

> I saw yesterday at the Capitol the dying Gladiator, the Lydian
> Apollo, the Amazon etc – all of them unspeakably simple and
> noble and eloquent of the breadth of human genius. There's
> little to say or do about them, save to sit and enjoy them and
> let them act upon your nerves and confirm your esteem for
> completeness, purity and perfection.[30]

Hawthorne in 1858 was enormously impressed with the COLONNA
PALACE, then occupied by the French ambassador:

> what chiefly interested me was the magnificent and stately hall
> of the palace [see ill. overleaf], fifty-five of my paces in length,
> besides a large apartment at either end, opening into it through
> a pillared space as wide as the gateway of a city. The pillars are
> of giallo antico, and there are pilasters of the same all the way
> up and down the walls, forming a perspective of the richest
> aspect, especially as the broad cornice flames with gilding, and
> the spaces between the pilasters are emblazoned with heral-
> dic achievements and emblems in gold, and there are Venetian
> looking glasses, richly decorated over the surface with beautiful
> pictures of flowers and Cupids, through which you catch the
> gleam of the mirror; and two rows of splendid chandeliers extend
> from end to end of the hall, which, when lighted up, if ever it
> be lighted up, now-a-nights, must be the most brilliant interior
> that ever mortal eye beheld. The ceiling glows with pictures in
> fresco, representing scenes connected with the history of the
> Colonna family; and the floor is paved with beautiful marbles,
> polished and arranged in square and circular compartments;
> and each of the many windows is set in a great architectural
> frame of precious marble, as large as the portal of a door. The
> apartment at the farther end of the hall is elevated above it, and

Palazzo Colonna, the main gallery; photographed c. *1850-80*

is attained by several marble steps, whence it must have been glorious in former days to have looked down upon a gorgeous throng of princes, cardinals, warriors, and ladies, in such rich attire as might be worn when the palace was built. It is singular how much freshness and brightness it still retains; and the only objects to mar the effect were some ancient statues and busts, not very good in themselves, and now made dreary of aspect by their corroded surfaces, – the result of long burial under ground.

Frances Elliot in 1869 gave more detail on the internal arrangements:

The gallery is more than two hundred and twenty feet long, terminating at the further end in a sort of tribune supported by vast columns, and raised on steps. Within this holy of holies, in aristocratic exclusiveness, are two beautiful Venuses by Bronzino, whom the extreme delicacy of the present prince has caused to be draped with an ill assorted garment painted in water colours, and therefore removable. This dressmaking spoils two fine pictures entirely. It would take pages to enumerate half the pictures and sculptures in this gallery. One fine portrait of the poetess Vittoria Colonna is very interesting; and another by Vandyke, of some family hero on horseback, very striking and noble.

The gallery, she admitted, was the finest room in all Rome, 'a perfect harmony of colour, luxury, size and grandeur'. One of the marble steps had been broken by a cannon ball in 1848, and the prince never allowed it to be repaired. In the garden she saw where the Quirinal Horsetamers had been found.

> Very picturesque gardens they are, ascending by double flights of steps through alleys of box and bay, along the margin of trickling streams and gushing fountains, to the hill above, where, from the grand terrace, one looks over Rome… Behind the terrace is a garden… Great orangetrees, loaded with fresh fruit, flung back the rays of the setting sun opposite, making one happy by the notion of having suddenly leaped into summer; for in these secluded nooks, embosomed in ilex and bay, within great orchards of the orange and lemon, not a vestige reminds one of the course of the seasons, and a perennial summer reigns.[31]

Melville declared the PALAZZO DORIA PAMPHILI gallery the 'most elegant one in Rome perhaps'. He appreciated the portrait of Lucretia Borgia, ascribed to Veronese (lost): 'no wicked look about her. Good looking dame – rather fleshy.' For Hawthorne the palace was the most splendid in Rome, but the rooms were 'colder and more comfortless than can possibly be imagined', but by this time he was suffering from 'gallery fatigue', and declared that one painting in a thousand 'ought to live in the applause of men'. Melville had been unimpressed with the landscapes of Claude here (for example, the *Marriage of Isaac and Rebecca*, and the *View of Delphi*), but Hawthorne did not doubt that they would be exquisite if they were kept by the National Gallery in London. Taine admired the great landscapes of Poussin and the women of Titian ('one adorned with pearls with a necklace is the most appetising of well fed servants'), but was most struck by the portraits: Veronese's *Lucretia Borgia*; del Piombo's *Andrea Doria*; Bronzino's (*Cristofano dell'Altissimo's) *Machiavelli*, revealing 'the humorist beneath the historian, philosopher and politician – crude, licentious, often bitter and finally desperate'; but the masterpiece was *Velázquez's *Innocent X* (see ill. Vol. I), revealing a 'poor simpleton, ill mannered, worn out', Was Taine mad? James noted only this painting and recalled Taine's 'memorable' comments. Wilde went to see that painting three times in a month in Rome: 'quite the grandest portrait in the world'.[32]

For Taine the PALAZZO FARNESE was 'the largest, most imposing, most noble and the most severely magnificent... alone in the middle of a darkish piazza, massive and high like a fortress, capable of receiving and returning a fusillade'.[33]

On the PALAZZO QUIRINALE Melville provided brief, sometimes enigmatic notes:

> Vast hall – cold splendor – Marbles, paintings, & c& c & c
> Gobelins – The Palm – Sèvres china – Guido's Annunciation
> (Raphael's) Fresco of the Swiss Guards looking down – boxes
> with ribands – *The Gardens* – A Paridise [*sic*] without joy – freaks
> & caprices of endless wealth – rhuematics [*sic*] in gardener – As
> stone is sculptured into forms of foliage, so here foliage trained
> into forms of sculpture –

Hawthorne's description a year later is remarkably similar concerning the interior, but he liked the gardens much better:

> They are very extensive, and laid out in straight avenues, bordered with walls of box, as impervious as if of stone, – not less than twenty feet high, and pierced with lofty archways, cut in the living wall...
> Marble sculptures, much weather stained, and generally broken nosed, stood along these stately walks; there were many fountains gushing up into the sunshine; we likewise found a rich flower garden, containing rare specimens of exotic flowers, and gigantic cactuses, and also an aviary, with vultures, doves, and singing birds.[34]

Garden steps of the Palazzo Rospigliosi, photographed by Pietro Dovizielli, 1859

The PALAZZO ROSPIGLIOSI, near the Quirinal, was still famous for its gardens and casino. Melville again provides staccato notes:

> The terraced garden – 200 years old – the garden stairway in hollow – mossy balustrades – The lemon walk tiled over – The fish pond & fountains & violets wet with spray – The Casino – bas releifs [*sic*] – Aurora – Floats overhead like sun dyed clouds – The Mirror – the lovers seated there. Sampson pulling down the temple – gigantic – unfortunate hint at fall of Aurora – The shot.

Hawthorne described the garden with its borders of box and ornamental shrubbery, with a fountain surrounded by a balustrade supporting eight classical statues, in poor condition. In the Casino, no fewer than four artists were copying the *Aurora*. The celebrated fresco by Reni (see ill. Vol. II) was a degenerate form for Taine. The painter was fashionable, and brought into a frivolous world 'the physiognomies and smiles of society. True energy, the internal force of genuine passion had disappeared in Italy; they no longer liked true virgins, primitive souls, Raphael's simple peasants, but the affecting inmates of the salon and the convent, well bred young ladies.'[35]

At the PALAZZO SCIARRA on the Corso Melville found 'fading splendour… closeness of a closet'. His attention was taken by Caravaggio's *Gamesters*, now lost ('the self possession and confidence of knavery – the irresolution and perplexity of honesty'), a landscape by Claude ('He paints the air'), the *Holy Family* by Dürer and a lady by Titian ('The crimson and white sleeves'). Hawthorne remembered Raphael's *Violin Player* (Rothschild), da Vinci's *Vanity and Modesty*, but liked best Titian's *Bella Donna*. Taine recorded that two paintings were under glass: the Raphael and the Titian. Of the former such paintings were more informative than his 'tarnished frescoes and peeling ceilings': 'the nobility and calm of this head are incomparable'. He compared Raphael in his tenderness and generosity to Mozart. The Titian woman was 'as noble and calm as a Greek statue'. Leonardo was 'the most thoughtful of all painters', and Taine found his *Vanity* 'incredible… more nobly elegant than the *Mona Lisa* and the abundance and refinement of her hair extraordinary'. The palace itself he described as dilapidated.[36]

The PALAZZO SPADA, finally, attracted the attention of Hawthorne. He was intelligently sceptical about the statue of Pompey ('much of the effect, no doubt is due to the solemn obscurity of the hall, and to the loneliness in which the great naked statue stands'), yet thought it worth monetarily the whole sculpture gallery of the Vatican! He noted a few paintings: Reni's *Judith*, family portraits by the same artist and Titian, and some good Guercinos.[37]

It seems, paradoxically, that interest in the great palaces declined dramatically among the visitors in the later nineteenth century. Detailed notes are found, for the most part, in the two Americans Melville and Hawthorne and the Frenchman Taine.

VILLAS

The years following 1870 were disastrous for the villas, which had for centuries been one of the glories of Rome. In the construction of ministries and housing, only the Albani, Borghese and Doria Pamphili were spared; the Aldobrandini, Altieri, Giustiniani Massimo, Ludovisi, Montalto and Negroni were utterly destroyed. The visitors before 1870 give us our last glimpse of these extensive parks and gardens and their accompanying collections of art.

At the VILLA ALBANI Herman Melville of course noticed the Antinoüs, and the Apollo Sauroctonos:

> Thence to villa Albani – along the walls – Antinoüs – head like moss rose with curls and buds – rest all simplicity – end of fillet on shoulder – drapery, shoulder in the mantle – hand full of flowers and eyeing them – the profile etc. The small bronze Apollo. Surprising how such a metal could be melted into such flexible looking forms.

The route to the villa taken by Nathaniel Hawthorne recreates a world destroyed:

> We set out between ten and eleven o'clock, and walked through the Via Felice, the Piazza Barberini, and a long, heavy, dusty range of streets beyond, to the Porta Salara, whence the road extends, white and sunny, between two high blank walls to the gate of the villa, which is at no great distance.

Hawthorne's reactions were quite the opposite of his countryman's: he could not feel the Antinoüs to be one of the finest antiquities, 'partly, I suppose, because the features… do not seem to me beautiful in themselves; and that heavy downward look is repeated till I am more weary of it than anything else in sculpture'. It was similar with the Apollo: 'I could not make myself in the least sensible of its merit.' The coffee house contained many statues and busts, mainly of important Romans. The then (1858) owner of the villa was Count Castelbarco,

The marble relief of Antinoüs *(Villa Albani),*
photographed by Robert Macpherson, 1860s

who resided at Milan. The grounds still retained, however, some of
their old glory:

The grounds are laid out in the old fashion of straight paths,
with borders of box, which form hedges of great height and
density, and as even as a brick wall at the top and sides. There are
also alleys forming long vistas between the trunks and beneath
the boughs of oaks, ilexes, and olives; and there are shrubberies
and tangled wildernesses of palm, cactus, rhododendron, and I

271

know not what; and a profusion of roses that bloom and wither with nobody to pluck and few to look at them. They climb about the sculpture of fountains, rear themselves against pillars and porticos, run brimming over the walls, and strew the paths with their falling leaves.

There are great lagunas; fountains presided over by naiads, who squirt their little jets into basins; sunny lawns; a temple, so artificially ruined that we half believed it a veritable antique; and at its base a reservoir of water, in which stone swans seemed positively to float; groves of cypress; balustrades and broad flights of stone stairs, descending to lower levels of the garden; beauty, peace, sunshine, and antique repose on every side; and far in the distance the blue hills that encircle the Campagna of Rome.

For Hippolyte Taine, the villa Albani was the first to teach him how to reconstruct a portrait of the ancient owners and their society. He was struck by the control and artificiality of the gardens, which allowed 'no freedom to nature'. Secondly, Albani was an antiquarian, who collected indiscriminately every fragment he could find, even trumpery. Thirdly, the architecture is southern in its openness. Taine described the gardens with their green oaks, plane trees, cypresses and aloes, with the mountains on the horizon; this indicated the appreciation of things externally, not internally. And the gardens were designed for large companies to wander in, just as the great salons were for receptions; only later did people learn to live alone or in a family. Turning to the art, Taine approved of the Antinoüs, 'this chest so strong, these virile lips, this appearance of a valiant wrestler[!]; an admirable pale cardinal of Domenichino, and the two little bacchanals, so lively, of Giulio Romano'. George Eliot, however, was also critical:

> Another drive was to the Villa Albani, where again the view is grand. The precious sculptures, once there, are all at Munich now, and the most remarkable remnants of the collection are the bas relief of Antinoüs, and the Æsop. The Antinoüs is the least beautiful of all the representations of that sad loveliness that I have seen – be it said, in spite of Winckelmann: attitude

Gardens and Coffee-House of the Villa Albani, photographed by Pietro Dovizielli, 1859

and face are strongly Egyptian[!]. In an outside pavilion in the garden, were some interesting examples of Greek masks.[38]

Ludwig of Bavaria had bought the best remaining pieces in 1815.

In the VILLA BORGHESE the brothers Goncourt described the hundred-year-old cypresses, and the intertwined green oaks, while on the grass were black cows with white muzzles, 'chewing the cud in their eternal pose as sphinxes'. Melville caught the 'peculiar odors' of the Italian garden, with its deep groves and the 'cold splendor of the villa'. When, on a second visit, he found the villa closed and the statues visible only through the railings, instead of complaining, he described 'the silence and enchantment'. Melville's disappointment was caused by the fact that, as Hawthorne reveals, the casino was open to visitors only on Saturdays. It was not the sculpture in the entrance

Oswald Achenbach, In the Park of the Villa Borghese, *1886*

hall which he praised: the Apollo, the Amazon, a Faun – 'none of them, I think, possess the highest merit' – but rather the floor and wall of the gallery covered with marble, especially *giallo antico*, and its alabaster pillars. Again the sculpture, porphyry busts of emperors, served only as 'upholstery'. On the floor above, *Pauline Bonaparte* was 'admirably done, and, I have no doubt, a perfect likeness', but it was amazing how, despite her nakedness, 'the artificial elegance of the woman of this world makes itself perceptible'. The Berninis he dismissed as 'freaks in marble'. Oscar Wilde, paradoxically, does not mention the art, only the gardens: 'too lovely for words'.[39]

The VILLA LUDOVISI in 1858 was owned by Prince Piombino. Hawthorne, as usual, referred to the masterpiece of the collection, the colossal head of Juno, and declared that he was not impressed. He preferred the face of Penelope (otherwise known as Electra, with her brother Orestes) (see ill. Vol. II), but declared the seated Mars and the 'Arria and Pætus' (see ill. Vol. II) also very fine. The gardens he found threatening, fearing malaria. In the second casino, he criticised Guercino's *Aurora* for its black shadows ('likely to turn to rain by and by'). Returning via the first casino he noted Bernini's *Pluto and Persephone*: 'it is very disagreeable, but it makes one feel that Bernini was a man of great ability'. Taine gives us one last view of the gardens:

> The villa is very cheerful: the lawns, intact and refreshed by the rains, were sparkling; the hedges of flowering laurel, the woods of green oak, the alleys of centuries old cypresses revived and restored the soul by their grace and size. This kind of landscape is unique; plants from opposite climates mingle and group: here are clusters of palms, of great variegated rushes which arise like a candle from their nest of shining interlacings, lower down a poplar, an enormous, greyish, naked chestnut which is budding. What is still stranger, it is the old walls of Rome, a natural ruin, which serve as an enclosure. The greenhouses are supported by the reddish arcades; the lemon trees, in pale rows, stand close to the dislodged bricks; all around new grass extends; from time to time, from the higher places, one sees the last circuit of the horizon, the blueish mountains, streaked with snow. All this is within the walls of Rome; no one comes here, I do not know if anyone lives here. This Rome is a museum and a museum where past forms of life survive in the silence.

Frances Elliot provides essentially the same picture, apart from the characteristic comment that 'one might fancy oneself at Sion or Chatsworth but for the sublimer features of the scene'. She found the absence of fountains puzzling. In the casino she accounted Guercino's Aurora 'a milkmaid' after Reni's goddess, although she greatly admired the figures of Night and Morning. Around the casino were thick groves of ilex, cypress and pine, and all the walks were bordered with high hedges. The glories of the sculpture gallery were completely lost on her: she thought the *Dying Gaul and his wife* was Verginius sacrificing his daughter in the Forum (450 BC), and Bernini's *Pluto and Persephone* was marred by his 'satyr like' look and her lack of grace.[40]

Villa Pamphili, photographed c. 1870

The VILLA PAMPHILI called forth a delicate evocation by the Goncourt brothers in February or March:

> The villa: the appearance of a chest by Benvenuto Cellini in burnished silver, and above its roof, in the blue of the sky, small white statues seeming like guardians of Olympus, amidst black trees leaning over indigo waters, and in the environs lawns, white with flowering marguerites. Under the umbrella pines, under these saplings, pretty and purplish – blue of sixty feet, and in their shadows stirring on the ground, a fragment of old terrace, with portly balustrades, topped by ribbed urns, bearing aloes with blueish foliage, and where, at intervals, an ox eye is almost masked by the great flowering camelias. In the centre, a little fountain, decorated with a Cupid, borne on a base of marble by four little fauns among bronze lilies attached to the wall.

With this we may compare Melville's impressions:

> Great extent. – rich green – Paradise within Paradise. Yellow villa. – long vista of green & green water. The cedars & pines. Avenues of olives. View of St Peters. The terrace gardens – the

form of the parterres – flourishes of chr(omphits?). [chromatics? crisolites? chestnuts?]

Hawthorne noted that the Constable de Bourbon was killed near porta San Pancrazio in 1527. The dusty road to the villa passed through very high walls. The villa was open to the public and many carriages were parked by the entrance. Hawthorne was very impressed with the stone pines, with a flower strewn lawn beneath. It was early March: 'We found open fields and lawns, all abloom with anemones, white and rose coloured, and purple and golden, and far larger than could be found out of Italy, except in hothouses. Violets, too, were abundant and exceedingly fragrant.' George Eliot also described it as 'a beautiful spot', 'a place which has the beauties of an English park and gardens, with views such as no English park can show'.[41]

The VILLA TORLONIA, finally, was the scene for a 'most sumptuous lunch', given by the Torlonias, to Giovanni Battista de Rossi, Pietro Ercole Visconti, the historian Jean-Jacques Ampère, the painter Rudolf Lehmann, Johann Henzen, Heinrich Bruun and the historian Ferdinand Gregorovius in June 1857.[42] This was a most distinguished gathering, archæologists except where otherwise noted.

Prince Don Alessandro Torlonia, Prince of Fucino, Prince of Civitella-Cesi, Duke of Ceri (1800-1886) with his daughter Anna Maria, wife of Giulio Borghese

Rudolf von Alt, The Fishmarket, *1865*

ANTIQUITIES

Ernest Renan made a fundamental observation about Roman anti-quities, in contrast to those of France:

> Here the monuments are in place. They are not monuments, they are real. In Paris, they would be surrounded by a balustrade, a guard would be placed over them, visitors would hand in their canes and umbrellas. The Baths of Julian, for example. Here one can come close, can touch as one likes. There are carts leaning up against the Pantheon of Agrippa. The chestnut sellers... rest their shops against it. Here there are no orders anywhere, no guards, except since the French, and they are still not constricting. The ancient monuments with us are dead, museum objects. Here they are living, true.

That was in 1849. Nearly a decade later, Nathaniel Hawthorne was less positive:

> The first observation which a stranger is led to make, in the neighbourhood of Roman ruins, is that the inhabitants seem to be strangely addicted to the washing of clothes; for all the precincts of Trajan's Forum, and of the Roman Forum, and wherever else an iron railing affords opportunity to hang them, were whitened with sheets, and other linen and cotton, drying in the sun. It must be that washerwomen burrow among the old temples. The second observation is not quite so favourable to the cleanly character of the modern Romans; indeed, it is so very unfavourable, that I hardly know how to express it. But the fact is, that, through the Forum, ... and any where out of the commonest foot track and road way, you must look well to your steps... If you tread beneath the triumphal arch of Titus or Constantine, you had better look downward than upward, whatever be the merit of the sculptures aloft...

The last was a centuries-old complaint!

For more general impressions, George Eliot provides a summary by a responsive, if fleeting, visitor (she was in Rome for one month):

> Let me see what I most delighted in, in Rome. Certainly, this drive [note] from the Clivus [Capitolinus] to the Coliseum was, from first to last, one of the chief things; but there are many objects and many impressions of various kinds which I can reckon up as of almost equal interest: the Coliseum itself with the view from it; the drive along the Appian Way to the tomb of Cecilia Metella, and the view from thence of the Campagna bridged by the aqueduct; the Baths of Titus, with the remnants of their arabesques, seen by the light of torches, in the now damp and gloomy spaces; the glimpse of the Tarpeian rock, with its growth of cactus and rough herbage; the grand bare arched brickwork of the Palace of the Cæsars rising in huge masses on the Palatine; the Theatre of Marcellus bursting suddenly to view from among the crowded mean houses of the modern city, and still more the * and Temple of Nerva, also set in the crowded city of the present; and the exterior of the Pantheon, if it were not marred by the papal belfries:-- these are the traces of Ancient Rome that have left the strongest image of themselves in mind. I ought not to leave out Trajan's Column, and the forum in which it stands; though the severe cold tint of the grey granite columns or fragments of columns gave this forum rather a dreary effect to me. For vastness, there is perhaps nothing more impressive in Rome than the Baths of Caracalla, except the Coliseum; and I remember it was amongst them that I first noticed the lovely effect of the giant fennel luxuriant among the crumbling brick work.[43]

On the Capitol overlooking the Forum MARCUS AURELIUS' EQUES-TRIAN STATUE called forth James' admiration – and some comparisons:

> This work, by the way, is one of the things I have most enjoyed in Rome. It is totally admirable – the very model of the *genre*: – so large and monumental and yet so full of a sweet human dignity – stretching out a long thin arm in the act of mild

The Forum, c. 1880-1900, seen from the Capitol. The recently cleared Basilica Julia is on the right behind the temple of Saturn, which established the southern limits of the Forum. The northern side, on the left, is still covered by modern buildings and will not be excavated until the 1920s. The Colosseum is visible in the distance.

persuasive command – that affects you like an audible personal voice out of that stony Roman past. As you revert to that poor sexless old Pope enthroned upon his cushions – and then glance at those imperial legs swinging in their immortal bronze, you cry out that here at least was a *man*![44]

Few visitors ventured into the nearby MAMERTINE PRISON. Hawthorne did, and described it at length, concluding that 'there cannot be in the world another such an evil den, so haunted with black memories and indistinct surmises of guilt and suffering'.[45]

The FORUM in 1856 was depicted by the Goncourts:

grey oxen with long horns, restlessly chewing, one horn attached to heavy carts, amidst chickens which women chase by throwing stones. The Forum has thus, as Grosely noted more than a century ago, returned precisely to the state in which Æneas found it when he met Evander.

In other ways the Forum was too modern. The temple of Venus was 'once covered in bronze, with a gilded vault; now its columns lean over the abyss of the ravines dug around its foundations, and under its great niche, where once Venus stood, today split from end to end, a man has put his stockings'. Similarly, in the temple of Antoninus and Faustina, hung out to dry were the grey stockings and yellow blouse of a woman from Salara Vecchia. On the temple of Romulus, by contrast, tattered posters announced the 'Office of the Glorious Virgin'.

It was the Forum, naturally, which inspired Frances Elliot to attempt to depict various national reactions to Rome's antiquities:

> I returned into the Forum. The afternoon was now come, together with a heterogeneous crowd lounging about in all directions. The modern Romans are easily recognisable as they

Unknown photographer, The Forum, *1860s*

*Ippolito Caffi, The Forum, before 1866. The Colosseum is to the right,
the Meta Sudans (an ancient fountain) in the foreground,
and the Arch of Constantine to the left*

slowly saunter along, wholly regardless of the celebrated scene
of their ancestors' greatest triumphs. No wonder: they simply
consider it as a dirty space devoted to the sale of cattle. We are
not given to studying English history in Smithfield; and to
them the Forum presents as few attractions. As decidedly are
the English recognised by their trivial and restless curiosity, the
questions they ask, and the ignorance they betray. Carriage after
carriage may be seen driving up, and party after party of extravagantly dressed ladies may be seen dismounting in the dirt at
various points of peculiar interest, only to peep and peer about
as did the famous Davis for pickles in the vases of Pompeii.
This vexatious mass of nameless temples particularly engages
their attention, and they stand, 'Murray' in hand, resolutely
decided on understanding what is not understandable. When I
see these antiquarian butterflies, attended generally by a servant

Ferdinand Heilbuth, Excavations in the Forum, *c. 1873-75.*
*The painting is said to record an excavation in 1872, when the Plutei of Trajan
(one of which is seen behind the professor) were discovered*

in livery and a pet spaniel, I confess I am disgusted. Here and
there a quiet, unassuming party of plainly dressed Germans
appear, industriously working their way along, really seeming
to approach the place in a right spirit of earnest inquiry; or
some solitary traveller, *en grande barbe*, smoking a cigar – sure
to be a French *savant* – evidently absorbed and overwhelmed by
the rich tide of recollections rising around. A long procession
of *frati*, enveloped in black robes and hoods, streams along
towards the Coliseum, carrying a large black cross, chanting
sad and dismal hymns that echo harmoniously amid the fallen
and decaying precincts of the past. Americans abound, active,
talkative, and unsympathetic. What sympathy can youth have
with decrepitude? – the enterprising young world, springing
into life and greatness (rejoicing in liberty and freedom), with
the mouldering remains of former tyrants? But whether they
come to say they have seen, or in reality to worship art at the

fallen altars of false gods, they come kindly, Christianly. Neither *morgue*, reserve, nor pride marks their manners; nor do they affect the exclusive indifference of that young English lady who, visiting the Forum for the *first time*, is seated in her carriage deeply engaged in reading the *Times*.

A more serious response was excited in Adam Sienkiewicz in his *Letter from Rome*, 1879:

> I was moved to see open wide before my eyes the sublime book of the Roman epic, written in marble and ruins. Strange thoughts crowd into the traveller's mind when he is in this glorious place, face to face with the past. All the memories, everything he knows about the history of Rome, everything which he has read and learned, and which, despite an effort of the imagination, seemed to him confused, fantastic, legendary, then comes alive under his gaze, stands erect in clear and evident shapes, like an indubitable truth; he can see everything, touch everything...[46]

By now the southern border of the Forum had been found and identified: the BASILICA JULIA. The Goncourt brothers described it in 1856:

> some rare square paving stones, eaten by the grass, and on these stones which are not today tables in the Jewish fish market, a ruin of pieces of cornice and broken columns, showing in their breaks the green veins of cippolino or the red of porphyry, and fragments of pedestals and capitals returned to a rough state: sculptured stones now only stones, on which time has effaced the work of man's hand...

The remains of the BASILICA OF MAXENTIUS on the northern side were similarly evoked by the same brothers:

> its collapsed vaults have now only three gigantic arches, stretching out like hands which might seek to meet again in the void of heaven; entering through the great openings in this

monument without a top, and where some eggs or denticles in the remains of the corners of the ceiling indicate a flayed monument, like the satyr Marsyas, and of which there remains only the monstrous coarse brick armature.[47]

The ARCH OF TITUS, of course, captured their imagination:

> with its rocking mass supported, and the legs of the horses of the triumphal car cropped, and the heads of the bearers of the seven branched candelabrum rolled on the ground, and the Famous, one foot on the globe, appear in heaven in their attenuated forms as if they had been filed down by the air and the wind over eighteen centuries.

Attention is here drawn to the damaged state of the reliefs. On the

Unknown British painter, Basilica of Maxentius, *May 1850*

Tina Blau, The Arch of Titus, *c. 1879*

ARCH OF SEVERUS, which they realised was for Parthian victories, the brothers were struck by the representation of the ram, 'the ancient war machine'; swallows nestled in holes in the marble.[48]

The COLOSSEUM undoubtedly was the classical monument which evoked most comment. Its religious adaptation, not unexpectedly, was noted by Renan:

> Sermon in the Colosseum. Capuchins, fraternity in grey, heads all cowled. Women all dressed up, French, follow a woman carrying a cross. Each poor little thing has a veil on her head, worn with charming grace. Very well-dressed women following the cross, suckling their children. Each doing her housework, men looking for fleas, etc.

It was a wonder, Renan mused, that Sixtus V did not sheathe the theatre in marble, but that would have been in the worst taste, making the antique into modern ornament. The Goncourts provided the most

Interior of the Colosseum, showing the Stations of the Cross,
photographed by Pietro Dovizielli, c. 1855

memorable description: 'like a round dance, suddenly and violently
broken, with one side of the dancers fallen over on their backs'. The
outer walls opposite the Cælian had been thrown down in the great
earthquake in 1348. There always, of course, had to be the disappointed. Hawthorne was one. 'The general aspect of the place is
somewhat bare, and does not compare favourably with an English
ruin, both on account of the lack of ivy, and because the material is
chiefly brick'! He noted the many people who kissed the iron cross in
the centre to win seven years' indulgence. The Colosseum was,
however, to play a leading role in his *Marble Faun*:

> There was much pastime and gayety just then in the area of
> the Coliseum, where so many gladiators and wild beasts had
> fought and died, and where so much blood of Christian martyrs
> had been lapped up by that fiercest of wild beasts, the Roman

populace of yore. Some youths and maidens were running merry races across the open space, and playing at hide and seek a little way within the duskiness of the ground tier of arches, whence now and then you could hear the half shriek, half laugh of a frolicsome girl, whom the shadow had betrayed into a young man's arms. Elder groups were seated on the fragments of pillars and blocks of marble that lay round the verge of the arena, talking in the quick, short ripple of the Italian tongue. On the steps of the great black cross in the centre of the Coliseum sat a party singing scraps of songs, with much laughter and merriment between the stanzas.

It was a strange place for song and mirth. That black cross marks one of the special blood spots of the earth where, thousands of times over, the dying gladiator fell, and more of human agony has been endured for the mere pastime of the multitude than on the breadth of many battlefields. From all this

Jean-Léon Gérôme, Ave Caesar! Morituri te salutant, *1859*
One of a series of famous paintings by Gérôme that established the Hollywood style for Roman epics. Gérôme himself took pains over the archæological accuracy of his work

crime and suffering, however, the spot has derived a more than common sanctity. An inscription promises seven years' indulgence, seven years of remission from the pains of purgatory, and earlier enjoyment of heavenly bliss, for each separate kiss imprinted on the black cross. What better use could be made of life, after middle age, when the accumulated sins are many and the remaining temptations few, than to spend it all in kissing the black cross of the Coliseum!

Besides its central consecration, the whole area has been made sacred by a range of shrines, which are erected round the circle, each commemorating some scene or circumstance of the Saviour's passion and suffering. In accordance with an ordinary custom a pilgrim was making his progress from shrine to shrine upon his knees, and saying a penitential prayer at each. Light footed girls ran across the path along which he crept, or sported with their friends close by the shrines where he was kneeling. The pilgrim took no heed, and the girls meant no irreverence; for in Italy religion jostles along side by side with business and sport, after a fashion of its own, and people are accustomed to kneel down and pray, or see others praying, between two fits of merriment, or between two sins.

To make an end of our description, a red twinkle of light was visible amid the breadth of shadow that fell across the upper part of the Coliseum. Now it glimmered through a line of arches, or threw a broader gleam as it rose out of some profound abyss of ruin; now it was muffled by a heap of shrubbery which had adventurously clambered to that dizzy height; and so the red light kept ascending to loftier and loftier ranges of the structure, until it stood like a star where the blue sky rested against the Coliseum's topmost wall. It indicated a party of English or Americans paying the inevitable visit by moonlight, and exalting themselves with raptures that were Byron's, not their own.

Henry James was another novelist in whose works the Colosseum was featured. He told his sister Alice

The Colosseum is a thing about which it's useless to talk: it must be seen and felt. But as a piece of the picturesque – a province of it – it is thoroughly and simply delightful. The grassy arena with its circle of tarnished shrines and praying strollers – the sky between the arches and above the oval – the weeds and flowers against the sky etc – are as charming as anything in Rome.

Of the nearby ARCH OF CONSTANTINE the columns of *giallo antico* were, the Goncourt brothers observed, 'ill restrained by iron frames, like hunchbacks, and the Victories had lost the arms which inscribed the glory of the victors on the bronze shields'.[49]

In the FORUM BOARIUM, Hawthorne observed that the 'TEMPLE OF VESTA' by the Tiber was 'so small that, in a suitable locality, one would take it rather for a garden house than an ancient temple'. It was the roof which bothered him: it 'looks like wood, and disgraces and deforms the elegant little building. This roof resembles, as much as anything else, the round wicker cover of a basket, and gives a very squat aspect to the temple.' Behind this lies the tragic story of the failed attempt to restore the temple envisaged by Giuseppe Valadier in 1810.[50]

Franz von Lenbach, The Forum Boarium, *1858-59*
The temple of 'Vesta' (Hercules) is to the left, that of 'Fortuna' (Portunus) on the right,
and in the background is the House of Crescentius

In the same forum few visitors shared James' experience. He was looking at the 'Janus' monument.

> A man sallied forth from the neighbouring shades with an enormous key and whispered the soul stirring name of the CLOACA MAXIMA. I joyfully assented and he led me apart under a series of half buried arches into a deeper hollow, where the great mouth of a tunnel seemed to brood over the scene and thence introduced me into a little covered enclosure, whence we might survey a small section of the ancient sewer. It gave me the deepest and grimmest impression of antiquity I have ever received. He lit a long torch and plunged it down into the blackness. It threw a red glare on a mass of dead black traver- tine and I was assured that I was gazing upon the masonry of Tarquinius Priscus. If it wasn't I'm sure it ought to have been.[51]

The nearby THEATRE OF MARCELLUS elicited from Renan two words: 'horrible shops'. The same impression was given by Melville: 'black- smiths shops etc in arches – black with centuries grime and soot – built upon above and inhabited'. It was, indeed, the Orsini palace. Hawthorne noted the different orders: Doric on the ground floor, Ionic above, 'but the whole once magnificent structure now tenanted by poor and squalid people, as thick as mites within the round of an old cheese'.[52]

The FORUM OF TRAJAN remained as left by the French excavations after 1814. The Goncourt description is memorable as always: 'The Forum Traianum, with its column of twenty feet [in reality 38 m!] is in the midst of thirty nine others, reduced to ten, five or two feet, and which give the effect of the trunks of a felled forest.'[53]

On the hill behind this forum, the QUIRINAL HORSETAMERS were considered by Renan in bad taste, because they were antiquities serv- ing as modern ornament, one of his bugbears. Melville, on the other hand, was highly impressed: 'colossal horses from ruins of baths – like finding the bones of the mastadon – gigantic figures emblematic of gigantic Rome… most imposing group of antiques in Rome – People those Caracalla baths anew with these colossal figures'.[54]

The dominating monument of the Campus Martius was the

The Theatre of Marcellus, photographed by Robert Macpherson in c. 1860
showing the lowest arcades filled with shops

PANTHEON. Renan noted that there were carts leaning up against it, and chestnut sellers supported their shops there. Attempts to free the most beautiful classical monument of Rome had been going on since the seventeenth century, but Renan approved of the 'informality'. Such efforts had been entirely unsuccessful, as Taine revealed in 1864:

> The Pantheon of Agrippa is in a dirty, baroque piazza, where miserable cabs wait, spying out foreigners; the vegetable booths

The Pantheon, photochrom made after the 1880s when the belfries were demolished

throw their refuse on the blackish pavement, and bands of peasants in great gaiters, a sheepskin over their shoulders, watch and look, unmoving, with shining eyes. The poor temple itself has suffered everything which a building can suffer: modern structures cling to its back and sides; it is flanked by two ridiculous bell towers; they have stolen its beams and nails of bronze to make the columns of the baldaquin of St Peter's; hovels encrusted between the columns have long blocked its portico; the earth has so encumbered it, that to reach the interior, instead of stepping up, one steps down. Even today, as restored as it is, under its blackish shades, with its cracks, its mutilations, and the half effaced inscription of its architrave, it has a lame and sick look.

James, of course, saw beyond that:

By far the most beautiful piece of ancientry in Rome is that simple and unutterable Pantheon to which I repeated my devotions yesterday afternoon. It makes you profoundly regret that you are not a pagan suckled in the creed outworn that produced it. It's the most conclusive example I have yet seen of the simple sublime. Imagine simply a vast cupola with its drum, set directly on the earth and fronted with a porch of columns and a triangular summit: the interior lighted by a hole in the apex of the cupola and the circumference furnished with a series of altars. The effect within is the very *delicacy* of grandeur – and more worshipful to my perception than the most mysterious and aspiring Gothic.[55]

The BATHS OF CARACALLA were still on the visitor's itinerary. Hippolyte Taine mused on Rome of the Cæsars, when Rome exploited the whole Mediterranean basin for the profit of 'one hundred thousand lazy people'. They were entertained in the Colosseum, the Circus Maximus and the Theatre of Marcellus. The baths, on the other hand, were for relaxation:

Here they bathed, came to chat, to look at statues, hear an orator, spend the hot hours in the cool. Everything found until then which was convenient, pleasing or beautiful, everything one could gather in the world which was curious or magnificent, was for them... Its form cannot be compared to anything... It is a human work which time and accidents have deformed and transformed so as to make it natural.

Taine described at length the vast fallen vaults, and those that were in danger of falling; others intact rose in tiers one above the other. It was like a whole city. The vegetation was, of course, a focus of attention:

There are suspect depths where the humid shade lingers among the strange blackness. Ivy descends here; fennel, anemones and mallows abound on the margins; half-buried under the pieces of fallen stone, the shafts of columns plunge under a confusion of

George Howard, 9th Earl of Carlisle, The Baths of Caracalla, *1890s*

climbing plants; the clover with thick leaves carpets the slopes. Small round green oaks, green shrub trees, thousands of wall-flowers perch on the ledges, cling to the hollows, decorate the bricks with their yellow flowers. All this sounds in the wind, and the birds sing in the deep silence.

The grand purpose of the baths fascinated him: the Greeks and Romans loved athletics and speech. 'We no longer have any idea of this physical and pagan life, idle and speculative; people have been transformed by putting on clothes and becoming Christian.' Henry James, amazing to say, had the baths all to himself, about sunset. 'Even more than the Colosseum I think they give you a notion of the Roman *scale.* Imagine a good second-class mountain in reduced circumstances – perforated and honeycombed by some terrestrial cataclysm.' Frances Elliot agreed:

Certainly it is the only Roman ruin above ground worthy of competing with the Coliseum, and may, perhaps, be preferred by those admiring a ruder and more chaotic mass of positively fabulous extent. All is desolation. One's footsteps echo mournfully under the great arches – grass grows in the vast halls – shrubs and creepers tapestry the roofless walls – wild roses bloom in the place where emperors have trodden.

Mrs Elliot referred, indeed, more than once to her fantasy over Caracalla or Heliogabalus wandering here. It was obviously the custom to point out various rooms of the baths and define their use: a vast swimming bath, an immense hall with mosaics which was the emperor's private baths, with galleries to observe gladiatorial combats, and the Pinacoteca (Picture Gallery), which she imagined to be a library, where the Farnese Hercules and the Belvedere Torso were found. She noticed young priests playing ball: the baths had been leased for centuries to the Roman Seminary for recreational purposes.

The great MAUSOLEA may be visited in chronological order. James declared that the TOMB OF CÆCILIA METELLA was 'at any rate one of the effective objects of the world'. Charles Norton revealed the state of the MAUSOLEUM OF AUGUSTUS in 1857:

Lawrence Alma-Tadema, The Baths of Caracalla, *1899*

The old walls still stand, but so surrounded by close packed houses, that but little of the ancient structure is to be seen. The central area, in which were the tombs of the Cæsars, is now hollowed out into an open amphitheatre, round which are ranges of seats to accommodate the common people of Rome, drawn thither in summertime by the attractions of circus riders or of Policinello. The dirty stairway which leads to the upper benches is lined with various marble slabs, bearing modern inscriptions. They are alike in character, – and one of them runs as follows: –

The wordy trumpet of fame falls silent where the name of Giovanni Guillaume does not reach, superb tamer of war horses, extraordinarily applauded by the city of the Tiber in the autumns of 1851 and 1852.

And Hawthorne made a long inspection of the MAUSOLEUM OF HADRIAN. It had a French garrison in 1858, and one of the soldiers acted as guide. The original entrance was walled up, and the circular ascending passage was only partly excavated. To show its length, the guide sent a large cannon ball crashing down it! In the upper levels Hawthorne was shown the prisons. 'All these prison vaults are more horrible than can be imagined without seeing them; but there are worse places here, for the guide lifted up a trap door in one of the passages, and held his torch down into an inscrutable pit beneath our feet. It was an *oubliette*, a dungeon where the prisoner might be buried alive, and never come forth again, alive or dead.' The commandant's quarters were, by contrast, declared comfortable![56]

The most particular tomb in Rome, however, was the PYRAMID OF CESTIUS, which was now indelibly associated with the so called Protestant Cemetery. No one expressed this better than Thomas Hardy, visiting, as so many others, the tombs of Keats and Shelley:

> Who, then, was Cestius,
> And what is he to me? –
> Amid thick thoughts and memories multitudinous
> One thought alone brings he.

Walter Crane, The Protestant Cemetery with the grave of John Keats, and the Pyramid of Cestius in the background, *1873*

I can recall no word
    Of anything he did;
For me he is a man who died and was interred
    To leave a pyramid

Whose purpose was exprest
    Not with its first design,
Nor till, far down in Time, beside it found their rest
    Two countrymen of mine.

Cestius in life, maybe,
    Slew, breathed out threatening;
I know not. This I know: in death all silently
    He does a finer thing,

In beckoning pilgrim feet
    With marble finger high
To where, by shadowy wall and history haunted street,
    Those matchless singers lie...

– Say, then, he lived and died
    That stones which bear his name
Should mark, through Time, where two immortal Shades abide;
    It is an ample fame.[57]

John Linton Chapman, The Appian Way, *1869*

Visitors, finally, paid attention to the great roads leading out of Rome. George Ticknor in 1857 noted the work on the VIA APPIA, 'opened quite out to Albano, and its tombs uncovered farther than we have yet driven'. The road had been surveyed by Alessandro Nibby and William Gell in 1824. Now Luigi Canina was clearing and restoring the tombs. Melville, on the other hand, was disappointed: 'Narrow – not like Milton's Way [ie. to Hell] – not suitable to dignity etc. Old pavement. Tomb with olive tree on it, sown in corruption, raised in olives.'[58]

James visited the recently discovered COLUMBARIA near the beginning of the Appian Way:

> a series of subterranean vaults recently discovered, in which the Romans *pigeon holed* or deposited on small concave shelves the vases containing the ashes of their dead. They stand in a great sunny rubbishy Italian vineyard, whence you descend into the dead moist air and the dim mildewed light of these strange funeral wells. Few things transport you so forcibly into the past. Their perfection is almost unimpaired. Tier upon tier the little pigeon holes sit yawning upon you, each subscribed with its original Latin statement.[59]

This is probably the tomb of the freemen of the Julio-Claudians in the vigna Codini, discovered in 1852.

Excavations were also in progress on the VIA LATINA. Ferdinand Gregorovius provided a formal note of the discovery of the basilica of S Stefano, built by Leo I, and of two tombs, decorated with stucco and paintings, and containing sarcophagi, one with the history of Phædra. The excavator was Lorenzo Fortunati. The tombs belonged to the Valerii and Pancratii. Hawthorne devoted some space to these discoveries; they excited great interest, and there were many visitors watching the work in progress. Hawthorne had to wait to enter such a tomb: it contained large sarcophagi, with unfinished portraits, in an outer Christian cemetery. The inner, pagan tomb was square, paved with mosaic, and the roof and walls were covered in frescoes. The sarcophagi were covered with 'the most delicately wrought and beautiful bas reliefs that I ever beheld'. Another tomb was ornamented with plaster medallions; here Hawthorne handled a thigh bone and measured it with his own! One of the visitors in the 1860s was Henrik Ibsen, who admitted: 'I often lie for half a day among the tombs on the via Latina, or on the old Appian Way.'[60]

Visitors in fact strangely paid little attention to excavations. An exception, as we have seen, was Ticknor. He noted recent uncovering of the remains of the so called wall of Servius Tullus, 'recently dug out, just where Dionysius of Halicarnassus said it would be found'. Remains of the wall had recently been found on the Quirinal.[61]

Part of the Columbaria at the vigna Codini, photographed by Lodovico Tominello in the 1850s

VIEW FROM CAMPIDOGLIO, ROME.

the Capitol

CONTEMPORARY ROME

There were many topographical features of the city which were noticed by travellers. The centre of the classical and modern city was the CAPITOL. Nathaniel Hawthorne noted the solidity with which the ancient Romans built. The foundations of the Capitol 'will make a sure basis for as many edifices as posterity may choose to rear upon it till the end of the world'. The modern piazza, on the other hand, did not please him:

> The architecture that surrounds the piazza is very ineffective; and so, in my opinion, are all the other architectural works of Michael Angelo, including St Peter's itself, of which he has made as little as could possibly be made of such a vast pile of material. He balances everything in such a way that it seems but half of itself.

It was the view that entranced George Eliot:

> Perhaps the world can hardly offer a more interesting outlook than that from the tower of the Capitol. The eye leaps first to the mountains that bound the Campagna – the Sabine and Alban Hills, and the Solitary Soracte farther on to the left. Then wandering back across the Campagna it searches for the sister hills, hardly distinguishable now as hills. The Palatine is conspicuous enough...

It was Henryk Sienkiewicz, not unexpectedly, for whom the Capitol came alive historically speaking:

> Here on the Capitol, the Mirabeau of ancient times, like Canuleius, and after him Licinius, amid the people's acclamations, uncaring of the furrowed brows and clenched lips of the aristocrats, declared their ultimatum: 'that one consul should be chosen from the plebs, and then an ædile and a censor...'

Opposite: The view from the Campidoglio, photographed by Giorgio Sommer in c. 1865

There by the via Sacra passed the chariots of the triumphators, and behind them in chains, the barbarian kings, mournfully thinking of their native forests, sad yet great in their defeat; around them came the lictors carrying the bundles of rods and axes: then followed the legions, the Roman eagles, the trophies, and behind, the applauding people. And in the days of disaster here the Gracchi fell, at the hands of their own compatriots. On the Capitol the senators paled and Sulla laughed when the groans of those being murdered rose up from the Mamertine prison...[62]

One other hill, the Pincian, is vividly portrayed for us in the later nineteenth century by Hawthorne:

In the morning, there are few people there except the gardeners, lazily trimming the borders, or filling their watering pots out of the marble brimmed basin of the fountain; French soldiers, in their long mixed blue surtouts, and wide scarlet pantaloons, chatting with here and there a nursery maid and playing with the child in her care; and perhaps a few smokers, ... choosing each a marble seat or wooden bench in sunshine or shade as best suits him. In the afternoon, especially within an hour or two of sunset, the gardens are much more populous, and the seats, except when the sun falls full upon them, are hard to come by. Ladies arrive in carriages, splendidly dressed; children are abundant, much impeded in their frolics, and rendered stiff and stately by the finery which they wear; English gentlemen, and Americans with their wives and families; the flower of the Roman population, too, both male and female, mostly dressed with great nicety; but a large intermixture of artists, shabbily picturesque; and other persons, not of the first stamp. A French band, comprising a great many brass instruments, by and by begins to play; and what with music, sunshine, a delightful atmosphere, flowers, grass, well kept pathways, bordered with box hedges, pines, cypresses, horse chestnuts, flowering shrubs, and all manner of cultivated beauty, the scene is a very lively and agreeable one. The fine equipages that drive round and

Peter Christian Skovgaard, View from Monte Pincio in Rome, *1861*

round through the carriage paths are another noticeable item. The Roman aristocracy are magnificent in their aspect, driving abroad with beautiful horses, and footmen in rich liveries, sometimes as many as three behind and one sitting by the coachman.[63]

The centre of the modern city was the CORSO. Frances Elliot had to set the record straight:

> Having so much abused the dirty streets, I must do justice to the grandeur and magnificence of the unique Corso – nearly a mile in length – where the eye wanders from palace to palace in a maze of astonishment as to what size the next stupendous structure will attain. Aladdin's palace, with its four and twenty windows in a row, would be quite put to the blush beside those amazing edifices that call the Doria, the Torlonia, the Schiarra, master. Less gloomy than the palaces of either Florence or Venice (which have a repulsive prison like aspect, spite of great picturesqueness), they exceed all others in size, splendour, and number.

She admitted the poetry of the Moorish style palaces in Genoa, the

majesty of the 'huge mediæval piles' in Florence, the French elegance
of the Milan palaces, and the 'Byzantine, eccentric, strange' charm of
the Venetian edifices, but they could not match Rome, where the
Corso was 'a street of palaces, a walk of state'. Then there were the
shops, 'Parisian in their elegance and display. Splendid vehicles chase
each other along, and crowds of pedestrians fill the remaining space,
recalling the busiest thoroughfares of Paris or London.' This was in
the late 1860s.

Tchaikovsky is one of the few visitors to comment on the changes
after 1870: 'Rome has changed very much. Much of it is quite unrec-
ognisable. For instance, the second half of the via del Tritino [*sic*] has
become wide and grand, and does not lead to the Trevi, but straight
into the Corso.'[64]

The most frequented piazza was, as always, the PIAZZA NAVONA.
Hawthorne admitted that it was also the most interesting piazza. He
quite failed to understand Bernini's virtuosity and was disturbed by
the market. The central fountain

> is an immense basin, over which is reared an old Egyptian
> obelisk, elevated on a rock, which is cleft into four arches.
> Monstrous devices in marble, I know not of what purport,
> are clambering about the cloven rock or burrowing beneath
> it; one and all of them are superfluous and impertinent, the
> only essential thing being the abundant supply of water in the
> fountain. This whole Piazza Navona is usually the scene of
> more business than seems to be transacted anywhere else in
> Rome; in some parts of it rusty iron is offered for sale, locks and
> keys, old tools, and all such rubbish; in other parts vegetables,
> comprising, at this season, green peas, onions, cauliflowers,
> radishes, artichokes, and others with which I have never made
> acquaintance; also, stalls or wheelbarrows containing apples,
> chestnuts (the meats dried and taken out of the shells), green
> almonds in their husks, and squash seeds – salted and dried in
> an oven – apparently a favourite delicacy of the Romans. There
> are also lemons and oranges; stalls of fish, mostly about the size
> of smelts, taken from the Tiber; cigars of various qualities, the
> best at a baiocco and a half a piece; bread in loaves or in small

Piazza Navona, with S Agnese dominating the eastern side and the space apparently covered with market stalls, photographed by Giorgio Sommer and Edmund Behles, c. 1867-74

rings, a great many of which are strung together on a long stick, and thus carried round for sale. Women and men sit with these things for sale, or carry them about in trays or on boards on their heads, crying them with shrill and hard voices. There is a shabby crowd and much babble; very little picturesqueness of costume or figure, however, the chief exceptions being, here and there, an old white bearded beggar. A few of the men have the peasant costume – a short jacket and breeches of light blue cloth and white stockings – the ugliest dress I ever saw. The women go bareheaded, and seem fond of scarlet and other bright colours, but are homely and clumsy in form. The piazza is dingy in its general aspect, and very dirty, being strewn with straw, vegetable tops, and the rubbish of a week's marketing; but there is more life in it than one sees elsewhere in Rome.[65]

The last glimpses can be caught of the TIBER, as it had been since the beginning of Rome; it was now to be changed forever by the vast embankments.

> Yesterday I crossed the ponte Sisto, and took a short ramble on the other side of the river; and it rather surprised me to discover, pretty nearly opposite the Capitoline Hill, a quay, at which several schooners and barques, of two or three hundred tons burden, were moored. There was also a steamer, armed with a large gun, and two brass swivels on her forecastle, and I know not what artillery besides. Probably she may have been a revenue cutter.

This is most interesting, because he does not refer to the two well known 'ports' of Rome, Ripa Grande by via Marmorata or porta di Ripetta, much further up river. The quay he describes must have been near the Tiber Island. In 1864 Hippolyte Taine gave a depressing picture:

Veronika Maria Herwegen-Manini, Scene on the Tiber, *1890s*

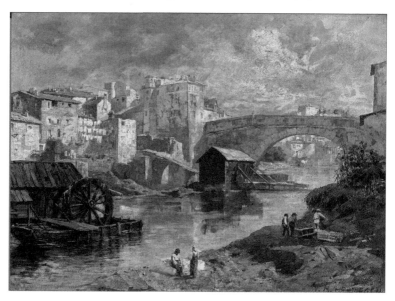

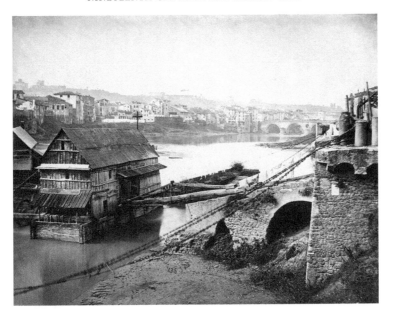

The Tiber, *taken by an unknown photographer in the latter half of the nineteenth century before the building of the embankments and showing the characteristic mills*

I returned on foot behind Castel Sant'Angelo, then along the Tiber, on the right bank. One cannot imagine such a contrast. The bank is a long strip of crumbling sand, bordered by spiny hedges. Opposite, on the other side, stretches a row of old, dirty houses, pitiful, battered, faded sheds, all stained by flooding and by contact with human vermin, some plunging into the river, their foundations worn away, others leaving a little space between them and it, polluted with rubbish... The Tiber rolls along, yellow and muddy between this desert and this decay.

In Hawthorne's time it was still possible to cross by the ponte Rotto: the piers had been connected by a suspension bridge. The toll was one *bajoccho.*[66]

There were two special districts in Rome. Of the GHETTO, Herman Melville gave his customary impressionistic account:

The Ghetto, in c. 1850, by an unknown photographer, showing the fish markets just inside the portico of Octavia. The street is bizarrely deserted

The market (butcher) in old temple alley leading through between columns. Filth & crowd. Old clothes – babies in basket & babies sewed up. Fountain of 7 branch candlestick. Way in which old temples are used – churches – shops – alleis [*sic*] – blacksmiths – markets & c & c & c. View from piazza of San Pietro in Montorio. Best in Rome.

The famous fountain in pizza Giudea was made of two basins, one above the other, and the water was carried away in troughs decorated with the seven branched candelabra. One has been accustomed in the travellers' accounts in preceding centuries to the inhuman conditions in which the Jews of Rome were confined. Now a new element enters. The Goncourts visited the ghetto on Good Friday 1856. The streets were deserted. Rubbish was piled everywhere. The shops were half closed with 'enormous, barbarous locks'. The only noise was the fountain. Their eyes slowly become accustomed to the dark, and they perceive old men and women, described without the slightest trace of pity, likened indeed to animals, turning over rags and old papers. Worse still is Taine, who is too repulsive to quote.[67] That was in 1864, only thirty years before the Dreyfus affair, and less than eighty years before the Holocaust, in which Vichy France was to play a far from negligible role.

The other special district was TRASTEVERE. Henry James did not describe it in his letters, but has an evocative passage in *Roderick Hudson*:

It happened some days later that, on a long afternoon ramble, Rowland took his way through one of the quiet corners of the Trastevere. He was particularly fond of this part of Rome, though he could hardly have expressed the sinister charm of it. As you pass away from the dusky swarming purlieus of the Ghetto you emerge into a region of empty, soundless, grass grown lanes and alleys, where the shabby houses seem mould-ering away in disuse and yet your footstep brings figures of startling Roman type to the doorways. There are few monu-ments here, but no part of Rome seemed more oppressively historic, more weighted with a ponderous past, more blighted with the melancholy of things that had had their day. When the yellow afternoon sunshine slept on the sallow battered walls and lengthened the shadows in the grassy courtyards of small closed churches the place acquired a strange fascination.[68]

The last special place to visit is, appropriately, the 'PROTESTANT' CEMETERY. George Eliot declared it 'the most attractive burying place I have seen'. Shelley was here 'for ever at rest from the unloving cavillers of this world', but Keats' tomb she found painful, because its inscription 'seems to make him still speak in bitterness from his grave'.[69] In 1877 Oscar Wilde wrote a poem for each, one for Keats ('Taken from life when life and love were new, The youngest of the martyrs here is lain') and one for Shelley ('Sweeter far for thee a restless tomb in the blue cavern of an echoing deep').

We now turn to institutions and customs. A very negative view was given of the GOVERNMENT, as usual, by Ernest Renan in 1849:

> It is certain that for centuries this country has been the worst governed in the whole of Europe. Industry is looked at askance; all normal knowledge, which produces engineers, mechanics, navigators, doctors even, is in a state of infancy. All the land is owned by the clergy and a few great papal families and is leased to the peasants, a kind of serfs who cultivate it without any enthusiasm. The fine fruit which one can buy here in dozens for a few *sous*, oranges, olives, grapes are the raw product of nature, and grow here with as little cultivation as the mulberries in our ditches in Brittany. All administration is in a deplorable state, theft is the order of the day and barely prosecuted. It is stated that there are 'licensed thieves' and that some brigands arrested near Albano by a French detachment showed the officer the letters authorising them to exercise their profession. Of all the abuses in this country, the most flagrant are without doubt those against justice. It is entirely arbitrary; the trial is secret; there is no code, there are no studies in civil law; everything is managed by money or protection. Privileged jurisdictions are very numerous: a lay person cannot summon a

cleric before the court in which he himself is liable to be tried, and there are certain crimes for which he will never obtain justice because the ecclesiastical tribunal does not recognise them. In sum, I do not believe that there is any country in Europe governed by more deplorable institutions, and if a revolution is anywhere desirable, it is surely in this unfortunate country. But alas, one is reduced to fearing this revolution as the final plague. A revolution is useful to a people only when it opens the way to a class which is intelligent, hard working, active, and anxious for the betterment of society. Where can one find such people in this country? The education of these people is completely lacking.

The same pessimism was exhibited by Lord Acton nearly a decade later:

The pontifical states can never be well governed according to modern ideas because it [sic] has not gone through that which has influenced other states. Many things are not done by the government because it has not acquired the power of doing it. The people besides have no great Trieb [urge] like the English for municipal self government. No great ends have caused all the powers of the state to be united for any common purpose. Besides men can do only one thing well – not both spiritual and temporal power. It can never be governed like the modern states – and one or the other must suffer...

The administration of Justice is the worst. The judges of 1st instance have only 40 sc[udi] a month – juges d'appel, 60 or 70. All the higher places are given to prelates, but they do not stay, but become nuncios &c. so that there is no good body of judges, and the laity is not applied to that as much as might be the case. [Gaspare] Grassellini wrote that it was impossible to govern these provinces because the people mistrust the govt and the govt the people – both with good cause. The finances are not the worst. They have been badly managed, but the resources are enormous, and might be greatly developed.

Taine, similarly, in 1864 stated that the first topic of conversation of any Italian was politics. He was told that the French occupation had made the government worse than ever.

> Before there were some cautions, and injustice stopped half way. Now, relying on a garrison of 18,000 men, they no longer fear the discontented. No one doubts, therefore, that the day the French leave will be the last for papal sovereignty…
>
> The laws are passable, but whim corrupts them and interferes with penalties and pardons. No one therefore counts on justice, or is willing to be a witness, or is revolted by stabbings, or feels safe from accusation, or is sure of sleeping tomorrow in his own bed and room.

Charles Norton provided an illustration of judicial corruption, with an interesting connection. In February 1856 he reported that gasworks had just been established under the Palatine (in fact, in the Circus Maximus), somewhat at variance with the revered surroundings. The contractor was English, and wanted to install gas in his rented apartment, but the owner was averse. The project went ahead. The court ruled in favour of the owner, the contractor appealed, and a second court upheld the first. The police then ordered the restorations to cease. The Englishman was rich.

As for the FRENCH GARRISON, in 1858 Hawthorne recorded clear impressions. Emerging from St Peter's, he saw a French sergeant drilling his men in the piazza:

> These French soldiers are prominent objects everywhere about the city, and make up more of its sight and sound than anything else that lives. They stroll about individually; they pace as sentinels in all the public places; and they march up and down in squads, companies, and battalions, always with a great deal of din of drum, fife, and trumpet; ten times the proportion of music that the same number of men would require elsewhere; and it reverberates with ten times the noise between the high edifices of these lanes than it would make in broader streets. Nevertheless, I have no quarrel with the

French soldiers; they are fresh, healthy, smart, honest looking young fellows enough, in blue coats and red trousers; ... and, at all events, they serve as an efficient police, making Rome as safe as London; whereas, without them, it would very likely be a den of banditti.

On another score, however, he noted that they were useless. Although very civil, they did not ever knew the name even of the palace or piazza where they stood guard![70]

Apart from justice – or the lack of it – the other main criticism was of the management of the ECONOMY. Renan's picture was horrific, especially with reference to

the deplorable measures taken by the government relating to the paper money of the Republic. This paper was secured on the property of the clergy. They had to give up 1.5% of their revenue to prevent a frightful bankruptcy. They refused, and the paper suffered a depreciation of 35%. This paper money consisted of promissory notes of 10, 15 and 20 *sous*, and were therefore all in the hands of small merchants and poor people. This was a frightful ruin... As for silver it is not seen here... Whatever is issued by the mint is cornered by an agiotage [speculation] which no one can identify... For the simplest purchases – to buy a pair of shoes or pay at a restaurant – require the most complicated calculations. When you ask the price, the merchant answers: so much in silver, so much in paper, so much in French money. Everything has three or four prices.

Norton gave further details in 1856:

This year some of the annual taxes were laid for fourteen instead of twelve months. A piece of absurd chicanery. The government did not wish nominally to increase the tax, and therefore ordered that the year should be considered as containing fourteen months, and the tax be reckoned by months, and paid accordingly.

No *employé* of government pays taxes.

Corruption rules supreme. It is acknowledged and permitted by the highest authorities. Many officials receive a salary so small as to be utterly insufficient for their support; they are told to depend for their livelihood on the *incerti* of their office – that is, on fees, whose very name shows that they are regulated by no fixed scale, but depend on the ingenuity and the impudence of him who demands them.

George Ticknor also noted the crisis, but admitted that so much of Europe was in the same position: Spain and Austria were bankrupt, and France was in the gravest danger. Taine quoted the extortionate rates of taxation: 5% on the sale price of a horse, 20-30% on the value of animals brought to market, 18% on fish, 22% on grain, while the land tax was 15-18%.

Norton commented on the long standing custom of tips for domestic servants of any Roman family with whom the visitor had had any dealings. Twice a year, at the beginning and in the middle, each expected to receive 30-50 *bajocchi* which, as he noted, could mount up. The same visitor commented on the prevalence of begging. 'Perhaps no city in Europe is furnished with more numerous or more wealthy institutions for the care of the poor, and yet few cities have a larger or more unblushing host of beggars.'

Renan was quite frank about the importance of tourists to the economy. Rome counted on 30-40,000 tourists each winter. The numbers were dramatically cut in 1849-50, during Pius IX's absence. Whatever antipathy the Romans had to their ecclesiastical government, they were hoping that tourist money would return when he did.[71]

As for foreign policy, the French garrison told half the story. The other was told to Renan by Pietro Visconti: 'The pope is the vassal of the king of Naples; the sovereign of the spiritual world allows himself to be exploited by the most abominable tyrant of modern times.'[72]

About SOCIETY in general, Taine in 1864 provided a depressing picture. He began with the bourgeoisie. People were very intelligent, but also very selfish: they smiled at the thought of a Frenchman placing himself in physical danger for country or glory. They were also very accommodating: not the least smile at the foreigner's barbarous pronunciation, only an anxiety to trick others. Laziness was a virtue: many people seemed to have no job, no income; others with 10 *scudi* income a month spent 30, but there were charity and gratuities. Anyone could fall into beggary. Taine referred on various occasions to 'households living off the beauty of their women'. The general effect of the government was depressing: 'people are accustomed to tremble, to kiss an ecclesiastic's hand, to be humble; over generations pride, strength and resistance have been pulled out, like weeds'. On the other hand, a 'Roman man or woman wears all the money they earn or are given. They eat little and badly – pastries, cheese, cabbage, fennel; no fire in winter; miserable furniture, all for appearance.' On the outside their clothing is all finery; Taine recommended no close examination of the linen. Alongside laziness ignorance flourished. He knew a noble family (living in two rooms, renting five others), where only one of four daughters was literate. The prospect for the sons was little better: a post in the Datery at 6 *scudi* a month; no commerce, no industry, no army, and no chance of return if they sought their fortune abroad. After a morning at their 'office', they walked continuously in the Corso, pursuing women. Younger women were kept secluded, dreaming of marriage. To a French person, their life would seem almost dead, but the Romans were content. Taine calculated the cost of living as being half that of Paris. 'Get your confession certificate, shun liberals, and prove your meekness and carelessness, and you will find the government patient, accommodating, paternally indulgent.' Pleasures were simple: a Sunday stroll in the villa Borghese or dinner in a country *trattoria* paid off a week's dreams. Taine found the Romans basically good humoured and affable, with paradoxically few class barriers, but lacking moral sense: their temperament aggravated the defects of the constitution.

He turned his attention next to the aristocracy. A few had some education, but because of inbreeding, almost all were dull and narrowminded. The character of Prince Lello in Edmond About's *Tolla* (1855) was taken from life. The few exceptions were liberals, the rest papists. There were few salons. To rise in the world, it was necessary to attach oneself to a cardinal and his household. There was a great lack of easiness and much suspicion, and passions ran high. Women spent the day on their balcony or going to church in the Corso. For men, similarly, 'the great misfortune is not having anything to do'. Rome in this sense was like a provincial town. The main topics of conversation were music and archæology; foreign journals and modern books were lacking. Their lands were leased to peasants.

Taine finally considered the people, the peasants. Their leading trait was a propensity to violence. He told various stories of the easy resort to knives. There were also horrendous stories of cruelty to animals. Those guilty of murder were condemned to prison or the galleys, but often returned to their village with honour. The government did not even try to civilise them, but asked only taxes and a confession ticket (which could be bought for 2 *paoli*). Society was seen as a struggle in which self-defence was essential; false witness was therefore normal, because any judge was seen as an enemy. Life being so hard, the people bore pain stoically. Taine nevertheless believed that, if treated properly, they were capable of affection, loyalty, intelligence and energy. In a physical sense, they were very healthy.

One thing linked all these classes: patronage. 'Everyone here has his protector: impossible to survive otherwise: it is necessary in order to obtain the slightest thing, to obtain justice, to gain access to income, to retain property. Favour rules. Have in your family or service a pretty and obliging woman, you will come out of the tightest corner white as snow… The able, well supported man can gain anything. Life is a league and a struggle, but underground.'[73]

Frances Elliot in the same decade had a very different way of classifying Roman society. It was made up of many sets. First came the ecclesiastics, 'dreaming away their lives', 'lazily driv[ing] about to each other's palazzi in big red coaches drawn by black horses, with a retinue of antiquated retainers in the most singular liveries, coats hanging down to their heels, and cocked hats on their heads'. In the afternoons they strolled outside the city walls. These higher ranks were, however, remarkable for their 'moral conduct, serious demeanour, and blameless lives'.

The second set was the princesses:

grand, haughty dames, proud of their descent from the

Cornelias, the Lucretias, and the Portias of the republic. They are, as a body, remarkable for correct conduct, extreme devotion, and a lamentable want of intellectual cultivation... They dislike strangers, unless especially introduced – particularly Protestants, who are not considered Christians – and clan and club together in a *noli me tangere* spirit very unusual among the Italians, who are in general an easy, hospitable, polite, and facile people. But the Romans generally, and especially the princes and princesses, are remarkable for their senseless pride. They are unceasingly haunted by the notion of their descent from the Fabiuses, the Maximuses, and Cæsars of old, and endeavour, very unsuccessfully, to ape the dignified and solemn bearing of those ancient pillars of the state.

Third came the 'diplomatic set', 'of necessity more hospitable and outwardly affable, but in reality excessively exclusive'. In fourth place came the Americans. They were 'a numerous body, extremely sociable, and remarkable for general intelligence, bustle and go ahead propensities, and for the fragile and delicate beauty of the younger ladies'. They were followed by a 'learned set, necessarily cosmopolitan, but decidedly Catholic'. That reminded her of the 'Protestant set', presumably visitors. It 'considers the Pope the abomination of desolation, and have [*sic*] been heard to stigmatise his blessing as a curse'. Elliot's scorn, however, was reserved for the English set, as we have seen.[74]

The RELIGIOSITY of the Romans was often commented on by visitors. The free-thinking Renan mused in 1849 on

this people, living calmly in its religion which satisfies and amuses it; a calm population, without any of the eighteenth century's political ideas. All this has led to a collapse, a horrible degradation. How well I understood Rome of the eighteenth century, nonchalantly extended in its devotion, playing with ceremonies, churches of Borromini. There is the price, and in a sense the beauty, of the architecture of ornamentation in bad taste, which is, however, well adapted to this cult.

Unknown Roman artist, Ex-voto painting offering thanks to the Virgin for the successful recovery of the person on whose behalf it is offered, 1851

Eight years later the educator Charles Norton declared roundly that the Roman people 'belong to the Dark Ages'. He was struck by 'the earnestness with which miraculous intervention is sought, the confidence in its frequent occurrence, and the ease with which stories of miracles are received'; these were proofs of the prevalence of superstition and false notions of the nature of God. The results were fascinating:

> From their infancy, the Romans are taught to believe that the Virgin and the Saints are not only their spiritual consolers and guides, but protectors from earthly perils, healers of bodily maladies, and guardians of worldly goods. Two plain results follow from this, – superstitious devotion, and blasphemous irreverence. The Virgin and the Saints who fail to answer the prayers that are made to them are cursed with a heartiness proportioned to the fervor of the previous petition.

The Goncourts told an amusing story of a friend who by mistake gave a boy a gold coin (20 francs) instead of 20 *sous* (1 franc or about 20 *bajocchi*). He kept asking the boy whether he had found the coin, until Easter came. The question was then rejected outright: the boy had confessed his dishonesty and received absolution. At the same time the Puritan Hawthorne was struck by the paradoxes:

> They spit upon the glorious pavement of St Peter's, and wherever else they like; they place paltry looking, wooden confessionals beneath its sublime arches, and ornament them with cheap little coloured prints of the crucifixion; they hang tin hearts and other tinsel and trumpery at the gorgeous shrines of the saints, in chapels that are encrusted with gems, or marbles almost as precious; they put pasteboard statues of saints beneath the dome of the Pantheon; in short, they let the sublime and the ridiculous come close together, and are not in the least troubled by the proximity. It must be that their sense of the beautiful is stronger than in the Anglo-Saxon mind, and that it observes only what is fit to gratify it.

He also recorded the nature of modern Roman funerals:

> Mr Story told us of the horrible practices of the modern
> Romans with their dead – how they place them in the church,
> where, at midnight, they are stripped of their last rag of funeral
> attire, put into the rudest wooden coffins, and thrown into a
> trench – a half a mile, for instance, of promiscuous corpses.
> This is the fate of all, except those whose friends choose to pay
> an exorbitant sum to have them buried under the pavement of
> a church. The Italians have an excessive dread of corpses, and
> never meddle with those of their nearest and dearest relatives.
> They have a horror of death, too, especially of sudden death,
> and most particularly of apoplexy; and no wonder, as it gives
> no time for the last rites of the Church, and so exposes them
> to a fearful risk of perdition for ever.[75]

Several visitors commented on EDUCATION. Norton was, naturally,
interested. Evening schools had begun in Rome in 1830, thanks to the
work of a lawyer, Michele Gigli. By 1856 there were thirteen such
schools in various parts of the city, catering to one thousand pupils,
but they were entirely dependent on private support. Most of the
teachers were young liberals; one of the few ecclesiastics involved was
abbate Fabiani. The students were all boys, aged from five or six to
eighteen or twenty. Each school was divided into four or five classes,
and each of those into two groups: the Carthaginians and the Romans,
competing for prizes. The main problem was textbooks, with no good
treatises on reading for beginners or geography or history (the books
that did exist were prepared by priests, and were 'of such a character
as to disgust children, not only with learning, but with religion'). The
supporters of these schools had to act with 'the utmost circumspec-
tion', because of 'the large and influential class of bigots, who regard
them with suspicion and distrust'.

At the top of the education system in Rome was the University, la
Sapienza. Taine stated that the professors were paid 300-400 *scudi* per
annum for giving five lectures a week, so that they had to supplement
this by other work. There were then (1864) forty seven chairs, and five
hundred students. Theology flourished, but there was no course in

secular history. The only two public schools otherwise remained the seminary and the Collegio Romano.[76]

The famous Collegio della Propaganda Fide was still an attraction for visitors, especially on 13 January, the Festa delle Lingue. Norton was present in 1856. In the previous year one hundred-and-thirty-three budding missionaries had been educated there. At the festival, each student made a speech in his native language on the same topic, this time the miraculous escape of Pius IX when the floor of a room at S Agnese fuori le mura gave way, in April 1855 (no one in fact was hurt). The speeches were made in thirty seven different languages! Norton found the topic uninspiring: the 'Tower of Babel' would have been much more appropriate!

SOCIAL LIFE on the other hand seems to have had its quality and attractions. Ticknor in 1857 characterised it thus:

> More or less distinguished and intellectual persons come here every winter from the different countries of Europe, and as there is really but one society, they must either live isolated, or among their own countrymen, or meet in the common places of exchange for all, and carry on, in the conversational language of all, an intercourse which never wants topics for agreeable conversation...
>
> Society has grown more luxurious, more elaborate, and less gay. The ladies' dresses, by their size, really embarrass it somewhat, and Queen Christina [Dowager Queen of Spain], with the ceremonies attending such a personage everywhere, embarrasses it still more this year. Above all, it costs too much. Three balls, therefore, are as much as anybody gave last winter, or will give this year. The rest is made up of tea and talk, ices and sideboard refreshments, which at Count Lutzow's and the Marquis Spinola's are very agreeable once a week, and pretty dull at the Roman Princesses of the race of Fabius Maximus. At *all* the other palazzos – and in sundry other places – a half hour or an hour may be spent pleasantly, whenever the inmates are not out visiting, a fact politely intimated by shutting half of the porte cochère. I go pretty often in this way, especially to the Borgheses', where there is of course much of a French

tone, and where, amidst all the luxury of Paris, and in grand old tapestried halls, such as Paris cannot show, you find the most simple and unpretending ways; the children and their playthings, in the third and fourth generation, mixed up with a stray cardinal or two, or a couple of foreign ambassadors and their wives, as I witnessed the last time I was there.[77]

MUSIC continued to have its charms, as attested by no less a judge than Franz Liszt. 'On Sundays I go regularly to the Sistine Chapel to bathe and reinvigorate my spirit in the sonorous waves of Palestrina's *Jordan*.' He admitted to being wholly enthralled by the music here, 'where everything is grand, majestic, permanent, equally sublime in its general effect and its radiance'. It transpires almost immediately that here was the exception to the rule:

> The musical diet known to me here is nowhere near as plentiful and substantial as the one I was used to. Thus far I have heard nothing which has given me the desire to listen to it more attentively – with the exception, however, of masses by Palestrina and his school, whose character of sublime permanence is fully revealed in the Vatican chapel. The number of choristers is rather restricted; but the acoustic proportions of the chapel are so excellent, and the choir so well placed (towards the middle of the nave, but a little nearer the altar), that those 24 – or 30 voices at most – produce a very impressive effect. It is a sonorous incense which carries prayer aloft on its clouds of gold and azure!
>
> …As for what in Germany are called Concerts – such as those of Löwenberg, to mention one of the best examples – the kind has not yet been imported into Italy; and if it ever did make its way here, I doubt that it would succeed in becoming acclimatized. This notwithstanding, one here and there comes across artistes who declare their high regard for the *classical* music of Haydn, Mozart, and Beethoven – but it is a little like the way in which in other capitals society ladies can occasionally be heard extolling the profundities of German philosophy, with which they will take good care not to become more closely acquainted.

The Tiber before embankment, which was started in 1876: the Apollo theatre is the large building centre right. It was demolished during the embanking processs

That was in 1861-2. In 1873 he noted that the autumn opera season opened with Gounod's *Faust* at the Apollo theatre, and Flotow's *Martha* at the Politeama in Trastevere.[78]

The CAFES, of course, remained a major centre of social life, for both Romans and visitors. Josef Kraszewski described the Greco in the 1850s:

> We are in the Caffè Greco in the first room, and if the doors were not open, one could not sit because of the smoke from cigarettes and cigars. There is an indescribable noise, and every now and then laughter bursts out which even increases it. Half of the artists are sitting in their shirt sleeves... Waiters serve coffee, and every while one hears 'Due... fe... e!' This is an abbreviation for caffe. Some are playing dominoes, the newly arrived are looking at the frescoes on the wall, one leans on the wall and looks at the street. The old stray dog, who for some hours sat, begging alms, outside the Lepre trattoria now lies in ambush on the doorstep of the Greco, being very well behaved.

Buffalo Bill and two members of his troupe, Jacob White Eyes and
Iron Tail, at the Caffè Greco in 1890. Bill's cowboys were beaten
in a cow punching contest by local horsemen

Taine in 1864 described it as 'a long room, low, smokey, not at all light or charming, but comfortable: it seems the same everywhere in Italy. This is the best cafe in Rome, but would seem third class in Paris. It is true that everything here is good and cheap: the coffee, which is excellent, costs 3 *sous* [c. 3 *bajocchi*] a cup.'

Melville gives his characteristic impression of the Cafe Nuovo, in the palazzo Ruspoli on the Corso: 'old palace. Deep recesses of windows. Crowd of orderly well dressed people. Musical guitarr [*sic*] man. Hush and applause.'[79]

The arts in Rome were still presided over by the ACCADEMIA DI S LUCA, in via Bonella. Hawthorne visited in 1858. He admired a *Virgin and Child* by Vandyke, but although Guido's *Fortune* was 'celebrated', it did not appeal to him. He saw the gallery of self-portraits by the academicians, 'most of whom, judging by their physionomies, were very common-place people'(!) The more erotic paintings by Titian disturbed him, notably *Calypso and her Nymphs*. His countryman, Norton, was much more direct:

> The utter sterility and impotence of mind which have long been and are still conspicuous at Rome, the deadness of the Roman imagination, the absence of all intellectual energy in literature and in Art, are the necessary result of the political and moral servitude under which the Romans exist. Where the exercise of the privileges of thought is dangerous, the power of expression soon ceases… The Roman artists of the present time have not, in general, the capacity even of good copyists. They can mix colors and can polish marble, but they are neither painters nor sculptors.

And yet, paradoxically, Rome was the mecca of so many FOREIGN ARTISTS. Melville mentioned the English sculptor John Gibson (1790-1866) in Rome from 1817, who had his studio near the Pincian and was famous for his *Tinted Venus* (Liverpool, Walker Gallery), the American sculptor Edward Bartholomew (1822-58), in Rome from 1850, famous for his *Eve Repentant*, and the Irish American sculptor Thomas Crawford (1813-57), in Rome from 1835, in whose studio he saw 'a colossal America and various statues' (a pediment for the Capitol in Washington). It is, however, Hawthorne who tells us most. He visited the studio of the American painter Cephas Thompson (1809-1888) in via Sistina, and in the same street that of William Story (1819-95), the American sculptor and writer, in Rome from 1856, working on his seated *Cleopatra*, and *Goethe's Margaret*. Hawthorne told stories against his fellow countrymen: visitors to Story's studio asked if he had decided yet whom the Cleopatra was to represent! Hawthorne revealed that the great sculptors had stonecutters to transfer the plaster cast to the marble in broad form, to which they added the finish. He visited Thompson again, and much admired his *St Peter Released from Prison* and his *Georgian Slave*. Crawford had died in 1857, so that Hawthorne was able only to visit his studio near the Baths of Diocletian, full of statues of American heroes such as Washington and Jefferson and mytholog- ical figures such as Orpheus. Hawthorne thought him much overrated. He particularly criticised the Washington monument, where a single step of the horse 'must precipitate him'. At a dinner party he met Gibson, now sixty-eight, but his hair still dark, his face unwrinkled, 'his eye undimmed'. His manner was 'quiet, self contained'; he was a bachelor, and he talked little, but his conversation was partly of India and partly of art: he roundly condemned the pre-Raphaelites. Other artists visited by Hawthorne were not named. One was the American sculptor Joseph Mozier (1812-70), who had produced among other things *Pocahontas* and the *Prodigal Son*: 'his cleverness and ingenuity appear in homely subjects, but are quite lost in attempts at higher ideality'. He was, moreover, accused of plagiarism. Another was Harriet Hosmer, whose portrait will be found under the appropriate section below. Hawthorne saw in her studio *Beatrice Cenci*, and a *Puck*. She was an associate of Gibson. Another American artist in Rome was George Loring Brown (1814-89), the landscapist, 'a plain, homely Yankee, quite unpolished by his many years' residence in Italy; he talks ungrammatically, and in Yankee idioms; walks with a strange awkward gait and stooping shoulders; is altogether unpicturesque; but wins one's confidence by his very lack of grace'. Hawthorne went so far as to declare that he preferred his work to that of Claude. The novelist finally extended his visits beyond his fellow countrymen. One was 'an elderly Swiss artist, named Müller, I believe,' who showed 'a great many water-colour and crayon drawings of scenes in Italy, Greece and Swit- zerland'. In 1860 George Eliot visited four artists' studios. With Gibson she was unimpressed ('feeble imitation of the antique') but she liked the same *Cenci* and *Puck* by his pupil Harriet Hosmer; Johannes Frey (1813-65), in Rome from 1843, was 'a very meritorious landscape painter'; Augustus Riedel (1802-83) in Rome from 1828 until his death, was intrigued by light and colour; and Johannes Overbeck (1789-1869) was in Rome from 1810 until his death: 'a benevolent calm and quiet conviction breathes from his person and manners. He has a thin, rather high nosed face, with long grey hair, set off by a maroon velvet cap, and a grey scarf over his shoulders.'[80]

George Peter Alexander Healy, Frederic E. Church, and Jervis McEntee,
Henry Wadsworth Longfellow and his daughter Edith under the Arch of Titus, with the
three artists in the foreground, *1871*

Robert Hillingford, Carnival in Rome, *1862*

The later nineteenth century saw the last days of the CARNIVAL celebrations after centuries of self-indulgence. Frances Elliot in the late 1860s described it as 'a perfectly contagious plague of folly, vulgarity, license, noise and ribaldry'. Masks had been forbidden and the supplication and humiliation of the Jews had been suppressed, but the general scene was anything but attractive:

> People are crushed into carriages and cars by dozens; streets overflow; the windows are crammed; the galleries and verandahs tremble with the weight; the dust flies like sand on the desert; the sun shines too hot; the wind blows too chill; and after all this *chiasso*, [noise] 'what come they out for to see?' A few dozen miserable ragamuffins of the lowest grade in dirty costumes hired in miserable slop shops (for none but the lowest ever dream of a regular costume) – crowds of the refuse of a great city – troops of half tipsy and much excited soldiers – gentlemen with a charming return to infantine simplicity, dressed in 'over all' pinafores of brown holland; and ladies wearing blue wire masks, which make them look particularly hideous. Then one is pelted with flowers so black and dirty that they seem the very corpses of themselves. Blinded with showers of lime (the *gesso* [plaster] of the studios put to such unholy abuses!) which every rascal may freely fling in one's face, and which descends also in deluges from above, making one's eyes intolerable for days (mine positively ache to write of it), screamed at, sworn at, stared at, by a vast crowd, where one recognises not a soul, so muffled up is every one in the aforesaid wire masks, veils, and great hats of the conspirator cut – all this martyrdom being occasionally rewarded by a tiny bag of sugar plums thrown by a compassionate male friend, or a bouquet of decent flowers, which is either lost in the street, or the next instant torn violently from one's grasp by a vile little street urchin, who makes a few *bajocchi* by its speedy sale!

Tchaikovsky in 1880 agreed:

> The Carnival is in full swing. I am not the least attracted by all

this excitement but am glad to have seen it. We have a balcony over the Corso from where we can see everything perfectly. It would be difficult for you to imagine how far this madness goes. It is quite an agony to walk along the Corso. From all sides you are being bombarded with little balls of flour, in your face, on your head. Some really hurt, but God preserve you from getting angry, for if you do you will be bombarded to death. I came back covered in flour like a flour merchant.[81]

The ultimate question, as always, was the quality of FREEDOM in Rome. Renan in 1849 declared 'Rome is the city in the world where one is freest, as regards small freedoms. No police.' Norton seven years later was, however, categorical:

To feel and to speak, to think and to act, independently, are privileges denied to Romans. They are privileges too dangerous to the Church, to be allowed by the ecclesiastical masters of the State. The less feeling and the less thought there are at Rome, the better for its rulers. The system of the Church cannot coexist with freedom in any direction. The claim of infallibility does not recognize that of individual opinion...

Such a government can be carried on only by secret and corrupt means. The confessional becomes an instrument of the State, the secret police an instrument of the Church. Suspicion is universal. 'We never talk openly together, we cannot trust each other,' is the common confession of Romans. My Italian servant is afraid of my Italian friend, and my friend fears lest my servant should overhear his talk. 'I cannot venture to have friends, except those of science,' says a Professor of the Collegio Romano. The nephew of one of the exiles of 1849 brings me a letter for his uncle, to send under an inclosure of mine, for he does not think it prudent to let it pass openly through the post office.

And at this point it seems, Norton did not yet know of censorship, about which he wrote in detail almost a year later. 'No book, no pamphlet, no placard is printed at Rome without the ecclesiastical imprimatur.' It was the fate of foreign journals, however, which must have most distressed him:

> The 'Athenæum' came to us the other day with the article on [Henry] Milman's 'History of Latin Christianity' carefully blotted out; from the 'Revue des Deux Mondes' of the fifteenth of January the article on 'Italie: Son Avenir', etc., is gone; and from the 'Revue' of the first of February three leaves are cut out of the middle of [Jean-Baptiste] Montegut's article on Michelet.

Such acts contrasted with the books which were encouraged: the most credulous accounts of saints and miracles.

Taine in 1864 noted that it was impossible to travel without a passport, which was often refused. And those who obtained one were often told not to return: it was feared that they would have imbibed liberal views. The police allowed one to do much as one liked – except dealing in matters close to religion or politics. Anyone known to be reading too much (!) was put under surveillance, and was subjected to raids on his home, or to a curfew.[82]

WITNESSED EVENTS

PIUS RETURNED TO ROME ON 12 APRIL 1850. Ernest Renan described the scenes:

> I never saw anything more strange, anything less able to be guessed. I was expecting demonstrations which were officially organised and paid for, like those of Carnival. What was my astonishment, when standing on the steps of S Giovanni in Laterano, I found myself, as the pope entered, in the midst of a crowd of possessed, screaming their heads off: 'Long live Pius IX', prostrating themselves on the ground, shouting 'Benediction! Benediction!' But this was nothing alongside the bizarre spectacle in the narrow, poor streets which the procession passed. I was following it in parallel in order to examine the

Karl Bryullov, Return of Pius IX to Rome, *1850*

various faces. It is difficult without having seen this strange scene really to understand Italy and the blind enthusiasm of the masses. Ordinary men, with distracted look and bare arms, threw themselves into the streets, under the horses' hooves, shouting: 'Command us, Holy Father, command us!' A word or a gesture misunderstood and that fanatical crowd would have rushed to murder and to burn as if they were holy works. The women especially were terrifying: true bacchants, in rags, hair flying, eyes starting out of their heads, fierce beasts... The three evenings which these holidays lasted were for me the most enjoyable and very fertile in moral observations. The Borgo especially, with its illuminations like day, strolling orchestras, singers of the people improvising in honour of Pius IX, restaurants of foliage in the open air where one could sit, choirs in the shops and at the corners in front of the madonna, offered a unique spectacle.[83]

We have seen especially the Germans keeping up their own anniversaries in Rome. On 21 February 1851, Americans celebrated GEORGE WASHINGTON'S BIRTHDAY, as Julia Howe recorded.[84] And Robert Browning noted that in December 1853 the CITY WAS LIT BY GAS for the first time.[85]

The Protestant historian Ferdinand Gregorovius recorded two very different events in 1854. In October he made a momentous decision, not unaware, surely, of Edward Gibbon:

> I propose to write the history of the city of Rome in the Middle Ages. For this work, it seems to me that I require a special gift, or better, a commission from Jupiter Capitolinus himself. I conceived the thought, struck by the view of the city as seen from the bridge leading to the island of S Bartholomew. I must undertake something great, something that will lend a purpose to my life. I imparted the idea to Dr Braun, secretary to the Archæological Institute. He listened attentively, and then said, 'It is an attempt in which anyone must fail.'

He was thirty-three years of age. His *Geschichte der Stadt Rom im Mittelalter* was to occupy him until 1873. Two months later he was highly unimpressed by the second event of 1854:

> On December 8, the solemn proclamation of the absurd dogma of the IMMACULATE CONCEPTION took place. I saw the procession of 250 bishops in S Peter's. Festivals and music in the churches every day.[86]

On 6 January 1856, PRINCE TOMMASO CORSINI (1767-1856) died. It was one of the last flourishes of the old aristocracy.

> To day the doors have been open, and every one who desired has been admitted to see the state apartments and the dead Prince. All sorts of persons have been going up the magnificent

double flight of stairs, – ladies and gentlemen, poor women with their babies in their arms, priests, soldiers, ragged workmen, boys and girls, and strangers of all kinds. There were no signs of mourning about the house, but in the first great saloon sat two men in black gowns, busily employed in writing, as if making inventories; and in each of the next two rooms were two priests in their showy robes, performing separate masses, while many people knelt on the floors, and others streamed through to the apartment in which the corpse was laid out. Here, on a black and yellow carpet, in the middle of the floor, surrounded by benches which were covered with a black cloth on which was a faded yellow pattern of a skeleton with a scythe, lay the body of the old man. He was eighty-nine years old; but here was nothing of the dignity of age, or the repose of death. The corpse was dressed in full court costume, – in a bright blue coat, with gold laces and orders upon the breast, white silk stockings, and varnished pumps. It had on a wig, and its lips and cheeks were rouged. At its feet and at its head was a candle burning; two hired mourners sat at each side, and two soldiers kept the crowd from pressing too near or lingering too long. The room, which was not darkened, was hung with damask of purple and gold, and the high ceiling was painted with gay frescoes of some story of the gods. It was a scene fit for the grave digger's grim jokes and Hamlet's sad philosophy.[87]

On 30 March 1856 as Gregorovius was going along the via Appia, all the bells in Rome began to ring. It was the news of the peace to end the CRIMEAN WAR, which arrived by telegraph.[88]

The dogma of the IMMACULATE CONCEPTION had been announced in 1854. Two years later on 18 December 1856, the commemorative COLUMN was erected in piazza di Spagna. It was drawn to the spot by galley slaves. It soon became the butt of Pasquino. The mouth of Moses was thought too small. 'Speak,' says Pasquino. 'I cannot,' replies Moses. 'Well, hiss,' orders Pasquino. 'Yes, I hiss the sculptor!'[89] This was the work of Giuseppe Obici. The most circumstantial account is provided by Charles Norton:

Piazza di Spagna with the column of the Immaculate Conception, photochrom of c. 1890

ROME, 18th December, 1856.
The old column for the new monument in the Piazza di Spagna, in honor of the Virgin of the *Immaculate Conception*, and in memory of the promulgation of the dogma, was raised to day and set upon its base. The architect who directed the work adopted much the same means of operation as Fontana employed for raising the obelisk in front of St Peter's, about which the famous story of 'Wet the Ropes' is told. For some weeks the Piazza has been blocked up at the end near the Propaganda with a clumsy and enormous inclined plane of timber, for the purpose of rolling the column up to a level with the top of the base of the monument. The immense extent of timber work gave rise to a pasquinade in which there was some humor: 'Lost, an architect, supposed to have missed his way in the forest in the Piazza di Spagna!'

There was no religious ceremony connected with the raising

of the column; and the Pope, although greatly interested in the work, was not present even as a spectator. The people say he stayed away on account of his evil eye. A large proportion of the spectators, both in the square and in the neighboring houses, were foreigners. The Romans do not like the monument; – it costs too much money, and their taxes are heavy. The windows of the Propaganda were occupied by cardinals, while Queen Christina [widow of Ferdinand VII of Naples], no fear being felt of her evil eye, was looking on from one of the windows of the Spanish palace.

A troop of soldiers was stationed around the board fence which inclosed the monument, to keep the crowd at a proper distance, and within the inclosure were the city firemen, in their blue dresses and brass topped caps, manning the windlasses by which the column was to be hoisted. Before the work began, the ropes, already damp with the morning rain, were well wet, and then, at the sound of a trumpet, the men began to turn the windlasses, and the great mass moved slowly. As the column rose and the creaking ropes bore the strain, the clouds broke, and, just as it settled down upon the base prepared for it, the sun came out brightly. A band played a march, the people quickly dispersed, the draperies were pulled in from the windows, and the workmen unwound the covering of ropes in which the pillar had been bound, showing the fine green veins of the *cipollino* marble. Next summer four statues of the prophets are to be set at its foot, and it is to be crowned with one of the Virgin *sine labe concepta*. It promises, when finished, to be as ugly as most of the public monuments of Rome. When will architects and artists learn that a column is not a proper pedestal for a statue?

Two facts connected with this column are curious. It once belonged to a building of the Empire, and has been lying for centuries on the Quirinal. In repolishing it for its present use, it was found not to be sound, and it has been cased, for security, nearly half way up, in bronze open work. The statue of the Virgin on its summit will afford a curious type of the Roman Church itself, based upon unsound supports derived from heathen times.[90]

In June 1857, the RUSSIAN EMPRESS, Marie of Hesse Darmstadt, wife of Alexander II, visited Rome. Gregorovius reported that the Colosseum and all the monuments of the Forum were illuminated with Bengal lights (blue fireworks) in her honour.[91]

Following the defeat of the Republic of 1848, the next major step towards Italian unification was GARIBALDI'S CALL IN 1860 FOR A NATIONAL ARMY which he would lead. The sequel was an oath of loyalty from the nobility to the pope:

> The Roman nobility have handed to the Pope an address of loyalty with 134 signatures, headed by the Marchese Antici, Senator of Rome, Prince Domenico Orsini, and Marcantonio Borghese. Several princes have seceded; such are the Gætani, the two Torlonias, Doria, Pallavicini, Gabrielli, Piombino, Buonaparte, Buoncompagni, Fiano, Cesarini, and others.

On 22 January there was then a great counter-demonstration in piazza Colonna. The people shouted Evviva Napoleone e Vittorio Emmanuele! The combination is intriguing. The rumour reported by Gregorovius was that it was all a French plot to force Pius to flee so that they could take over the government. Stimulus to further unrest was provided by the feast-day of St Joseph (19 March), Garibaldi's nameday, and the vote in Tuscany and central Italy in favour of union with Piedmont. At the church of the saint, students sang a Te Deum, there was a tumult, and troops occupied the via Nomentana and the Corso, and engaged and dispersed the crowd in the latter. It transpired that one hundred people were wounded and one died. The American consul had to be protected by an officer.

On 26 March Pius issued an excommunication against 'usurpers of papal rights in general'. The bull was posted on the Curia, the basilicas of St Peter and St John, and in the Campo de' Fiori. The bull included Napoleon III, whose troops protected the pope, and at the beginning of April the Republican Christophe Lamoricière was appointed commander of papal troops, and began vigorous recruiting. On 14 May came the news that Garibaldi had landed in Sicily (in actual fact, three days earlier). Pius seems to have been mostly occupied with canonisations, rather than cannon. 'Crosses, miracle working pictures,

Carlo Ademollo, The Slaughter of Giuditta Tavani Arquati and Her Family in 1867, *1880.*
Arquati was a committed patriot who was killed with her husband and children by papal forces,
while preparing ammunition for Garibaldi. She became a symbol for the liberation of Rome

processions, canonisations, all the decayed lumber of the superstition
of past centuries, is set in motion.' Gregorovius, for his part, was at
work on volume 4 and the proofs of volume 3.[92]

Of the momentous events of SEPTEMBER 1870, Harriet Hosmer had
a close view:

> yesterday at five o'clock in the morning began a cannonading
> which made us open our winkers pretty lively, and keep them
> open as big as saucers until near eleven o'clock, when a hole
> was knocked in the wall and in marched Victor Emmanuel's
> troops.
>
> All the fighting was at the Porta Pia, which you recollect is
> very near my house, so we had the full benefit of the noise and
> of the cannon balls too, as I found when I attempted to see
> a little of the fun outside my own walls. When the cry arose
> that Napoleon's Villa was on fire, my curiosity overcame my
> prudence and I went into the Via Pia, spyglass in hand; but I
> was soon brought to my senses, for a shell burst within a stone's
> throw of me and a piece fell not two yards from my feet. A

The breach of Porta Pia, 1870, from a magazine illustration of 1889

great cry arose of '*Indietro, indietro!*' [Back, back] and I, with the rest of the crowd, left for home, and had not turned the corner by more than a second and a half when another shell burst at the very corner and cut open a man's head who was so near me that he was touching my dress. Pretty lively, wasn't it?

So I concluded home was as good a place as any, and stayed here as long as I could, but presently sallied forth again, being hailed by two friends, and crept round corners till I got to Rossetti's house in the Porta Pinciana, where we had a grand view of things, with a ball whizzing round our ears every few minutes to add to the excitement of the occasion. We had, however, to make ourselves scarce again when a bomb fell three roofs from ours, and I then began to think I had had enough of the smoke and din of battle, and had better retire gracefully while I had a whole set of bones in my body.

No one thought the fighting would be so serious, as the Pope had declared he should make only a 'moral protest', for which five minutes of actual warfare was as good as five days. After just five-and-a-half hours, the cannonading ceased and Rome became *Italian*. We can scarcely believe it, and such rejoicings as the Romans are waking up to, are perfectly unnatural in this quiet Papal city. How many times I have thanked my stars that I was here! I wouldn't have missed it for the world. I write in a disjointed manner, for my head is entirely dazed with what I have seen and heard. You will have a better account than I can give you, in all the papers for the next month, probably, and this is only a sort of excuse for my telling you that I am here and not killed, but very lively indeed.

In the afternoon everybody went out to the Porta Pia, and you would never have recognized the place. The gate that the dear old Pope has been whittling at for years, his own pet portal, looks like a piece of perforated card, and a strange thing happened that set afloat all sorts of sensational stories. A shell took off the heads of two statues, each side of the gate, and sent them rolling along the pavement. The statues were those of St Peter and St Paul. The bodies were not injured. Of course those who so desired, read the omen as indicating that ecclesiastical rule was ended forever. The fresco of the Madonna is pretty well punched, and there are so many trenches to skip over that one wants four legs instead of two. The Napoleon Villa (just inside the gate) has suffered most. A bomb set fire to it so that all that was combustible went '*per aria*'. The iron gate is twisted into all kinds of shapes, and the garden wall riddled. I got into that garden and there saw a sight I shall never forget, – a dead Zouave all covered with dust, his hands and face like marble, and a most frightful gunshot wound in the lower part of his face, which must have killed him on the spot. There were very few killed, tho' a number were wounded. But it is so impossible to get at the truth of things in this confusion that I believe nothing as yet. The entry of the soldiers was most exciting, to the number, some say, of 40,000, some say 60,000.[93]

Harriet recorded that the following Christmas was the quietest ever in Rome. The tourists were not coming, and Cardinal Giacomo Antonelli urged the loyal Romans to go into mourning! Then came the terrible FLOOD, an omen to the reactionaries:

> That inundation was truly awful. It is said that for two centuries, such a visitation has not been known. The Corso, Ripetto, and portions of the Babuino were only navigable in boats, and most of the shops in the Corso have lost fifty thousand francs apiece, on an average. The waters rose with astonishing rapidity, yet I still think that in any other place than Rome, where people have a way of sitting down and expecting the Madonna to help them, they would have saved three-fourths of what was lost for want of a little energy and discretion.[94]

In the wake of that, Victor Emanuel finally made a flying visit to the city.

In October 1764 Gibbon had pondered the ruins of Rome. On 18 April 1876, the twenty-two years old LUDWIG PASTOR, on his last day in Rome, followed suit:

> Back to the Capitol. On the small terrace facing the Forum I sat for a long time, absorbed by the sight of the Forum and Palatine, until the departing sun made the Alban mountains glow in the most wonderful variation of colours.[95]

Three years later he gained access to the papal archives, and in 1886 began appearing his monumental *Geschichte der Päpste*.

In January 1878 VICTOR EMANUEL DIED. Julia Howe was there:

> I recall vividly the features of the king's funeral procession, which was resplendent with wreaths and banners sent from every part of Italy. The monarch's remains were borne in a crimson coach of state, drawn by six horses. His own favorite war horse followed, veiled in crape. Nobles and servants of noble houses walked before and after the coach in brilliant costumes, bareheaded, carrying in their hands lighted torches of wax. I stood to see this wonderful sight with my dear friend

The tomb of Victor Emmanuel II in the Pantheon, photochrom of c. 1890

Sarah Clarke, at a window of her apartment opposite to the Barberini Palaces. As the cortège swept by I dropped my tribute of flowers.[96]

He was followed closely by Pius IX, in February. A very short conclave elected LEO XIII. Julia saw his consecration in the Sistine chapel:

> Leo XIII was brought into the church with the usual pomp, robed in white silk, preceded by a brand new pair of barbaric fans, and wearing his triple crown. He was attended by a procession of high dignitaries, civil and ecclesiastic, the latter resplendent with costly silks, furs, and jewels. I think that what interested me most was the chapter of the Gospel which the Pope read in Greek, and which I found myself able to follow. After the elevation of the host, the new Pontiff retired for a brief space of time to partake, it was said, of some slight refreshment.[97]

She reported also that Leo revived old customs long superseded, such as that all persons presented to him should kneel and kiss his hand. He applied this rule even to a very stout brother, who was infuriated.

And in about December 1897, another famous historian took a momentous view of the city, this time from the Janiculum. GEORGE TREVELYAN was twenty-one:

> Another day my father took me up the Janiculum, to see all the roofs of Rome shining below in the winter sun. Standing there, he told a story that was quite unknown to me and little known then to English tourists in general, – the story of Garibaldi's defence of Rome on that spot in 1849. That morning we visited the Vascello and the Porta San Pancrazio. Something new had been planted in my mind and heart.[98]

His Garibaldi trilogy would be published between 1907 and 1911.

PORTRAITS

We have many impressions of the longest-ever-occupant of the papal throne. William Thackeray recorded meeting PIUS IX in 1854 in the street; he had 'a most comfortable bow from him'. George Ticknor recorded in 1857 Pius' disapproval of gambling by ecclesiastics: 'however much the people may dislike him – or rather his ministers – those near his person are sincerely attached to him, and all admit him to be a man of irreproachable character'. Lord Acton, who was in 1870 to be a bitter opponent of the doctrine of papal infallibility, had an audience with Pius in April 1857:

> The pope gave the impression of great kindness and suavity, well acquainted with religious questions, but not so with the state of other countries...
>
> When he thinks he is in the right way he is energetic and decided. So when the Cardinals voted with black and white

balls on the constitution [of Papal States, 1848] and the great majority were against it, he gathered the black balls together, and covering them with his white cap said, 'ecco! sono tutti bianchi' [There, they're all white]. His system at that time failed so completely that he has in reality abdicated all political power and authority, and leaves all that completely in Antonelli's hands. In religious questions he has an opinion and a will of his own, and is not so much influenced, but there also he is less free, as he must remain attached to so many traditions of his predecessors. Here he can only show his opinion by preferring one order or another, &c. and personally, but not in questions of things. He does not much like the Jesuits, and complains of their artfulness and intrigue.

Within a few days, however, Acton changed his view:

The Pope unfortunately has no knowledge whatever of theological matters, and this is very inconvenient in a personal point of view. Gregory XVI was a good theologian. Now nobody feels that the pope will think less of him because he knows nothing at all. Generally however it does little harm, as all things are so fixed and regulated, by congregations &c.

And there was another audience that day:

all greatly struck with his obesity and almost torpidity, and found him old and weak. He took a deal of snuff, and spoke very quietly distinctly and slowly, with no affectation whatever of impressiveness. My impression is not of any ability and he seems less banally good-natured, than his smiling pictures represent him to be.

Acton's summary was extraordinary: 'Everything here is done by word of mouth – as all things are settled by the pope, he dismisses them summarily, verbally. In this way he often gives audiences till past midnight.' Nathaniel Hawthorne saw Pius at St Peter's in March 1858:

Then, in the midst of the purple cardinals, all of whom were

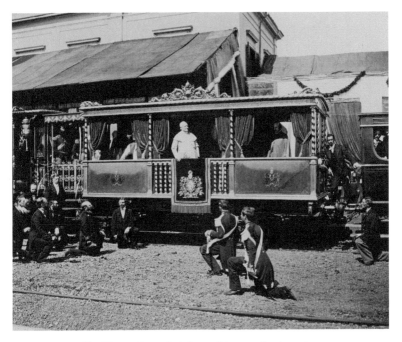

Pius IX appearing at the balcony of his personal train carriage,
by an unknown photographer, 1863

grey haired men, appeared a stout old man, with a white skull
cap, a scarlet gold embroidered cape falling over his shoulders,
and a white silk robe, the train of which was borne up by an
attendant. He walked slowly, with a sort of dignified movement, stepping out broadly, and planting his feet (on which
were red shoes) flat upon the pavement, as if he were not
much accustomed to locomotion, and perhaps had known a
twinge of the gout. His face was kindly and venerable, but not
particularly impressive.

In the late 1860s Frances Elliot seconded these judgements of Pius'
affability and informality. The last impression was provided by Ludwig
Pastor: 'The beatific appearance of the pope, his tender, pure look will
never be forgotten by me. His look is serious, the power of his voice
unbelievable.'[99]

William Kennedy-Laurie Dickson, Leo XIII, in a still from a film made in 1896.
The Pope is thought to have been the earliest born person to have been filmed.
When Dickson showed him the images: 'He was delighted, and exclaimed
'Wonderful! wonderful! See me blessing!' and turning to Mons della Volpa
[to the left above] , he added, 'How splendid you look!'

Pius' successor was LEO XIII (1878-1903). Oscar Wilde was in St
Peter's on 15 April 1900:

> He was wonderful as he was carried past me on his throne,
> not of flesh and blood, but a white soul robed in white, and
> an artist as well as a saint – the only instance in History, if the
> newspapers are to be believed.
> I have seen nothing like the extraordinary grace of his gesture,
> as he rose, from moment to moment, to bless – possibly the
> pilgrims, but certainly me.[100]

One cannot say that Wilde exactly vouchsafes us any impression of
KING UMBERTO, but a remarkable encounter occurred in April 1900,
only three months before the king's assassination:

> Yesterday a painful thing happened. You know the terrible,
> the awe inspiring effect that Royalty has on me: well, I was

outside the Caffè Nazionale taking iced coffee with *gelato* – a most delightful drink – when the King drove past. I at once stood up, and made him a low bow, with hat doffed – to the admiration of some Italian officers at the next table. It was only when the King had passed that I remembered I was *Papista* and *Nerissimo*! I was greatly upset: however I hope the Vatican won't hear about it.[101]

Pius' right hand man was the reactionary and corrupt Cardinal GIACOMO ANTONELLI (1806-76), Secretary of State from 1848. Visitors were deceived. Ticknor in 1857 found him 'an accomplished person, with winning manners, but with much more the air of the world than that of the church... The pope occupies himself very sincerely and earnestly with the spiritual condition of the church. Cardinal Antonelli does all the rest...' As we saw above, Acton agreed that Pius had 'abdicated all political power and authority', which were entirely in Antonelli's hands. He saw another side of the cardinal. After listing the ablest members of the cardinal's college, he stated: 'Antonelli gets rid of the better heads among them. He and the rest in general seem

Cardinal Antonelli, portrait by an unknown photographer, 1852

to have no idea of the very critical state in which they are.' Frances Elliot in the late 1860s was, of course, swept away. She described him as 'a very remarkable man, on whose shoulders rests the entire responsibility of the papal government... Secretary of State, Minister also of Finance, of Police, of Justice, of everything... I cannot positively assert that Antonelli is handsome, but he has a fine Roman face, also zingaro [gypsy] in character, with brilliant black eyes, and that rich, sunburnt complexion common to Italians. The expression of his countenance is excellent; and the suavity and kindness of his manner in receiving a party of ladies (who must have been a great nuisance to him) admirable.' She remarked on the luxury of his apartments, his admiration for the English and his phenomenal memory (he described the interior of a duchess's London mansion by recalling what he had read years before). Franz Liszt saw him in 1873: he had not been outside the Vatican since September 1870.[102]

Acton in 1857 met PETER BECKX (1795-1887), General of the Jesuits 1853-1887. 'Very quiet, amiable, almost timid man, handsome, pleasing countenance, high spirits – slow, low conversation. He said he could not hope to travel, because a general always had to be in Rome.'[103]

One of the most famous characters of Rome was the BEGGAR OF THE SPANISH STEPS. Hawthorne gave a vivid portrait:

> He is an unlovely object, moving about on his hands and knees, principally by aid of his hands, which are fortified with a sort of wooden shoes, while his poor, wasted lower shanks stick up in the air behind him, loosely vibrating as he progresses. He is grey, old, ragged, a pitiable sight, but seems very active in his own fashion, and bestirs himself, on the approach of his visitors, with the alacrity of a spider when a fly touches the remote circumference of his web. While I looked down at him he received alms from three persons, one of whom was a young woman of the lower orders, the other two were gentlemen, probably either English or American. I could not quite make out the principle on which he let some persons pass without molestation, while he shuffled from one end of the platform

to the other to intercept an occasional individual. He is not persistent in his demands; nor, indeed, is this a usual fault among Italian beggars. A shake of the head will stop him when wriggling towards you from a distance.[104]

In the middle of the century a very impressive figure was COUNT FRANZ COLLOREDO (1799-1859), the Austrian ambassador from 1856 to 1859, after having previously served in Stockholm, Copenhagen, Dresden, Munich, St Petersburg and London. Ticknor, of course, knew him:

> The ablest man I meet is, I suppose, Count Colloredo, the Austrian Ambassador, living in great state and luxury in the vast old Palazzo di Venezia. He is a spare man, looking much like a Yankee, quick and eager in all his motions, yet unmistakably a grand seigneur, both by the dignity and by the attentive politeness of his manners. We knew him very well twenty years ago, just beginning his career as Austrian Minister at Dresden with auguries of great success, which have been fully justified; for he satisfied his government during five years of trouble and anxiety in England, including the Russian war, and has been sent here now, – much to his own satisfaction, – on account of the preponderating influence of France. His wife – whom we also knew in Dresden, though he was not then married to her – is a Polish lady, very rich, and by her talent fit to do half the work of his Embassy, any day. Both are very agreeable, courtly people, who have the fame of giving the best dinners that are given in Italy.[105]

In 1857 Ticknor also provided a note – would that it were more extensive – on FERDINAND GREGOROVIUS (1821-91), working for the last four years on his history of Rome in the Middle Ages (from 410 to 1527, to be precise). He calculated the work would take him another six years. It took twice as long. Ticknor described him as living 'in straitened circumstances, but with a very bright cheerful nature, that seems to gild his dark hours as they move on'.[106]

Another case of one of the visitors whose account we are using being

Harriet Hosmer with her assistants and carvers in the courtyard of her Roman studio,
by an unknown photographer, 1867

described by another visitor is HARRIET HOSMER (1830-1908), the
sculptor, who worked in Rome from 1852. Hawthorne described her
to a tee – but, incredible to say, anonymously:

> She has a small, brisk, wide awake figure, not ungraceful; frank,
> simple, straightforward, and downright. She had on a robe, I
> think, but I did not look so low, my attention being chiefly
> drawn to a sort of man's sack of purple or plum-coloured broad-
> cloth, into the side pockets of which her hands were thrust as
> she came forward to greet us. She withdrew one hand, however,
> and presented it cordially to my wife (whom she already knew)
> and to myself, without waiting for an introduction. She had on
> a shirt front, collar, and cravat like a man's, with a brooch of
> Etruscan gold, and on her curly head was a picturesque little

cap of black velvet, and her face was as bright and merry, and as small of feature as a child's. It looked in one aspect youthful, and yet there was something worn in it too. There never was anything so jaunty as her movement and action; she was very peculiar, but she seemed to be her actual self, and nothing affected or made up.[107]

HENRY MANNING (1808-92), later cardinal (1875), gave a series of three sermons in 1857 at S Carlo al Corso. They were attended by Charles Norton, who wrote:

He is a man of tall and striking presence, with an intellectual head, dark eyes, and the look of an ascetic. His personal influence is great, and his reputation at Rome very high. The church was filled with a large audience...

Dr Manning's simple and finished manner, his careful and occasional poetic diction, his quiet fervor, and his fine voice, give him uncommon power as a pulpit orator. His style of thought is subtle, he is an acute pleader, and he makes much use of the forms of logical reasoning. 'In strictest truth' is a phrase which he frequently uses. There was, however, no attempt in his discourse to avoid those doctrines of the Church which are most repugnant to reason and most contrary to Christianity. He spoke of the Eucharist as 'the real, actual, living, breathing, palpable presence of the Lord'. He spoke of the *deification* of the Saints. 'Do not startle', said he, 'at the word; it belongs to them by participation in the nature of Jesus Christ.' He argued, that, as the Virgin was the mother of Christ, and Christ had called us his brethren, she was our actual mother. He urged that she deserved reparation for the past neglect with which she had been treated, and for the scoffs of those who did not honor her. He declared that the Church had not pronounced the doctrine of the Immaculate Conception to be *true*; but that it announced this dogma as revealed from Heaven, through the Divine Spirit which dwells always infallible in it. 'I know', said he, 'that it is often objected that there is very little about all this in the Gospels. Very little of this in the Gospels? In a spark that darts from a burning mass there is the whole essence of fire. If there were but one word in the Gospels concerning the Blessed Virgin, in that word would be concentrated the whole force and spirit of the New Testament. If I found only the words "And the mother of Jesus was there" I should find enough to learn devotion, reverence, and worship for her.'[108]

A famous political figure was the DUKE OF RIGNANO, Prince Mario Massimo (1808-1873), with whom Ticknor dined in 1857:

a dinner yesterday, unlike any I have seen here. It was at the Duc de Rignano's, a statesman who was in poor Rossi's excellent cabinet, and one of the ablest and most respectable men in Rome. He lives with great luxury in his palace on the declivity of the Capitol, and had at his table yesterday the President of the French Academy [Victor Schnetz] here, a professor from the Sapienza, [Arthur Auguste] de la Rive, [Jean-Jacques] Ampère, [Pietro Ercole] Visconti, [Joseph] Pentland, – who wrote Murray on Rome [the famous guidebook], and is more than half Italian – the Duc [Michelangelo] de Sermoneta, – who is accounted the pleasantest man in society here, and who has a great deal of literary cultivation, – with two or three members of the family, including the Duchess, who was the only lady at table. The service was silver, as in most great Roman houses, and the dinner *recherché*, after the Paris fashion. But it was really a dinner for *talk*, and in this particular was very brilliant.

The curious circumstance about it, however, was that at the end of the regular two hours, we went into the *salon* for coffee, and there continued the conversation on French politics, Italian literature, etc., near two hours more, *with cigars*, to the full content of the Duchess, – a Piombino, – who enjoyed it very much, talk, cigars, and all. Ampère, de la Rive, and Sermoneta – especially the first and the last – were admirable. I have not been present at so agreeable and brilliant a dinner in Europe. Don't you think the Italians are improving?'[109]

The man who succeeded Pietro Ercole Visconti as briefly the leading archæologist in Rome was PIETRO ROSA (1810-91). His reputation now is not high, but Liszt reported that he retained 'a feeling of profound gratitude towards the Emperor Napoleon, and that he had wept bitterly on learning of the disaster of Sedan'. He had worked for him on the Palatine in the 1860s. Liszt also revealed the vicious campaign against Rosa following 1870:

> A few right thinking newspapers, such as the *Osservatore*, the *Voce della verità*, are publishing articles inspired by Visconti and [the architect Virginio] Vespignani (they say) reminding Rosa of his lowly origins – which circumstances would seem conducive to excavating – of his former breadwinning job at the Borghese Gallery, where Visconti claims to have given him *la mancia*; and they bury him far deeper than any past, present, or future excavations with this triumphal quip: 'M. Rosa has achieved far more through the sweat of his feet than through the sweat of his brow!'[110]

Ticknor had already mentioned the DUKE OF SERMONETA, Michelangelo Caetani (1804-82). He was a writer, sculptor, goldsmith, and scholar of Dante, known to Scott, Gregorovius, Liszt and Chateaubriand, a moderate liberal, minister of police in 1848, and president of the commission on the plebiscite in 1870, who handed the favourable results to Victor Emanuel II. Liszt provides the most detailed impression of this eccentric but talented man:

> Among the most distinguished personalities that can be met with in the European aristocracy he has his own distinct individuality, and one finds really great delight in following the sallies and meanderings of his exceptional and lively mind. While 'not believing in geography', as he said to silence someone who was persisting in charging him very dearly for an atlas he didn't need, the Duke doesn't for that reason surrender to 'le vague des passions'; and in practising with as much assiduity as success Benvenuto Cellini's art, so that he has, as it were, created a kind of archæological jewellery in excellent, exquisite, and erudite taste, he is by no means out of his depth.

Unknown painter, Michelangelo Caetani, Duke of Sermoneta, *1870*

Furthermore, he cultivates equally successfully another branch of art – that of Bernard Palissy – by maintaining the pottery of Urbino, with as fellow workers, his wife and his daughter, the most gracious Donna Ersilia Caetani, Contessa Lovatelli, about whom a woman that I should feel almost ashamed to praise for her mind, but whom Herr von Humboldt named with good reason *die vielbegeistigte Fürstin*, has said: 'The noble and expressive type of her beautiful features is at once part Juno and part Titania.'

I do not know if Monseigneur has seen samples of this artistic pottery that the Duke sometimes further ennobles by Greek inscriptions; but, convinced that you would take great pleasure in them, I urge you to call for a dessert service from this most illustrious workshop, which would certainly make a splendid show on your table.

Your library probably already contains the Duke of Sermoneta's work on Dante and his *Atlas transmondain de la Divine*

Comédie, which, as it seems to me, only too well exempted him from 'believing in geography'. It is regrettable that only a small number of copies of this work has been printed and is not available commercially. Very competent judges give it sincere praise and state that the author deservedly has the reputation of being Rome's outstanding authority on the works of Dante – indeed, that he has mastered the *Divina Commedia* to the point of being able to recite every canto from memory. How humbling for a poor ignorant musician like me who has ventured to publish a cacophonous mish mash adorned by the title of '*Dante*' Symphony![III]

A famous scholar known to a generation was JOHANNES THEINER (1799-1860), librarian at the Chiesa Nuova and prefect of the Vatican archives. Ernest Renan could not praise him highly enough: he not only opened up the treasures of his own library completely to Renan and his companion, Charles Daremberg, but introduced them to all the other libraries. 'Theiner is at Rome one of the finest, purest, most unexpected types, and knowing him is not one of the least sweet pleasures which I have found in this celestial city.' A decade later Acton knew him:

Theiner is more in the Pope's confidence than anybody. He has obtained permission to publish the acts of the Council of Trent. The pope resisted at first saying that none of his predecessors had done it. But Theiner answered that none of them had defined the Imm[aculate] Conception. A commission was appointed, led by the Domin. Cardinal and reported favourably. It was chiefly led by the Dominican divines – so that it is much to their glory. The Jesuits have vigorously opposed it, partly out of opposition to Theiner. His quarrel with them is of ancient date. He had joined them at one time, and was obliged to leave them in order to avoid expulsion. Roothaan [then General of the Order] signified to him that perfect obedience was requisite. He says that he urged the General to pursue a new path, saying that their old system was no longer effectual. But Roothaan answered that it was to their system they owed all their success, and could not abandon it for an uncertain experiment. T[heiner]'s book [*Life of Clement XIV*] is very unjust. His authorities do not prove his case at all – and he is utterly wrong in saying that the Jesuits had any hand in their own fall. The book is only a lesson to popes not to be influenced by diplomatic agents, and fully proves the case against the pope.

There was, however, a sinister side to him. He refused to show Acton the proceedings of Galileo's trial, but asserted that there was no question of torture. We now know that Theiner lied: Galileo was threatened with torture. Liszt met him 'in his turret, formerly inhabited by Galileo'[!] and was particularly impressed with his publications of Hungarian and Polish documents. Theiner made a remarkable confession to the composer:

– 'Well!' he went on, 'since you speak of glory, there is one to which I am not indifferent. It is that given to me by the happy awareness of having done by myself alone, in a dozen years, more work than about fifty of my colleagues in Germany (under the direction of Pertz, I believe) have done in more than thirty years, and thus of having lit for Poland and Hungary two torches which will shine in perpetuity for those two nations.'[112]

The man who presided over Roman archæology from 1836 until 1870 was the last Commissioner of Antiquities, PIETRO ERCOLE VISCONTI (1802-80). Renan provides a valuable picture in 1849:

Every Thursday evening we find in his salon the whole artistic and literary society of Rome, and as well incomparable music and an art collection of which our poor bourgeois France can give no idea. Visconti is personally one of the finest models of the union of science, art and the noblest character. He says that he is half-French, and he is in fact out of place in the midst of this deplorable people. For having merely agreed to receive French officers, he was threatened with fire and dagger.

His hospitality to the French was in 1848. Ticknor had the good

Pietro Ercole Visconti, by an unknown photographer, c. 1860

fortune to have Visconti as a guide in 1857: 'With Visconti, who is in all societies, as he always has been, we went to the excavations he is superintending at Ostia, and to the Lateran Museum, which he is arranging, and found him full of knowledge, inherited and acquired.' The 'inherited' knowledge presumably refers to his famous family, especially Ennio Quirino Visconti. All that changed in 1870, when, as we have seen, Pietro Rosa took over. Liszt found Visconti at a papal audience 'in the guise of "the courtier of misfortune" (as he styles himself). *Roma capitale* has deprived him of everything save the honour of his imperishable glory'.[113]

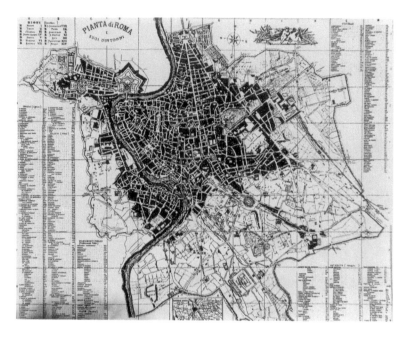

Map of Rome in 1870. *One of the most remarkable of many maps of Rome, this is not well known, but shows that in 1870 inhabited Rome was limited to the north-west third of the city that in the 270s had been enclosed by the Aurelianic walls*

The end of old Rome came in the later nineteenth century. The changes were momentous, as signalled by the name Roma seconda. Rome became the capital of new Italy, but it was less than it was before. It was henceforth essentially the home of an enormous bureaucracy. The old head of state, not only of the city itself but also of the Papal States since the Middle Ages, was now the 'Prisoner of the Vatican'. The state of war which broke out in 1870 and was so quickly won by the new monarchy was not to be concluded by a peace treaty until 1929.

The 1870 map tells everything. Until that time 'modern' Rome occupied about one third of the area of the third-century imperial city when the emperor Aurelian built the walls. Within a few years after 1870 it surged out to engulf all that space and far beyond. And within the city the old topography was devastated. The great villas which had been one of the defining marks of Rome were sold to building speculators and the green spaces which had been a delight and a boon became covered with brick, concrete and asphalt. The heart of classical and mediæval Rome was demolished to construct one of the ugliest imaginable monuments to the new king. The unruly Tiber was caged within huge concrete embankments, the construction of which was plagued with the usual corruption; floods no longer occurred, but the old river was gone and its famous ports.

Even in 1860 George Eliot referred to 'ugly modern Rome'. St Peter's began to lose its charm for the visitor in the later nineteenth century, and there seemed little to enthuse about any more in any of the other churches. Pre-Unification Rome is, however, vividly described with all its old vices: endemic corruption in the justice system, a primitive economy, and rampant superstitition. Many travellers commented on the parlous lack of freedom after 1848. The palaces at least seemed to retain their attraction.

Antiquities continued in the nineteenth century essentially in the state in which they had been left by the French in 1814 until new work began in 1870, but the great transformations were to be owed to

Giacomo Boni from 1898 and then the Fascists in the 1920s and 1930s. The last great collections of art – the Corsini by gift (1883), the Borghese by purchase (1902) – were acquired by the state. This was at least an improvement on the way in which they had previously been exported, such as that of the Farnese collection to Naples and the Medici to Florence, both in the late eighteenth century.

The whole nature of travel changed in the later nineteenth century. The era of mass travel had begun. There were new modes of arrival and movement, notably the railway from the 1850s. Drawing, painting and engraving as means of record were replaced by photography. There was severe inflation.

Now in the twenty-first century the traveller usually arrives by train from the airport into the Marshall Plan station at Termini. The city is ruled by chaotic traffic. The elegant shops along the Corso, still to be seen until after the Second World War, have been replaced by garish purveyors of mass consumerism. The palaces into which they are set, however, remain the elegant edifices they always were. The city's antique past is more on show than ever before, with the recent extensions in the excavated area of the fora and the splendid new museums. And for all the 'gutting' (*sventramento*) of old Rome by the Fascist city-planners, there are many streets which preserve elements going back to the Middle Ages. The glory of Rome, however, remains her Baroque palaces and churches. And for those who desire still to recapture some of the magic of a vanished past, there is the walk up the road between fields in a walled estate from Quo Vadis to the catacomb of St Callistus, or a quiet stroll on the Cælian, the hill largely unchanged for centuries. Rome in short, is a palimpsest which allows one to find traces of every century over almost three millennia.[114]

Rome in the twenty-first century is still unique, as millions of visitors each year attest. Dr Johnson said that the man who was tired of London was tired of life. He had never been to Rome. He did not understand that his dictum applied many times more to another city.

Opposite: Maurice Brazil Prendergast, Steps of Santa Maria d'Aracœli, Rome, *c. 1898-9*

SOURCE NOTES

1. Tchaikovsky, 232.
2. Ibsen, 121; Liszt (2), 97; Renan, *Lettres*, 9.1253; James, *Letters*, 1.168; Eliot, *Letters*, 3.285, 287; Liszt (1), 678.
3. Browning (1), 68; Melville, 206, 211; Liszt (1), 579.
4. Hawthorne, *Notebook*, 1.269.
5. Taine, 1.351.
6. Browning (2), 31; Melville, 190; Hawthorne, *Notebook*, 1.67; Ferronays, 149; Eliot, *Letters*, 3.286; Eliot, *Journals*, 341; Taine, 121-2; Tchaikovsky, 85-6; Hardy, *Letters*, 1.163; Ibsen, 111; James, *Letters*, 1.160; Pastor, 76.
7. Elliot, 1.201-2, 248-9.
8. Renan, *Voyages*, 81; Thackeray, 3.326; Melville, 190; James, *Letters*, 1.164; Eliot, *Journals*, 344.
9. Hawthorne, *Notebook*, 1.87-8; Eliot, *Letters*, 3.289; Taine, 1.306-7.
10. Eliot, *Journals*, 345; Liszt, (1), 574, (2), 162.
11. Taine, 1.304-5.
12. Hawthorne, *Notebook*, 1.112; Renan, *Voyages*, 43; Taine, 1.312; S Clemente: Eliot, *Journals*, 344; James, *Letters*, 1.176; Quo Vadis: Hawthorne, *Notebook*, 1.250; Gesù: Taine, 1.280; S Luigi: Hawthorne, *Notebook*, 1.293.
13. Hawthorne, *Notebook*, 1.104-6; Taine, 1.295; œli: Renan, *Voyages*, 33-5 (see also *Lettres*, 9.1247); Howe, 192; S Maria della Concezione: Taine, 1.291-4; Florence Hardy, 248; Hawthorne, *Marble Faun*, chap. 21; S Maria della Pace: Taine, 185; James, *Letters*, 1.180; S Maria del Popolo: Taine, 1.290-1; 1.293.
14. Melville, 207; Hawthorne, *Notebook*, 1.208; Eliot, *Journals*, 345-6; James, *Letters*, 1.181; Renan, *Voyages*, 61.
15. Norton, 36-7.
16. Ibid., 39-43.
17. Goncourt, 208; Elliot, 2.60-3; Ferronays, 224f.
18. Norton, 204-210.
19. Hawthorne, *Notebook*, 1.261-3; Tchaikovsky, 232; Eliot, *Journals*, 345; Taine, 221, 225.
20. Hawthorne, *Notebook*, 1.198-9; Taine, 186-8; James, *Letters*, 1.165; Hawthorne, *Notebook*, 1.200; Taine, 173-4.
21. Norton, 63-9.
22. James, *Letters*, 1.166; Taine, 172-3; Pastor, 80.
23. Hawthorne, *Notebook*, 1.151; Eliot, *Journals*, 344; James, *Letters*, 1.166.
24. Goncourt, 204-5; Ibsen, 82; Goncourt, 213f.
25. Hawthorne, *Notebook*, 1.224.
26. Wilde, *Letters*, 826.
27. Taine, 1.257; Hawthorne, *Notebook*, 1.71.
28. Melville, 200-1; Hawthorne, *Notebook*, 1.109, 168-9; Taine, 1.272.
29. Hawthorne, *Notebook*, 1.131-4; Taine, 1.265-8; James, *Letters*, 1.177; Pastor, 78. – There are Visitations by Piombo in Venice and the Louvre, but neither came from the Borghese.
30. Thackeray, 3.340; Melville, 191; Hawthorne, *Notebook*, 1.120, 135-8, 218-20; Eliot, *Journals*, 348; James, *Letters*, 1.167.
31. Hawthorne, *Notebook*, 1.204-5; Elliot, 1.42-5.
32. Melville, 208; Hawthorne, *Notebook*, 1.151-3; Taine, 1.263-5; James, *Letters*, 1.177; Wilde, *Letters*, 823.
33. Taine, 1.255.
34. Melville, 204-5; Hawthorne, *Notebook*, 1.197.
35. Melville, 204; Hawthorne, *Notebook*, 1.110-11; Taine, 1.271.
36. Melville, 203; Hawthorne, *Notebook*, 1.148; Taine, 1.257-60. – The most likely candidate for Titian's 'bella Donna' is his Laura dei Dianti now in Switzerland, previously owned by Queen Christina and then the Odescalchi, but they sold it in 1721. And there is a Titian of a woman with red and white sleeves, but it has been in the Pitti since 1631.
37. Hawthorne, *Notebook*, 1.265-7.
38. Melville, 195-6; Hawthorne, *Notebook*, 1.255-9; Taine, 1.231-7; Eliot, *Journals*, 347.
39. Goncourt, 212-3; Melville, 195, 210; Hawthorne, *Notebook*, 1.210-15; Wilde, *Letters*, 826.
40. Hawthorne, *Notebook*, 1.178-81; Taine, 1.241-2; Elliot, 1.51-8.
41. Goncourt, 202-4; Melville, 212;

Hawthorne, *Notebook*, 1.175-7; Eliot, *Journals*, 347.
42. Gregorovius, 36.
43. Renan, *Voyages*, 60-1; Hawthorne, *Notebook*, 1.102; Eliot, *Journals*, 343.
44. James, *Letters*, 1.165.
45. Hawthorne, *Notebook*, 1.122.
46. Goncourt, 192-5; Elliot, 1.28-9; Sienkiewicz in Bilinski, 442.
47. Goncourt, 191-2, 194. Cf. Ridley, *The Eagle and the spade*, Cambridge 1992, 205-16.
48. Goncourt, 193, 195.
49. Renan, *Voyages*, 37, 59 (see also *Lettres*, 9.1229); Goncourt, 194; Hawthorne, *Notebook*, 1.164; Hawthorne, *Marble Faun*, chap. 17; James, *Letters*, 1.163, Goncourt, 193-4.
50. Hawthorne, *Notebook*, 1.161.
51. James, *Letters*, 1.175-6.
52. Renan, *Voyages*, 59; Melville, 194; Hawthorne, *Notebook*, 1.127.
53. Goncourt, 195.
54. Renan, *Voyages*, 60; Melville, 196-7.
55. Renan, *Voyages*, 61; Taine, 1.158-9; James, *Letters*, 1.164.
56. James, *Letters*, 1.175; Norton, 291; Hawthorne, *Notebook*, 1.170-4.
57. Hardy, *Poems of Pilgrimage*: 'Rome at the Pyramid of Cestius near the graves of Shelley and Keats'.
58. Ticknor, 282; Melville, 209.
59. James, *Letters*, 1.174.
60. Gregorovius, 44; Hawthorne, *Notebook*, 1.241-6; Ibsen, 82.
61. Ticknor, 282. This seems to be a reference to Dionysios Halikarnassos, 9.68. – *Ann.Inst.* 1852, 324.
62. Hawthorne, *Notebook*, 1.220-1; Eliot, *Journals*, 342; Sienkiewicz in Bilinski, 443.
63. Hawthorne, *Notebook*, 1.233-4.
64. Elliot, 1.6-7; Tchaikovsky, 455.
65. Hawthorne, *Notebook*, 1.235-7.
66. Hawthorne, *Notebook*, 1.126; Taine, 1.157; Hawthorne, *Notebook*, 1.162.
67. Melville, 212-3; Goncourt, 210-11; Taine, 1.255.
68. James, *Roderick Hudson*, chap. 14.
69. Eliot, *Journals*, 348-9.
70. Renan, *Lettres*, 9.1242-3; Acton, 192, 200; Taine, 1.356-7; Norton, 84-5;

Hawthorne, *Notebook*, 1.75, 136.
71. Renan, *Lettres*, 9.1244; Norton, 72; Ticknor, 285; Taine, 1.360; Norton, 73, 85; Renan, *Lettres*, 9.1243.
72. Renan, *Voyages*, 47.
73. Taine, 1.317-35, 345-55, 320.
74. Elliot, 1.243-8. For the English, see pp. 194-5.
75. Renan, *Voyages*, 29-30; Norton, 237-9; Goncourt, 211; Hawthorne, *Notebook*, 1.103 and 1.246-7.
76. Norton, 32-6; 93-6; Taine, 1.318-9.
77. Ticknor, 280.
78. Liszt (1), 567, 572, 573-4; Liszt (2), 97.
79. Kraszewski in Bilinski, 311; Taine, 1.120; Melville, 213.
80. Hawthorne, *Notebook*, 1.207-8; Norton, 292-3; Melville, 208, 212; Hawthorne, *Notebook*, 1.83-6, 154-9, 187-9, 215-7, 227-30. Müller is not listed in Murray's *Rome and its environs*, 1862, 284f; Eliot, *Journals*, 346.
81. Elliot, 1.226-9; Tchaikovsky, 233.
82. Renan, *Voyages*, 41; Norton, 163-4 and 229-36; Taine, 1.317-8.
83. Renan, *Lettres*, 9.1293-5.
84. Howe, 203.
85. Browning (1), 1.69.
86. Gregorovius, 16-17.
87. Norton, 29-30.
88. Gregorovius, 26f.
89. Gregorovius, 17, 34, 37, 39.
90. Norton, 201-3.
91. Gregorovius, 36.
92. Gregorovius, 77-90.
93. Hosmer, 283-5.
94. Hosmer, 288.
95. Pastor, 82.
96. Howe, 423-4.
97. Howe, 426.
98. Trevelyan, 28.
99. Thackeray, 3.343; Ticknor, 283; Acton, 190, 192, 193, 194; Hawthorne, *Notebook*, 1.182; Elliot, 1.64-5; Pastor, 77.
100. Wilde, *Letters*, 821.
101. Wilde, *Letters*, 824.
102. Ticknor, 285; Acton, 190, 191; Elliot, 1.281; Liszt (2), 100.
103. Acton, 193.
104. Hawthorne, *Notebook*, 1.90-1.
105. Ticknor, 281.
106. Ticknor, 282.

107. Hawthorne, *Notebook*, I.190.
108. Norton, 239-41. The phrase 'And the mother of Jesus was there' is striking. If there is anywhere she is most remembered for being, it is at the foot of the Cross – but for that there is no Gospel evidence!
109. Ticknor, 283-4.
110. Liszt (2), 19, 24.

111. Liszt (1), 568-9.
112. Renan, *Lettres*, 9.1231; Acton, 190-1, 198; M. Finocchiaro, *The Galileo affair: a documentary history*, Berkeley 1989; Liszt (1), 569.
113. Renan, *Lettres*, 9.1231-2; Ticknor, 284; Liszt (2), 24.
114. See Ridley, *Rome, Twenty-nine centuries*.

LIST OF POPES

REGNAL NAME	BIRTH NAME	DATES OF REIGN
Pius VII	Barnaba Niccolò Maria Luigi Chiramonti	14 March 1800 to 20 August 1823
Leo XII	Annibale Francesco Sermattei della Genga	28 September 1823 to 10 February 1829
Pius VIII	Francesco Saverio Castiglioni	31 March 1829 to 30 November 1830
Gregory XVI	Bartolomeo Alberto Cappellari	2 February 1831 to 1 June 1846
Pius IX	Giovanni Maria Mastai-Ferretti	16 June 1846 to 7 February 1878
Leo XIII	Gioacchino Vincenzo Raffaele Luigi Pecci	20 February 1878 to 20 July 1903

LIST OF ILLUSTRATIONS

pp. 102-3: Christoffer Wilhelm Eckersberg, *A View through three arches of the Third Storey of the Colosseum*, 1815; Statens Museum for Kunst, Copenhagen

p. 105: Joseph Severn, *Posthumous portrait of Shelley composing Prometheus Unbound*, 1819, 1845; Keats-Shelley Memorial House, Rome

p. 106: Ippolito Caffi, *Fireworks inside the Colosseum lit by fireworks*, c. 1844-45; Museo di Roma

p. 107: Luigi Rossini, *The Arch of Constantine*; engraving published 1827

p. 109: Sir Charles Lock Eastlake, *The Forum of Trajan*, 1821; Yale Center for British Art

p. 111: Bartolomeo Pinelli, *The Mausoleum of Augustus*, c. 1810; location unknown

p. 113: Jakob Alt, *The Pantheon and the Piazza della Rotonda*, 1836; Albertina, Vienna

p. 114: J. M. W. Turner, *Lecture sketch of the column of Marcus Aurelius, after Piranesi*, c. 1810; Tate, London

p. 115: Unknown artist, *Micromosaic after the mosaic of the Capitoline Doves*, c. 1835; Mayfair Gallery, London

p. 117: Benedetto Boschetti, *Reproduction of The Dying Gladiator*, c. 1830, Regent Antiques, London

pp. 118-9: Lorenzo Scarabello, *The Villa Campana*, c. 1847; private collection

p. 120: Ernst Meyer, *A smoke in Rome*, 1828-32; Statens Museum for Kunst, Copenhagen

p. 123: Ippolito Caffi, *Via del Corso,*

at night, c. 1835-1860; location unknown

p. 124: Giacomo Caneva, *Piazza Navona*, 1850; Rijksmuseum, Amsterdam

p. 127: Edward Lear, *Piazza di Spagna*, after 1837; Tate, London

p. 128: John Ruskin, *The Trevi Fountain*, 1841; The Ruskin, Lancaster

p. 131: Hieronymus Hess, *Study for 'The Conversion of the Jews in Rome'*, 1821; Städel, Frankfurt am Main

p. 132: Giacomo Lenghi, *The 'Cinque Scole (Five Synagogues under One Roof) in the Ghetto*, c. 1839; Museo Ebraico di Roma

p. 135: Invitation to the wedding of Prince Mario Gabrielli to the daughter of Lucien Bonaparte, 1816; British Museum, London

p. 140: Ludwig Pasini, *Artists in the Caffè Greco*, 1856; Kunsthalle, Hamburg

p. 143: Alexander Clemens Wetterling, *Domani? Sicuramente!*, 1827; private collection

p. 145: Jean-Auguste-Dominique Ingres, *Jacques Norvins*, 1811-12; National Gallery, London

p. 146: Dietrich Wilhelm Lindau, *A street altar in Rome, hung with votive offerings, attended by itinerant pipers watched by locals*, 1835; Wellcome Collection, London

p. 149: Antoine Thomas, *Loges de théâtre*, engraving published 1820

p. 151: Bartolomeo Pinelli, *Romans scanning theatre posters;* engraving published 1832

p. 153: Bartolomeo Pinelli, *Laying out the corpse*, 1832; private collection

p. 154: Isaac Weld, *Funeral procession*

Library of Congress, Washington, DC

p. 231: Albert Bierstadt, *Roman Fish-market*, 1858; Fine Art Museums, San Francisco

p. 232: Aleksandr Gierymski, *Street in Rome at night, c.* 1890; Lviv Picture Gallery

p. 234: Unknown photographer, *Pius IX and members of the papal court*, 1868; Wellcome Collection, London

p. 243: Unknown photographer, *Santa Maria della Concezione, c.* 1900; Wellcome Collection, London

p. 249: Unknown photographer, *The choir of the Sistine Chapel*, 1898; Wikipedia

p. 221: Unknown photographer, *Benediction of the Pope on Easter Sunday*, 1880s; collection the publisher

p. 253: Léon Bonnat, *Interior of the Sistine Chapel, c.* 1880; Musée d'Orsay, Paris

p. 255: Léon Bonnat, *Study after one of Michelangelo's ignudi, c.* 1860; Louvre, Paris

p. 257: James Anderson, *View of the display of classical statues in the Vatican*, 1859; J. Paul Getty Museum, Los Angeles, CA

p. 260: Enrico Fanfani, *Guido Reni paints Beatrice Cenci in prison*, 1855-60; private collection

p. 263: Unknown artist, *British Tourists and the Dying Gladiator*; magazine print published 1872

p. 265: Unknown photographer, *Palazzo Colonna, the main gallery, c.* 1850-80; Rijksmuseum, Amsterdam

p. 215: Pietro Dovizielli, *Garden steps of the Palazzo Rospigliosi*, 1859;

Victoria and Albert Museum, London

p. 271: Robert Macpherson, *The marble relief of Antinoüs (Villa Albani)*, 1860s; J. Paul Getty Museum, Los Angeles, CA

p. 273: Pietro Dovizielli, *Gardens and Coffee-House of the Villa Albani*, 1859; Victoria and Albert Museum, London

p. 274: Oswald Achenbach, *In the Park of the Villa Borghese*, 1886; Museum Kunstpalast, Düsseldorf

p. 276: Unknown photographer, *Villa Pamphili, c.* 1870; private collection

p. 277: Unknown photographer, *Prince Don Alessandro Torlonia, Prince of Fucino, Prince of Civitella-Cesi, Duke of Ceri with his daughter Anna Maria*; Wikipedia

p. 278: Rudolf von Alt, *The Fishmarket*, 1865; Princely Collections, Liechtenstein

p. 281: Unknown photographer, *The Forum, c.* 1880-1900; collection the author

p. 282: Unknown photographer, *The Forum*, 1860s; collection the author

p. 283: Ippolito Caffi, *The Forum*, before 1866; private collection

p. 284: Ferdinand Heilbuth, *Excavations in the Forum, c.* 1873-75.; Wallace Collection, London

p. 286: Unknown British painter, *Basilica of Maxentius*, May 1850; private collection

p. 287: Tina Blau, *The Arch of Titus, c.* 1879; private collection

p. 288: Pietro Dovizielli, *Interior of the Colosseum, showing the Stations of the Cross, c.* 1855; Metropolitan Museum of Art, New York, NY

LIST OF ILLUSTRATIONS

Matania, *The breach of Porta Pia*, 1870; magazine illustration published 1890

p. 344: Unknown photographer, *The tomb of Victor Emmanuel II in the Pantheon*, c. 1890; Library of Congress, Washington, DC

p. 347: Altobelli & Molins, *Pius IX appearing at the balcony of his personal train carriage*, 1863; J. Paul Getty Museum, Los Angeles, CA

p. 348: William Kennedy-Laurie Dickson, *Leo XIII*, still from film, 1896; private collection

p. 349: Unknown photographer, *Cardinal Antonelli*, 1852; collection the author

p. 352: Unknown photographer, *Harriet Hosmer with her assistants and carvers in the courtyard of her Roman studio*, 1867; National Gallery of Art, Washington, DC

p. 356: Unknown painter, *Michelangelo Caetani, Duke of Sermoneta*, 1870; Galleria d'Arte Moderna, Rome

p. 359: Unknown photographer, *Pietro Ercole Visconti*, c. 1860; collection the author

p. 360: Unknown cartographer, *Map of Rome*, 1870; collection the author

p. 363: Maurice Brazil Prendergast, *Steps of Santa Maria d'Aracœli, Rome*, c. 1898-9

Images courtesy holding institutions.

SOURCES

Acton, Lord John: 'Journal of Lord Acton: Rome 1857', ed. H. Butterfield, *CHJ* 8 (1931), 186-204

Andersen, *Hans Christian: Diaries*, ed. Patricia Conroy and Sven Rossel, Seattle 1990
¬— *The fairy tale of my life*, New York 1975

Baedeker, Karl: *Central Italy*, Leipzig 1909

Balzac, Honoré de: *Correspondence*, ed. Roger Pierrot, 5 vols, Paris 1960-9. See also Cesare

Berlioz, Hector: *Memoirs*, trans. Rachel and Eleanor Holmes, rev. Ernest Newman, New York 1935

Bilinski, Bronislaw: *Gli anni romani di Cyprian Norwid*, Warsaw 1973
—*Figure e momenti polacche a Roma*, Wroclaw 1992

Bonstetten, Charles Victor de: *Voyage sur le scène des six derniers livres de l'Énéide*, Geneva 1805

Browning, Robert: (1) *New letters of Robert Browning*, ed. William de Vane and Kenneth Knickerbocker, London 1951
—(2) *Browning to his American friends*, ed. Gertrude Hudson, London 1965

Burckhardt, Jacob: *Briefe*, ed. Max Burckhardt, 9 vols, Basel 1949-94

Byron, Lord George: *Letters and journals*, ed. Leslie Marchand, 12 vols, London 1976

Cesare, Raffaele de: 'Balzac a Roma', in *Studi in onore di Carlo Pellegrini*, Torino 1963, 609-48

Champollion, Jean François: *Lettres*, ed. Hermine Hartleben, 2 vols, Paris 1909

Chateaubriand, François-René: *Voyage en Italie*, in *Œuvres complètes*, 16 vols, Paris 1851-2 (vol.4, 1436f)

Cooper, James Fenimore: *Excursions in Italy*, 2 vols, London 1838

Corot, Jean Baptiste: *Corot raconté par lui-même et par ses amis*, Vesenaz-Geneve 1946. See also Galassi, Moreau

Deakin, Richard: *The flora of the Colosseum*, London 1855

Dickens, Charles: *Pictures from Italy*, London 1973

Dictionary of national biography, 2nd ed. 60 vols, Oxford 2004

Dictionnaire de biographie française, Paris 1933-

Dizionario biografico degli italiani, Rome 1960-

Dizionario enciclopedico universale della musica e dei musicisti, ed. Alberto Basso, 16 vols, Torino 1983-9.

Eliot, George: *Journals*, ed. Margaret Harris and Judith Johnston, Cambridge 1998
—*Letters*, ed. Gordon Haight, 9 vols, Yale 1954-78

Elliot, Frances: *Diary of an idle woman in Italy*, 2 vols, Leipzig 1871

Emerson, Ralph Waldo: *Journals*, 10 vols, Boston 1909-14

Ferronays, Pauline (= Mme Augustus Craven): *Reminiscences. Souvenirs d'Angleterre et d'Italie*, Paris 1879

Fuller Ossoli, Margaret: *At home and abroad*, ed. Arthur Fuller, Boston 1856

Gogol, Nicolai: *Impressioni romane*, Rome 1945

—*Letters*, ed. Carl Proffer, Ann Arbor 1967

Goncourt, Edmond and Jules: *Italie d'hier*, Paris 1894

—*Journal des Goncourts*, 3 vols, Monaco 1956

Gregorovius, Ferdinand: *Roman journals*, trans. Mrs Gustavus Hamilton, London 1911.

—*Tombs of the popes*, trans. R.W. Seton-Williams, Westminster 1903

Grove Dictionary of Art, ed. Jane Turner, 34 vols, London and New York, 1996.

Hardy, Thomas: *Collected letters*, ed. Richard Purdy and Michael Millgate, 7 vols, Oxford 1978-88

—*Poems of pilgrimage*, in his *Complete Poems*, ed. James Gibson, London 1981

Hauteville, Jean George: *Voyage en Italie dans l'année 1815*, Paris 1817

Hawthorne, Nathaniel: *The marble faun* (1860)

—*Passages from the Italian notebook*, 2 vols, London 1870

Hazlitt, William: *Complete Works*, ed. P. Howe, 21 vols, London 1930-4

Hillard, George: *Six months in Italy*, 6th ed. Boston 1858

Hosmer, Harriet: *Letters and memories*, ed. Cornelia Carr, New York 1912

Howe, Julia Ward: *Reminiscences*, Boston 1900

Ibsen, Henrik: *Correspondence*, trans. Mary Morrison, London 1903

Indice biografico italiano (fiche)

Irving, Washington: *Notes and journal of travel in Europe 1804-5*, 3 vols, New York 1921

James, Henry: *Letters*, ed. Leon Edel, 4 vols, Cambridge 1974-84

—*Roderick Hudson* (1876)

Kotzebue, Augustus von: *Travels through Italy in the years 1804 and 1805*, 4 vols, London 1806

Lamartine, Alfonse: 'Carnet de voyage en Italie' publiée par Rene Doumic, *Le Correspondent* 80 (1908), 263-279

—*Mémoires inédites*, ed. L. Ronchaud, Paris 1909

Liszt, Franz: (1) *Selected Letters*, ed. Adrian Williams, Oxford 1998.

(2) *Liszt-von Meyendorff :etters,* trans. William Taylor, 1979

Longfellow, Henry: 'Outre-mer. Rome in mid summer' in *The writings of Henry Wadsworth Longfellow*, 11 vols, London 1881 (Riverside ed.), vol.1

Macaulay, Thomas Babington: *Life and letters*, ed. George Trevelyn, London 1881

Melville, Herman: *Journal of a visit to Europe and the Levant*, ed. H. Horsford, Princeton 1955

Mendelssohn, Felix: (1) *Letters from Italy and Switzerland*, trans. Lady Wallace, London 1865

—(2) *Felix Mendelssohn, a life in letters*, ed. Rudolf Elvers, New York 1986

Michelet, Jules: *Journal*, ed. Paul Vialleix and Claude Digeon, 4 vols, Paris 1959-76

Mommsen, Theodor, *Viaggio in Italia 1844-45*, ed. A.Verrecchia, Torino 1980

Montcashell, Stephen, 2nd Earl: *An Irish peer on the Continent 1801-3 as related by Catherine Wilmot*, London 1920

Müller, Wilhelm: *Rom, Römer und Römerinnen*, 2 vols, Berlin 1820

Nightingale, Florence: *Florence Nightingale in Rome*, ed. Mary Keele, Philadelphia 1981

Norton, Charles Eliot: *Notes of travel and study in Italy*, Boston 1860

Pasquin, Antoine Claude: *Voyages historiques et lettéraires en Italie pendant les années 1826, 1827 et 1828*, Brussels 1835

Pastor, Ludwig: *The history of the popes*, 40 vols, London 1938-67

— *Tagebücher – Briefe – Erinnerungen*, Heidelberg 1950

Petit-Radel, Philippe: *Voyage historique, chronographique et philosophique dans les principales villes d'Italie en 1811 et 1812*, 3 vols, Paris 1815

Ranke, Leopold von: *Briefwerke*, ed. W. Fuchs, Hamburg 1949

— *The secret of world history*, New York 1981 (his autobiography!)

Recamier, Jeanne: *Souvenirs et correspondence*, 2 vols, Paris 1860

Recke, Elise von: *Voyage en Allemagne, dans le Tyrol et en Italie pendant les années 1804, 1805 et 1806*, 4 vols, Paris 1819

Renan, Joseph Ernest: *Lettres de famille* in *Œuvres complètes*, ed. Henriette Prichari, 10 vols, Paris 1947-61, vol.9

— *Voyages*, Paris 1927

Shelley, Percy Bysshe: *Letters*, ed. Frederick Jones, 2 vols, Oxford 1964

Staël, Mme Anne Louise: *Correspondence générale*, ed. Beatrice Jasinski, 6 vols, Paris 1960

Stendhal (Marie-Henri Beyle): *Correspondence* in *Œuvres*, ed. Henri Martineau, 79 vols, Paris 1927-37, vol. 56

— *Journal* in *Œuvres intimes*, ed. Henri Martineau, Paris 1955 (Pléiade ed.)

Taine, Hippolyte: *Voyage en Italie*, 2 vols, Paris 1930

Tchaikovsky, Piotr Ilyich: *Letters to his family*, trans. Galina von Meck, London 1981

Thackeray, William Makepeace: *Letters*, ed. Gordon Ray, 4 vols, Cambridge 1946

Ticknor, George: *Life letters and journal*, 2 vols, London 1876

Wilde, Oscar: *Letters*, ed. Rupert Hart-Davis, London 1962

— *Poems* (1881)

Wordsworth, William: *The letters of William and Dorothy Wordsworth*, ed. Alan Hill, vols, Oxford 1982

— *Memorials of a tour in Italy* in *The poems*, 2 vols, New Haven 1981, 2.839f

First published 2023 by
Pallas Athene (Publishers) Ltd.,
2 Birch Close,
London N19 5XD

Reprinted 2024

© Ronald T. Ridley 2023, 2024
Layout © Pallas Athene (Publishers) Ltd 2023, 2024

The author has asserted 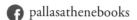 his moral right

For further information on our books please visit
www.pallasathene.co.uk

 pallasathenebooks   PallasAtheneBooks

 Pallasathene0

ISBN 978 1 84368 140 3

Printed and bound in Great Britain by
TJ Books Limited, Padstow, Cornwall

MIX
Paper from
responsible sources
FSC
www.fsc.org   FSC® C013056